Elizabeth Sharman

[across cultures]

culture | literature | music | language

Longman

Across Cultures is divided into eleven modules looking at eleven different aspects of life in the English-speaking world.
Modules 1-10 are each divided into 6 main units, plus a language practice page.

In each module you will find:

AN OPENING PHOTO PAGE ▶

This acts as an introduction to the theme of the module, presenting the topics that will be featured in the units that follow. It includes warm-up activities to help you discover and express what you already know about the subject.

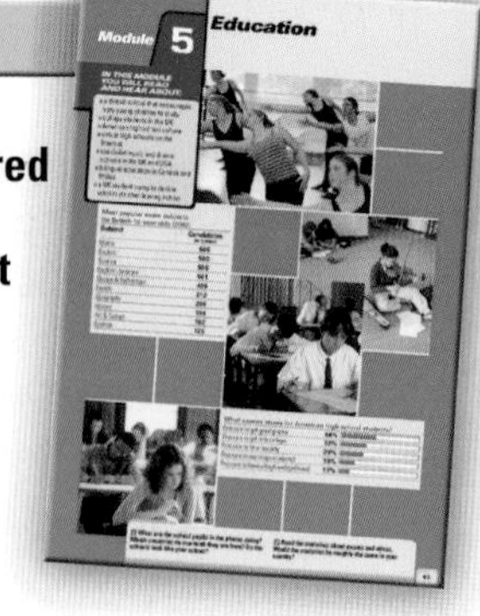

FIVE DOUBLE PAGE SPREAD UNITS (a-e) ▶

These contain reading, listening, speaking and writing activities connected to a different theme for each unit.

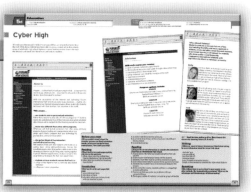

In Modules 1, 3, 5, 7 and 9 you will also find:

◀An *ENGLISH EVERYWHERE* spread (unit f)
These give information about an English-speaking country outside of Britain and the USA.

In Modules 2, 4, 6, 8 and 10 you will also find:

A *SOUNDTRACK* spread (unit f) ▶
These look at music and song lyrics from the English-speaking world.

◀A LANGUAGE & CULTURE PAGE (unit g)

Another text relevant to the module presents grammar and skills connected to the general theme.

Module 11 – Links to literature ▶

Module 11 looks at extracts from plays, poems or novels written in English, from Shakespeare to the modern day. The texts connect to the themes of the units in Modules 1-10.

▼ This box tells you the topic of the unit, the countries you will look at, and the vocabulary that you will practise. There is also a list of links to other units connected to this one.

▼ This is the number of the module (1-11) and the unit (a-g).

▼ This is the title of the module.

▼ This is the topic of the unit.

▼ This tells you the meaning of difficult words in the texts.

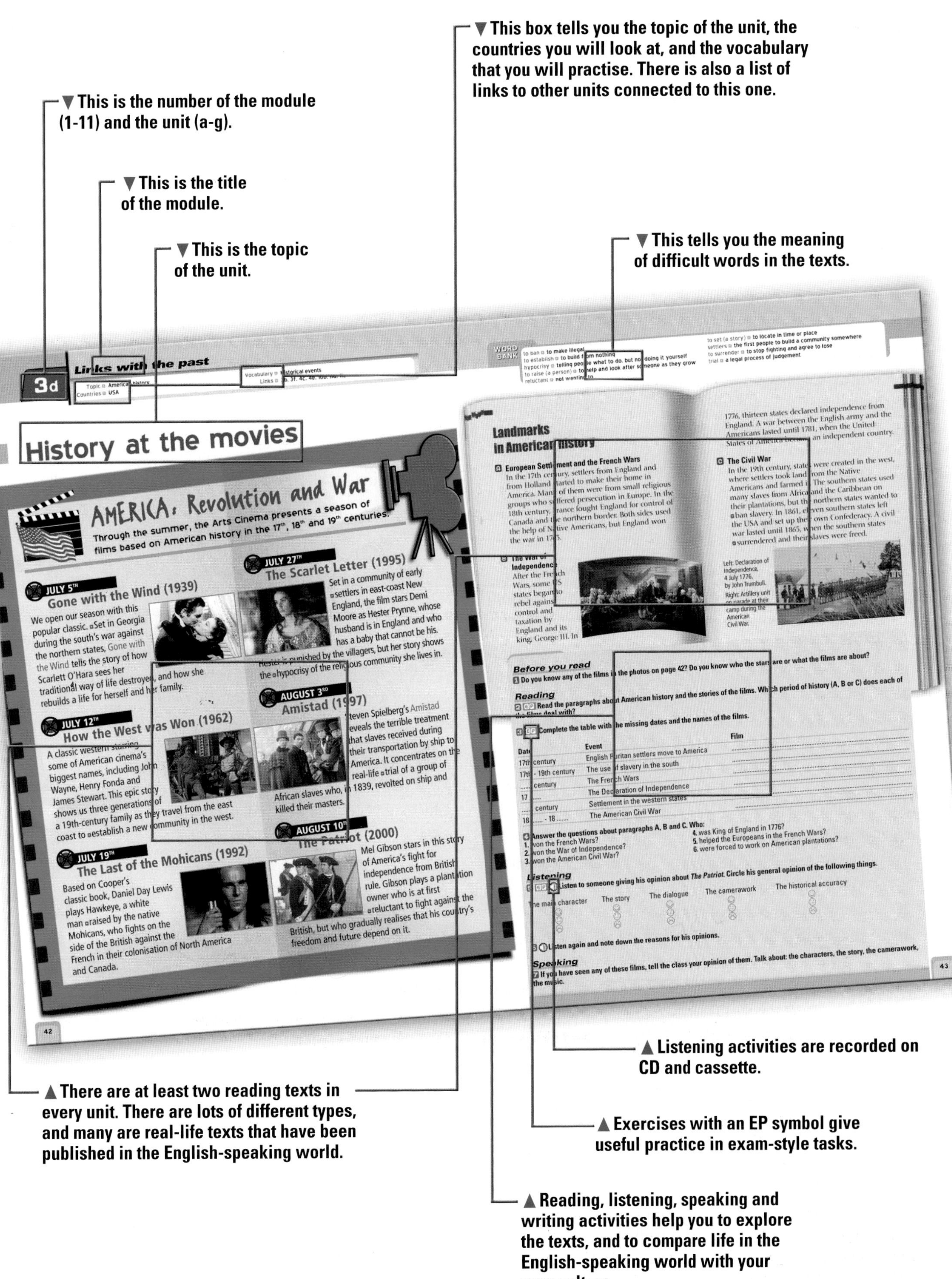

3d
Links with the past
History at the movies
AMERICA: Revolution and War
Through the summer, the Arts Cinema presents a season of films based on American history in the 17th, 18th and 19th centuries.
JULY 5TH Gone with the Wind (1939)
JULY 27TH The Scarlet Letter (1995)
JULY 12TH How the West was Won (1962)
AUGUST 3RD Amistad (1997)
JULY 19TH The Last of the Mohicans (1992)
AUGUST 10TH The Patriot (2000)
Landmarks in American history
Before you read
Reading
Listening
Speaking
42
43

▲ There are at least two reading texts in every unit. There are lots of different types, and many are real-life texts that have been published in the English-speaking world.

▲ Listening activities are recorded on CD and cassette.

▲ Exercises with an EP symbol give useful practice in exam-style tasks.

▲ Reading, listening, speaking and writing activities help you to explore the texts, and to compare life in the English-speaking world with your own culture.

Table of contents

Module 1

Everyday life

IN THIS MODULE YOU WILL READ AND HEAR ABOUT:

- everyday routines in the UK and the USA
- homes in the UK and the USA
- modern families in the UK, the USA and Australia
- food shopping in the UK and the USA
- leisure time in the USA
- everyday life for a teenager in South Africa

1 Which of the photos on this page do you think were taken: in the USA? in the UK? in South Africa?

2 What do you know about homes, schools and food in those countries? How are they different to life in your own country?

Two ordinary days

33, Regent Avenue
Leeds
West Yorkshire
LE3 5DX
UK

3rd March

Dear Tracey

Thanks for your letter – I've finally found an American penfriend! To answer some of your questions: I'm 16. My dad's a computer technician and my mum works in a ■factory. I've got two younger sisters – Kirsty and Laura. You say that you don't know anything about life in the UK, so I'm going to tell you about a typical day in our house.

My mum gets up really early, before 6.00, because she has to leave the house at 6.45. The rest of us get up at 7.00. We don't sit down together for breakfast – it's too chaotic. We leave the house at 8.15. Dad drives to the centre of town, and I walk with my sisters to the bus stop. School starts at 9.00. We have lunch at school at 12.30, and lessons finish at 3.30. Sometimes we walk home. We get home at the same time as Mum – 4.00. She gives us something to eat at about 6.00, because we're ■starving, but Dad doesn't get home until after 7.00, because the traffic can be really bad. She and Dad eat a meal at about 8.00, while we're watching TV or doing our homework. Mum and the girls go to bed at about 10.00 and Dad and I ■stay up watching films on ■SKY. I have to go to bed at 11.00. I don't know why Dad doesn't go to bed then too, because he always falls asleep in the middle of a film and goes to bed at about 1am!

Tell me about a typical day in your house.
You can email me on ssmith.3@freemail.co.uk

Best wishes

Simon

So you're visiting Britain for the first time?

Make sure you follow our EVERYDAY SURVIVAL GUIDE!

1. Look right before you cross the road – British traffic drives on the left.
2. If you're travelling by bus, you don't have to buy a ticket in advance. Just pay on the bus.
3. If you order something to eat or drink in a café, remember to pay for it when you're given it.
4. If someone introduces you to someone new, greet them by saying "Hello". Don't kiss them!
5. Use "please" and "thank you" a lot, to avoid sounding rude.
6. If you want to send postcards, you need to look for a red postbox.
7. You shouldn't have any problems changing your money because banks stay open all day – they don't close at lunch time.
8. Most large shops are open between 10am and 4pm on Sundays.

Before you read

1 Look at the photos of the people and their houses. Which countries do you think they live in? What time do you think they: start school? come home?

Reading

2 Read Simon's letter to Tracey and complete the table with the correct times.

	Simon	Simon's mum	Simon's dad
Get up	....	....	....
Leave the house	....	....	....
Get home	....	....	....
Have dinner	....	....	....
Go to bed	....	....	....

WORD BANK

factory ▪ a building where things are manufactured
pretty ▪ quite
SKY ▪ a satellite TV company
starving ▪ extremely hungry (literally, dying of hunger)
to stay up ▪ to not go to bed

Send Mail: Message Composition

Send Quote Address Attach Options Spelling Save Security Stop

To Simon Smith < ssmith.3@freemail.co.uk>

From Tracey Garofalo <garofalot@aol.com>

Priority: Normal

Subject: Our day

Hi Simon!

OK – you asked for it! Here is a normal day with my family. My mom and dad get up at 6.30, and Mom makes breakfast for us all. My brother Tom and I get up at 7.00. We're lucky, because the school bus stops right outside our door! We leave the house when we see it coming around the corner! That's at eight o'clock. Our school day starts at half past eight, and we eat lunch at school too – at 12 o'clock. Lessons finish at half past three, but we don't usually get home until 5.00, because Tom and I stay at school to do sport and music after the lessons. Dad leaves for work at 7.30 (he's a dentist), and he gets home at 6.00. My mom doesn't work. We all eat dinner together at about half past seven. Then we do homework, play computer games or surf the Internet until bedtime (10.00). We don't watch much TV in our house.

So that's it – ▪pretty boring, huh?

Tracey :)

3 **Now read Tracey's email to Simon and find:**

1. four ways in which their school days are the same.
2. other ways in which their school days are different.

Vocabulary

4 **Read the *Everyday survival guide.* Find words that mean:**

1. to ask for food or drink in a café, restaurant, etc.
2. to tell someone who another person is.
3. to speak to someone, or make a gesture, when you meet for the first time.
4. the opposite of 'polite'.
5. the box that you put letters in when you want to send them.

5 **Which of the tips in the text deal(s) with:**

a. buying things and using money?
b. how to behave with other people?
c. how to use public transport?
d. how to avoid an accident?
e. the postal system?

Listening

6 EP **Listen to a conversation between a foreign student staying in Britain and his host. Tick the topics from the survival guide that he mentions.**

1. driving ☐
2. paying for things in cafés ☐
3. kissing ☐
4. talking politely ☐
5. finding a postbox ☐
6. buying bus tickets ☐
7. bank opening hours ☐
8. shopping on a Sunday ☐

7 **Listen again. Note down how the topics you ticked in exercise 6 are different in the foreign student's country.**

Speaking

8 **How is life in the UK and the USA different or similar to life in your country? Discuss with the class.**

Home swap

Our 'Home Swap' this month concentrates on the Keane family from England, and the Miller family from South Carolina, USA. As usual, our families had a two-week holiday in each other's houses, and we interviewed them at the end of the stay. So how did they ▪cope?

The Millers

George and Sandy Miller and their children, Helen (17) and Daniel (8), had a shock when they first saw the Keanes' three-bedroom ▪terraced house in Gloucester. "It's so small!" said Sandy. Where will we all sleep?"
But inside, the house was more ▪welcoming. "It's bigger than it looks from the outside, and we were pleased to find that there were three bedrooms," said George. But the kids ▪weren't impressed. "Mum and Dad's room was OK, but our bedrooms were really small!" ▪complained Daniel. The Millers found it difficult to live in a house with only one bathroom. At home they have two bathrooms and three toilets! "And we have a study, where we keep the computer, and a playroom in the basement," said Helen. "In Gloucester we had to all stay in the living room together or go to our bedrooms." So was there anything positive about the experience? "The house was beautifully decorated," said Sandy, "and it was very ▪cosy. It was April when we stayed in the house, but the weather was terrible. We were very grateful for the carpets, the central heating and a real fire in the living room." Another good point for George was the garden. "We were very surprised by the large,

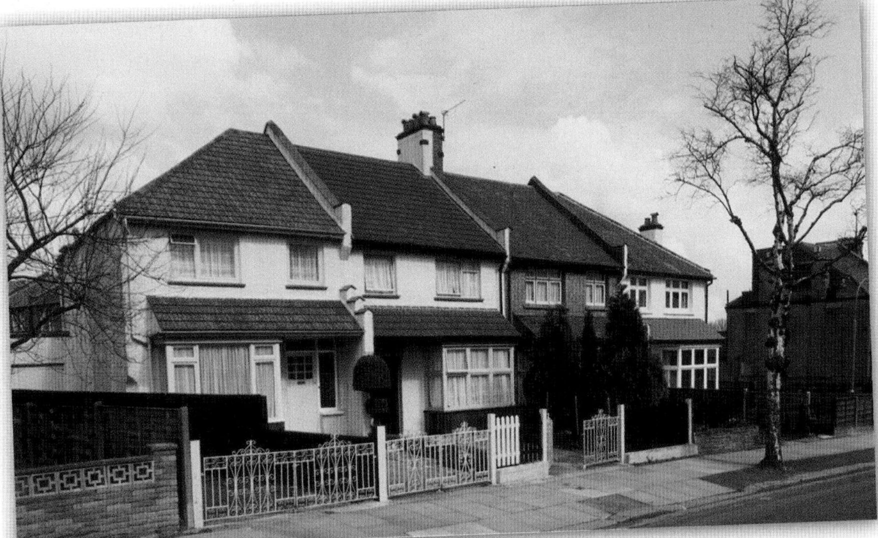

Before you read

1 Which things are common in houses in your country?

- ☐ *a study*
- ☐ *a basement*
- ☐ *carpets*
- ☐ *central heating*
- ☐ *a real fire*
- ☐ *a garden*
- ☐ *a barbecue*
- ☐ *a swimming pool*
- ☐ *an air-conditioning system*
- ☐ *a security system*

Reading

2 EP Read the magazine article. Which house (the English one or the American one) has got:

1. other houses attached to it?
2. the most bedrooms?
3. small bedrooms?
4. a room just for games?
5. a feeling of warmth inside?
6. lots of colours inside?
7. a pretty garden?
8. a lot of electronic systems?

3 EP Match the people with their opinions of the house they stayed in.

1. George Miller
2. Sandy Miller
3. Helen Miller
4. Daniel Miller
5. Tim Keane
6. Katy Keane
7. Bethany Keane

a. "It was strange not having separate rooms for using the computer and playing games."
b. "I loved playing and eating outdoors!"
c. "The house was so big it looked like it belonged to a famous person!"
d. "I was really impressed by the garden."
e. "Two of the bedrooms were too small."
f. "The house was warm and colourful."
g. "I didn't like the garden or the décor much."

WORD BANK

to be impressed ▪ to be have a positive reaction
to cope ▪ to succeed in doing something difficult
to complain ▪ to protest
cosy ▪ warm and comfortable
dull ▪ plain and boring
en-suite (bathroom) ▪ a bathroom that is attached to a bedroom and not shared with the rest of the house
to fiddle with ▪ to try with difficulty to operate something complicated
huge ▪ very big
terraced house ▪ a house that is joined together with others in a row
welcoming ▪ pleasant, making you want to stay
yard ▪ the open area around an American house, consisting of lawn, garden, patio, etc

long garden at the back of the house. We couldn't really enjoy it because of the weather, but it was obvious that the Keanes had put a lot of work into it. It was well designed and full of beautiful plants and flowers. Actually, I think British people have a bit of an obsession with houses and gardens – there are so many TV programmes about them!"

The Keanes

Tim and Katy Keane and their children, Bethany (8), Charles (9) and Joe (16), couldn't believe their luck when they arrived at Washington Drive, Greenville. "The houses were all enormous," said Tim. "I expected to see film stars coming out of them!"

The Millers' house has five bedrooms, a study, two bathrooms and an extra downstairs toilet. "Our bedroom was ▪huge, and it was lovely having an ▪en-suite," said Katy. "It was like staying in a hotel!" "We didn't see much of the children for two weeks!" says Tim. "They were either in the computer room, in the basement or outdoors." The weather was fine for the Keanes' visit to South Carolina, so they made good use of the Millers' ▪yard. "The Millers had sports equipment and a permanent barbecue in their yard," said Joe. "And their neighbours had a swimming pool, which we used once. It was great!" "The children really enjoyed the yard," said Katy, "but I found it a bit ▪dull. I like nice English gardens with lots of flowers. All the Millers had were a few trees." And Katy didn't think much of the décor, either. "It was all very smart and clean," she said, "but it wasn't very colourful. It's obvious that Americans spend more time outdoors than the British! We had good weather, but luckily we didn't need to use the air-conditioning system. The Millers had lots of security systems and alarms that we had to ▪fiddle with every night and morning – that was complicated enough!"

4 Look at the tables of scores for the two houses. Which house scored the most in each category?

Speaking

5 Discuss these questions with a partner.

1. Which house sounds nicer to you – the English house or the American one?
2. Would you like to try living in another family's house for two weeks?
3. How do the Millers' and the Keanes' houses differ from homes in your country?

6 Think about your ideal house. How many rooms would it have? Would it be old or new?

The Millers' scores for the Keanes' house

Space:	4/10
Comfort:	6/10
Decoration:	8/10
Garden:	10/10
Total	**28/40**

The Keanes' scores for the Millers' house

Space:	8/10
Comfort:	7/10
Decoration:	6/10
Garden:	5/10
Total	**26/40**

Topic ◘ Families
Countries ◘ UK, USA and Australia
Vocabulary ◘ Family members
Links ◘ 10d, 10e, 11c, 11i, 11l

Modern families

What is a "traditional" family nowadays? With more and more couples choosing not to get married, and with the number of divorces and second marriages increasing, the idea of the "traditional family" (two married parents, an average of two children, grandparents living nearby) is rapidly disappearing in some countries. Here are some personal examples and statistics from the English-speaking world.

Families	in the USA	in the UK
Marriages that end in divorce	50%	33%
Families with only one parent	25%	25%
Children who live in a single-parent home at some time	50%	33%
Children whose parents aren't married	33%	40%
Single parents who are men	10%	10%

I'm Callum, and I live with my parents in Cambridge, in the east of England. We moved here when I was five because of Dad's job, but my mum comes from the north of England, and Dad comes from Scotland. I've got a grandma in Edinburgh and a granddad in Yorkshire. And I've got two cousins who live near London, because that's where Dad's sister and her husband live. We see my cousins about three times a year, and we go up to Edinburgh every New Year, but I can't remember when I last saw my granddad in Yorkshire. He always sends me presents, though!

My name's Meera, and I live in Wolverhampton, near Birmingham, in England. I live with my parents, my brother and my sister. My grandmother lives next door. My mum was born here in Britain, but my grandmother moved here from India in the 1960s when my dad was a little boy. My dad has two sisters – Auntie Sunita and Auntie Rani. Auntie Sunita lives in the same street as us, and Auntie Rani lives in Birmingham, which is only 15 miles away. They're both married, and I've got five cousins. We see them almost every week. Someone is always visiting our house, or we go to Birmingham to see them. And two years ago we all went to India to see our family there.

Before you read

1 Who do you live with? Do other members of your family live near you, or do you have to travel to see them?

Vocabulary

2 Match the words to the definitions.

1. ex-wife/ex-husband
2. late wife/late husband
3. second wife/second husband
4. stepmother/stepfather
5. stepsister/stepbrother
6. half-sister/half-brother

a. someone that is married to one of your parents, but isn't your parent
b. someone who has the same mother, or the same father, as you, but not both parents
c. someone that you were married to in the past who is now dead
d. the child of someone that is married to one of your parents
e. someone that you were married to in the past but are now divorced from
f. someone that you marry when you have already been married to someone else before

WORD BANK every other ▫ alternate

suburbs ▫ residential areas around the edge of a town or city

I'm Ben, from Portland, Oregon, and my family is a bit complicated! I've got a sister called Ella, but three years ago my parents got divorced and now both of them are re-married. We live with my mom, Julie, and my stepfather, Bob. Bob's got a daughter called Daisy, but she doesn't live with us, she lives with her mom. My father's name is Pete. He and his second wife have just had a baby boy, Charles, so I've got a new half-brother!

My name's Trudi, and I've got a sister called Beth. Our mum and dad are divorced, so we live with just our mum in the ▫ suburbs of Melbourne, Australia. Our dad has an apartment in the centre of town, and we spend ▫ every other weekend there. After school every day we go to our grandma's house and have a meal there, because our mum doesn't finish work until six o'clock. She collects us at half past six, except on Wednesday evenings when we go swimming with our dad.

Reading

3 Read the texts and find out how many people Callum, Meera, Ben and Trudi share a house with.

4 EP Underline the correct alternatives to complete the sentences.

1. Callum's *aunt and uncle / grandparents* live near London.
2. Callum *often / sometimes* sees his cousins.
3. Meera's aunts both live *near / far away.*
4. Meera *often / rarely* sees her cousins.
5. Daisy is Ben's *half-sister / stepsister.*
6. Julie is Pete's *ex-wife / stepmother.*
7. Trudi's mum and dad live *in different places / together.*
8. Trudi *never sees her dad / sees her dad regularly.*

Speaking

5 Read the statistics about families in the USA and the UK. Which of the children in this unit lives:
- **in a single-parent family?**
- **in a stepfamily?**

6 How do you think that the same statistics would be different in your country?

7 What are the advantages and disadvantages of the four family situations in the texts? Discuss with a partner.

Listening

8 Listen to James describing his family situation and answer the questions.

1. Who are: Rachel? Louise? Richard?
2. What is James's opinion of Richard?
3. Who is the oldest child in the house?
4. Why doesn't James like Louise's behaviour?
5. What does their mum say when James and Rachel complain about Louise?
6. What happens when they have an argument with Louise?

Speaking

9 Discuss what you think James should do about his family situation.

What's in your basket?

New markets – shopping for food in the 21st century

A stall at a farmer's market.

Home deliveries are common these days.

Making a long trip to the supermarket and queuing for hours used to be the normal weekly routine for British and American shoppers. But since the 1990s, there is a better way to get your groceries. Supermarket shopping on the Internet has boomed in the UK and the USA.

The major supermarkets have their own websites, and if you order on-line with them, for a small extra sum such as $8/£5 the supermarkets will do your shopping for you and deliver it to your door. If you shop with them regularly, they'll 'remember' your favourite items so you can order them next time without searching for them! These days thousands of people in the UK and the States regularly do their supermarket shopping in this way.

In contrast, in many rural areas of Britain there has been a return to the traditional outdoor market. Farmers' markets, where farmers sell their products directly to the customer, had practically died out in Britain because of the attraction of the large supermarkets, but they have been resurrected recently, both to help farmers make more profits, and to provide customers with 'real' food again, such as fresh meat, eggs, vegetables and preserves. Organic food has become very popular, and some producers run a 'box service', where they deliver a weekly box of fruit and vegetables to your door. Customers can't select the food – they just receive whatever is in season – but it is guaranteed to be fresh and free from chemicals, and now you can often order these on-line too!

Before you read

1 Who shops for food in your family? How often do they go shopping? Where do they buy the food from?

Reading

2 Read the text about food shopping. Which different ways of shopping for food does it mention?

3 EP Underline the correct alternatives in these sentences about the text.

1. It is *cheap / expensive* to order your supermarket shopping on-line and have it delivered.
2. Supermarket websites *can / can't* remember what you have ordered in the past.
3. Farmers' markets *have always been well-supported / have recently become popular again.*
4. Organic food has a *lot of / no* chemicals in it.
5. The *customer / producer* decides what fruit and vegetables are used in a 'box service'.

4 Look at the websites and answer the questions.

1. From how many different countries do the frozen ready meals come? What do you think a ready meal is?
2. How much does a box from the organic food company cost?
3. What sort of food does it contain?
4. What food is depicted on the delicatessen web page?
5. Imagine you are having a picnic at the weekend. Which of the foods would you like to order?

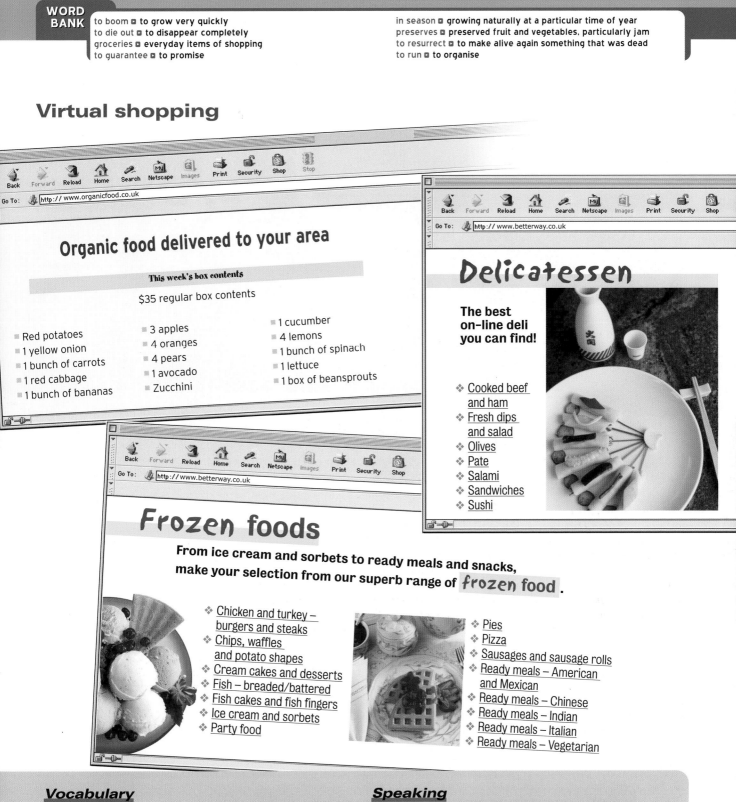

WORD BANK

to boom ▪ to grow very quickly
to die out ▪ to disappear completely
groceries ▪ everyday items of shopping
to guarantee ▪ to promise
in season ▪ growing naturally at a particular time of year
preserves ▪ preserved fruit and vegetables, particularly jam
to resurrect ▪ to make alive again something that was dead
to run ▪ to organise

Virtual shopping

Back Forward Reload Home Search Netscape Images Print Security Shop

Organic food delivered to your area
This week's box contents
$35 regular box contents
Red potatoes
1 yellow onion
1 bunch of carrots
1 red cabbage
1 bunch of bananas

4 oranges

1 avocado
Zucchini
1 cucumber

1 bunch of spinach
1 lettuce
1 box of beansprouts
Go To: http://www.betterway.co.uk
The best on-line deli you can find!
Cooked beef and ham
Fresh dips and salad

Frozen foods

From ice cream and sorbets to ready meals and snacks, make your selection from our superb range of frozen food.

- Chicken and turkey – burgers and steaks
- Chips, waffles and potato shapes
- Cream cakes and desserts
- Fish – breaded/battered
- Fish cakes and fish fingers
- Ice cream and sorbets
- Party food

- Pies
- Pizza
- Sausages and sausage rolls
- Ready meals – American and Mexican
- Ready meals – Chinese
- Ready meals – Indian
- Ready meals – Italian
- Ready meals – Vegetarian

Vocabulary

5 Which of the foods on the websites can you put under these categories?

Meat and fish: __________

Vegetables: __________

Fruit: __________

Bread and pastry: __________

Sweets: __________

6 Write a shopping list in English of twelve of your favourite items of food.

Speaking

7 Discuss in pairs. What are the advantages and disadvantages of getting your food from: a) a supermarket b) a smaller shop or a market? Think about:

> price.
> choice of products.
> quality of products.
> convenience.
> service.
> ecological reasons.
> who gets the profit.

Speaking/Reading

8 Have you ever tried to do virtual shopping? Are there any supermarkets in your area where it is possible to buy on-line? With your teacher's help visit an English-language supermarket website with the shopping list that you compiled in exercise 6.

Topic ▫ Leisure activities
Countries ▫ USA
Vocabulary ▫ Leisure activities
Links ▫ 1a, 5c, 7c, 8e

Time out

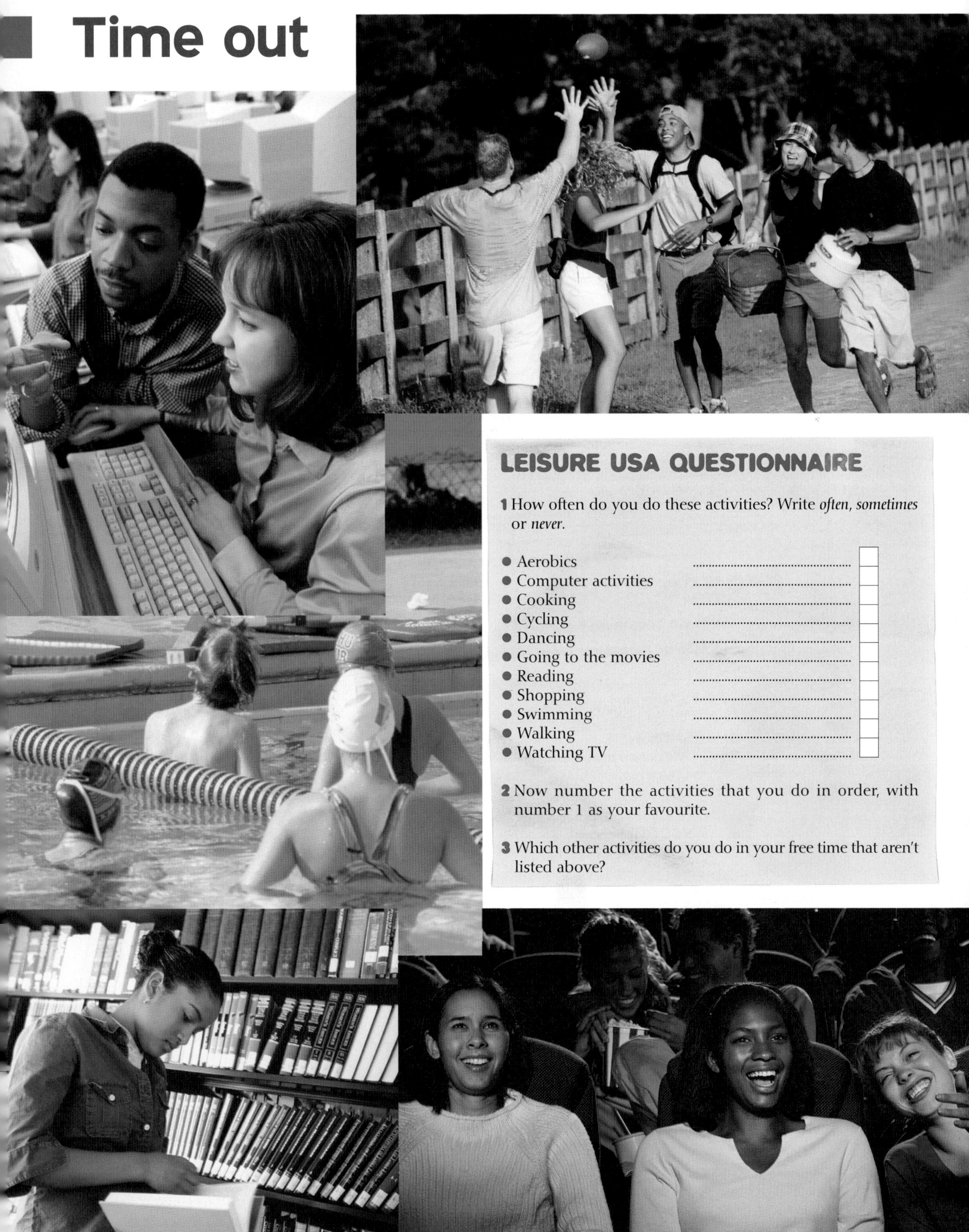

LEISURE USA QUESTIONNAIRE

1 How often do you do these activities? Write *often*, *sometimes* or *never*.

- Aerobics ....
- Computer activities ....
- Cooking ....
- Cycling ....
- Dancing ....
- Going to the movies ....
- Reading ....
- Shopping ....
- Swimming ....
- Walking ....
- Watching TV ....

2 Now number the activities that you do in order, with number 1 as your favourite.

3 Which other activities do you do in your free time that aren't listed above?

WORD BANK

body-molding ▪ that make the body slimmer and more attractive
elite ▪ top, first class
fee ▪ cost
to hail ▪ to welcome
precedent ▪ something that sets an example to be copied in the future
sedentary ▪ sitting down
set ▪ group
skinny ▪ very thin
stationary ▪ not moving, fixed
workout ▪ a session of physical exercise, usually in a gym

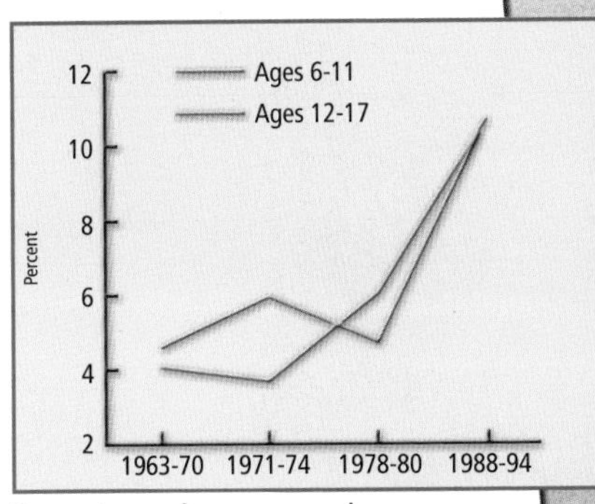

Percentage of young people who are overweight (1963-1994).

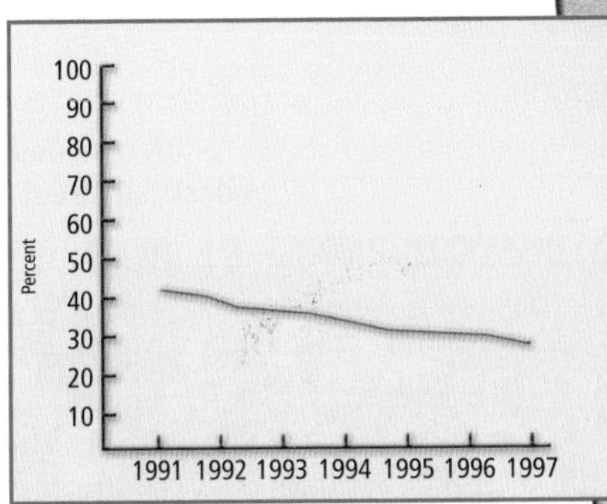

Percentage of teenagers taking daily physical exercise.

The New York Times

Kids need exercise, but what kind?

by Randi Hutter Epstein

Haley Moran-Wollens is not an elite athlete. She is a 13-year-old who, like lots of other teenagers, wants to be fit. And, like a growing number of teenagers whose parents can afford it, she has a personal trainer.

In her case, the trainer is Rodica Vranceanu, who charges $75 an hour for after school workouts at Radu Physical Culture, a gym in Midtown Manhattan.

"I don't want to be the skinniest," Haley said. "I just want to work out. But a lot of people do it for the nice bodies, even at my age."

Though personal training is by no means the norm for American children, a small but growing number of their parents are paying the membership fees to private gyms for aerobics, weight lifting, and body-molding activities once considered for adults only.

At the Spectrum Club in Valencia, California, children aged 13 to 17 can become Teen Fit members. They tend to go for the stationary bicycles and weights, said Cindy Breakfield, sports manager, who added that personal trainers were available for the younger set.

The Eastcoast Athletic Club in Port Washington, N.Y., has a program called Excel, which offers personal training at $45 an hour to children aged 12 to 17, said Christopher Patti, the fitness director.

Some health experts hail the trend, saying that too many children do not get enough exercise. But others disagree.

"It's a sad precedent," said Richard Killingsworth, a scientist at the Centers for Disease Control and Prevention in Atlanta. "We are teaching a behavior that it's O.K. to be sedentary all day except for the one-hour exercise class. In the past decade, our children have lost the idea of what it is to enjoy being young and physically active."

...

Before you listen

1 Look at the questionnaire. Are the activities on the list popular in your country?

2 Complete the questionnaire for yourself.

3 Work with a partner. Decide how you think an American teenage girl would complete the questionnaire.

Listening

4 EP Listen to Kirsten, an American 16-year old, completing the questionnaire and fill in her answers. Are her answers the same as you expected?

Speaking

5 EP Look at the graphs. What do they suggest about the leisure activities of young Americans?

Reading

6 Read the newspaper article and answer the questions.

1. When does Haley go to the gym?
2. How much does her personal trainer cost?
3. How old are the Teen Fit members of the Spectrum Club?
4. How old are the members of the Excel program at the Eastcoast Athletic Club?
5. How much does a personal trainer cost at the Eastcoast Athletic Club?
6. Who is Richard Killingsworth?
7. Why does he disagree with personal training for kids?
8. Do all health experts think that personal training for kids is a bad idea?

Speaking

7 With a partner, write five questions designed to find out if your classmates enjoy sports, and how much exercise they get each week. Ask your questions to the class and note down everyone's answers. Then present the results in the form of graphs or diagrams.

Topic ▪ Everyday life in South Africa
Countries ▪ South Africa
Vocabulary ▪ Everyday activities
Links ▪ 2f, 7a

English everywhere South Africa

PRETORIA
JOHANNESBURG
DURBAN
BLOEMFONTEIN
CAPE TOWN

A crowded pedestrian street.

Multi-racial colleges are quite common these days.

Panoramic view of Cape Town, one of South Africa's capitals.

South African landscape.

INFORMATION FILE

South Africa

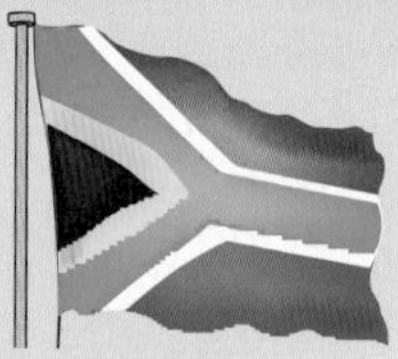

Total area ▪ 1.2 million sq. km
Total population ▪ 43 million
Ethnic mix ▪ 75% Black
14% White Afrikaans
3% Indian
Capital ▪ Pretoria (government)
Cape Town + Bloemfontein (law)
Popul. of capital ▪ Pretoria: 650,000
Cape Town: 1,000,000
Bloemfontein: 150,000
Government ▪ A republic with a president
Climate ▪ West coast: dry and arid
East coast: wetter, with forest vegetation

Before you read

1 Do you know anything about South Africa? Can you name any South African cities or any famous South Africans? What sports is the country famous for?

Reading

2 Look at the map and read the Information File on South Africa, then answer the questions.

1. What is the second biggest ethnic group in South Africa?
2. How many capital cities does South Africa have?
3. Which is the largest of the capital cities?
4. Where is it in the country?
5. Which part of South Africa gets the most rain?

3 Read the website. Complete the table with the correct information about Izak.

WORD BANK

apartheid ▪ the political system in South Africa from 1948-1994, involving an all-white government and almost complete racial segregation

multi-racial ▪ involving people from different ethnic groups

suburbs ▪ residential areas outside cities

Back Forward Reload Home Search Netscape Images Print Security Shop Stop

Go To: http:// www.swanepoel.co.za

Hi! My name's Izak Ford. I go to Swanepoel Boys School in the ▪suburbs of Cape Town, and this is my school's website. Here's a picture of one of our classrooms. There are 25 students in my class. Before 1994, when we had the ▪apartheid system, black students and white students were educated separately, but my school is now ▪multi-racial.

We go to school from Monday to Friday. Our school day starts at 7.40 am, so I get up at about 6 o'clock, but that's OK, because it's hot and sunny then. We have to wear a uniform. I hate it! We study the usual subjects – Science, History, Geography, etc., but we also study Afrikaans (which is our first language), English and Xhosa, a local African language. We have two short breaks, one at half past ten and one at half past twelve. The school day finishes at 2.15. After lessons we can do sports such as rugby, hockey and swimming, or artistic activities like music and photography. In the evening we do homework and watch TV. My favourite shows are ER and Friends. For dinner we always have meat or chicken with rice and vegetables such as sweet potato. At the weekends we go to Tyger Valley, which is a huge shopping mall in Cape Town, and we often have braais (barbecues). South Africans eat a lot of meat!

Tell me about your typical day!

You can email me at i.ford@netmail.co.za

Name:	Izak Ford
Nationality:	South African
Town/City:	....
Name of school:	....
Number of schooldays per week:	....
School day:	From .... a.m. to .... p.m.
First language:	....
Other languages studied:	....
Evening activities:	....
Favourite TV programmes:	....
Usual dinner:	....
Weekend activities:	....

4 Answer the questions.

1. Is Izak's school for white students only?
2. What time does Izak get up?
3. What does he think of his school uniform?
4. When does he have breaks at school?
5. What can students do at his school after lessons?
6. What is a braai?

Writing

5 Fill in the table in exercise 3 for yourself. What similarities and what differences are there between you and Izak?

6 In groups, write a text to go on a website for your school. Describe your school and the daily routine there. Remember to mention everything that might sound interesting or different to a student from another country.

Grammar ◘ Present tense review (present simple, present continuous, present perfect)
Skills ◘ Using sequencing words to order sentences in a paragraph

Language & Culture

Diana's day

My name's Diana. I'm 17 years old and I live with my mum in Brighton on the south coast of England.
I'm studying English, French and Spanish. I've just started Spanish this year and I'm really enjoying it!
My day starts at 7.00am. First, I get up and I have a shower. Then my mum and I have breakfast together. I usually have toast and a cup of coffee for breakfast and my mum has a cup of tea and a bowl of cereal.
My mum works in an office in town and she leaves for work at 8.15am. I leave at 8.30am and walk to the bus stop. I usually catch a bus at about 8.40am and it's only a ten minute ride to college. My classes start at 9.00am and finish at 3.30pm. After my classes, I usually go to the library for about an hour and after that I walk home.
I get home at about 5.00pm and I usually prepare a meal for my mum and me. She gets back at about 6.30pm and we eat our meal together.
After our meal, I usually do my assignments while my mum's doing the washing up. I've just begun an assignment on the French Revolution which is quite interesting. Then I text my friends or call them on my mobile for a chat. Finally, I go to bed between 11.00 and 11.30 every night but sometimes I'm still texting at midnight!

GRAMMAR

1 Read the text quickly. How is Diana's day different to yours?

2 Look at the verbs highlighted in the text. Write them in the correct column in the table. Then say why each tense is used each time.

Present simple	Present continuous	Present perfect
live	....	....
....	....	....
....	....	
....	....	
....		
....		

3 Present simple, present continuous or present perfect? Complete the text with the correct form of the verbs in brackets.

My school day (1) *starts* (start) at 8.00am but I (2) ...... (get up) at 6.30am. First, I (3) ...... (get dressed) and then I (4) ...... (have) breakfast. Every day I (5) ...... (catch) a bus to school. It (6) ...... (leave) at 7.30am.
This year I'm in 10th grade and I (7) ...... (study) a lot of subjects. I (8) ...... (just start) Italian this year. It (9) ...... (be) really interesting. School (10) ...... (finish) at 1.00pm and I always (11) ...... (have) lunch with my friends.
Sometimes we (12) ...... (play) football while we (13) ...... (wait) for the school bus. I (14) ...... (just win) a football competition with my school team.

SKILLS

4 Read the text and underline the sequencing words (*First* ..., etc). What do you think the man's job is?

My dad gets up every day at 4.00am.
First he has a shower and puts on his uniform. Then he goes downstairs and has breakfast. He always has a cooked breakfast with bacon, eggs, sausages and beans!
Next, he checks his bike and makes sure there are no problems.
After that, he cycles to work and sorts everything for the day.
Finally, he cycles round lots of houses and delivers things to people.

5 Put the sentences a-e in the correct order to make a paragraph. Then rewrite the paragraph using these sequencers to improve it.

After that   Finally   First   Next   Then

a. I go to bed at midnight.
b. I drive to work.
c. I get dressed and have breakfast.
d. I get up at 7.30am.
e. I work until 5.30pm.

6 Choose your favourite popstar, film star or sports star. Imagine their daily routine and write a paragraph about it. Remember to use sequencers.

Module 2

Habitats and homelands

IN THIS MODULE YOU WILL READ AND HEAR ABOUT:

- the four nations of the United Kingdom
- small and remote British islands
- the natural wonders of the USA and Canada
- extreme weather in the USA and Australia
- life in London and in an English village
- popular music in the USA, Ireland, Jamaica and South Africa
- a British city

1 Look at the pictures of the different environments. Which one do you think is of: the USA? Australia? England? Scotland?

2 In groups, make a list of as many British cities and American states as you can think of. Then compare lists. Which group has the most?

Topic ▪ British national identity
Countries ▪ UK
Vocabulary ▪ National symbols
Links ▪ 2b, 3a, 4a, 4e, 5f, 6e, 9f, 11a

Four nations

INFORMATION FILE

Scotland

Total population ▪ 5 million
Capital ▪ Edinburgh
National day ▪ November 30th (St Andrew's Day)
National symbols ▪ ▪Thistle, ▪tartan

Northern Ireland

In 1922 the south of Ireland was made independent from Great Britain (England, Scotland and Wales) and became the Republic of Ireland. Northern Ireland remained joined politically to Britain, and the United Kingdom was born. While this was a popular decision with most Irish Protestants, it was unpopular with most of the Catholic population, who wished Ireland to remain a united country. Conflict between these two groups came to crisis point in the 1970s with the terrorist activities of the IRA and the arrival of British soldiers. Even today, the Northern Irish population remains divided between Unionists (or Loyalists), who want to remain a part of the United Kingdom, and Republicans, who oppose it.

INFORMATION FILE

England

Total population ▪ 49 million
Capital ▪ London
National day ▪ April 23rd (St George's Day)
National symbols ▪ Red rose, lion, bulldog

INFORMATION FILE

Wales

Total population ▪ 2.5 million
Capital ▪ Cardiff
National day ▪ March 1st (St David's Day)
National symbols ▪ Dragon, ▪leek, ▪daffodil

Before you read

1 What's the difference between England, Great Britain and the UK?

Vocabulary

2 List the national symbols from the Information Files under these categories.

Plants:

Real animals:

Mythical animals:

Abstract patterns:

Reading

3 EP Read the Information Files on England, Scotland and Wales. Which of the countries:

1. has the largest/smallest population?
2. has a national day in the spring?
3. has a national day in the autumn?
4. has a blue and white flag?
5. has a red, green and white flag?

4 Read the text about Northern Ireland and answer the questions.

1. How many countries are there in Great Britain?
2. When did the south of Ireland become independent from Britain?
3. How many countries are in the UK?
4. What do Northern Irish Republicans want?
5. What do Northern Irish Unionists want?

Speaking

5 Look at the photos in the magazine article. What specific countries do the people in each photo come from? How can you tell?

Reading

6 EP Read the article. Match the beginnings and the endings of the sentences.

1. Welsh and Scottish sportspeople get annoyed when
2. If England and Scotland play a rugby match,
3. People enjoy St Andrew's Day and St David's Day now, but
4. Some buildings in England used to display the Union Jack, but now

WORD BANK

daffodil ▪ yellow spring flower (narcissus)
leek ▪ winter vegetable from the onion family
pitch ▪ sports field
tartan ▪ checked, coloured pattern used on textiles
thistle ▪ plant with sharp leaves and a purple flower
Union Jack ▪ the red, white and blue flag of the United Kingdom

Who are the British?

The UK is a confused nation when it comes to national identity, especially in relation to major sporting events. Commentators proudly refer to the country's internationally successful sportspeople as 'English' if they come specifically from England. Welsh and Scottish athletes, however, are usually given the general label 'British' without any recognition of their individual homelands.

But it's when the countries compete individually, especially against each other, that the idea of a 'united kingdom' becomes completely lost. At football and rugby matches there has been a strong revival of the individual flags, songs and symbols of England, Scotland and Wales – and there often isn't a ▪Union Jack to be seen.

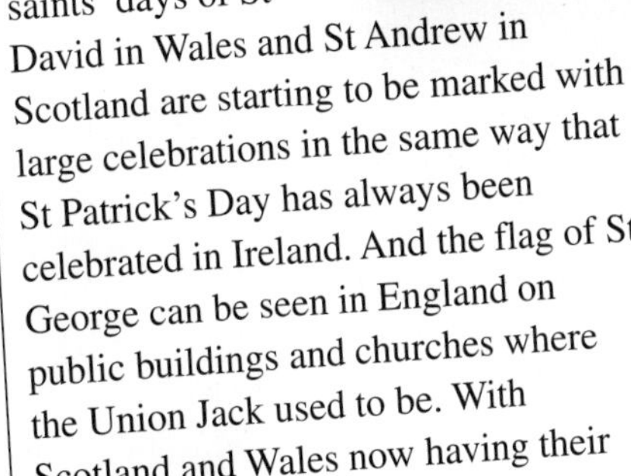

Away from the sports ▪pitch, the national saints' days of St David in Wales and St Andrew in Scotland are starting to be marked with large celebrations in the same way that St Patrick's Day has always been celebrated in Ireland. And the flag of St George can be seen in England on public buildings and churches where the Union Jack used to be. With Scotland and Wales now having their own parliaments, there is even extreme talk of an 'English Independence Movement', and some people are wondering if the United Kingdom will last into the next century.

a. they display their own symbols and flags, not British ones.
b. they show the English flag.
c. they aren't referred to as 'Scottish' or 'Welsh'.
d. they didn't use to celebrate them much.

Listening

7 EP **Listen to teenagers from each of the four countries. Note down where they come from and their ages.**

Name	Country	Age
Dean	....	....
Claire	....	....
Jason	....	....
Emma	....	....

8 **Listen again. Who feels that they are:**

British? ....

Irish? ....

English? ....

Scottish? ....

European? ....

Welsh? ....

Writing

9 **Write a paragraph about your country. Write about the national flag, the national day and the national symbols. Is your country 'united', or are there some parts of it that have a separate identity?**

Topic ▫ The geography of the smaller British islands
Countries ▫ UK
Vocabulary ▫ Features of a landscape
Links ▫ 2a, 3c, 5f, 6b, 7e

British islands

Did you know that 'the British Isles' doesn't just mean the two large islands of Britain and Ireland, but hundreds of other small islands around their coasts? Many of these islands are inhabited, and a lot of them are popular tourist destinations.

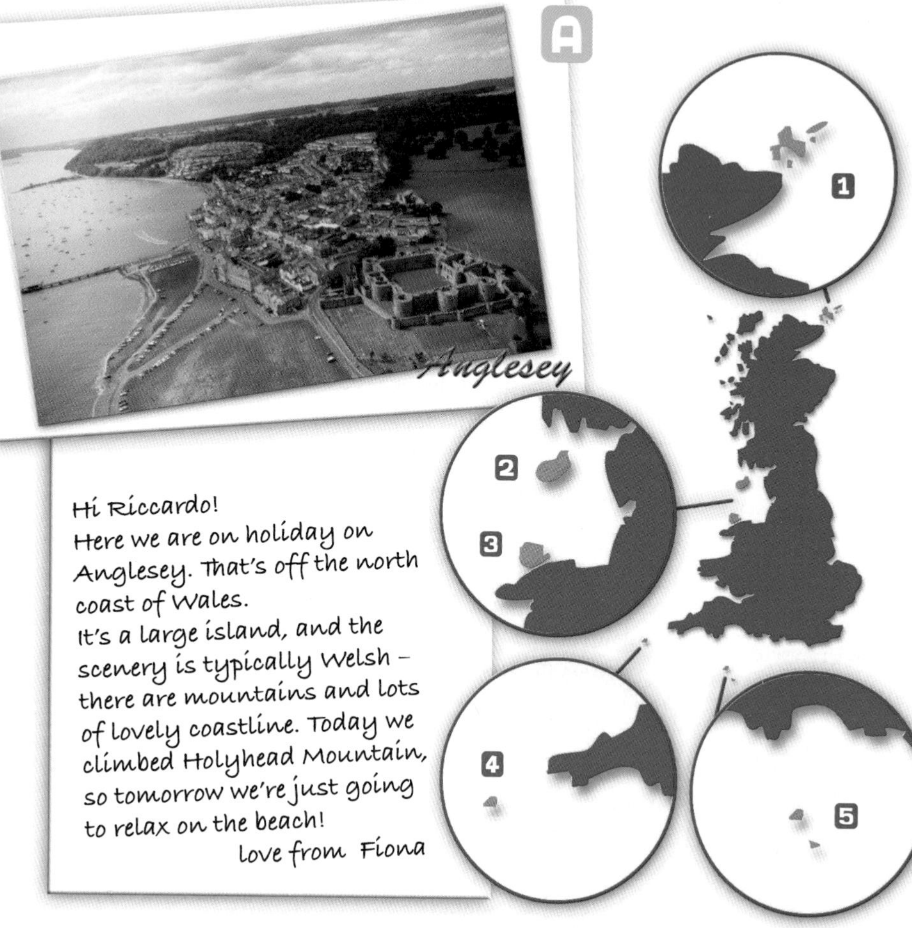

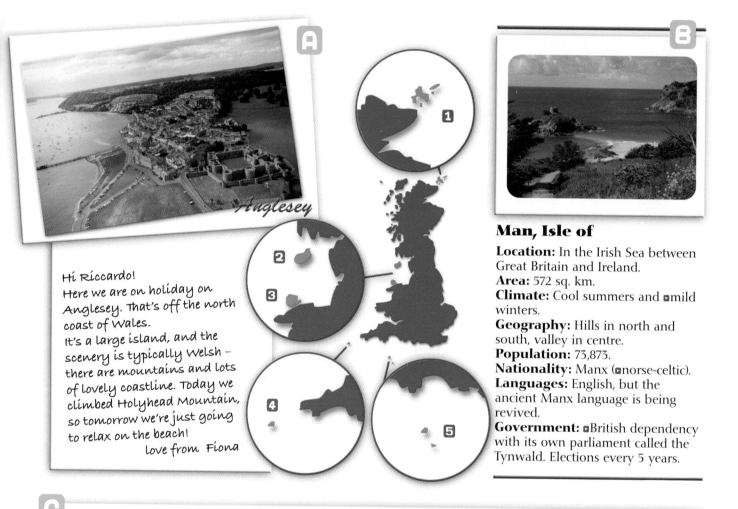

Hi Riccardo!
Here we are on holiday on Anglesey. That's off the north coast of Wales.
It's a large island, and the scenery is typically Welsh – there are mountains and lots of lovely coastline. Today we climbed Holyhead Mountain, so tomorrow we're just going to relax on the beach!
Love from Fiona

B

Man, Isle of

Location: In the Irish Sea between Great Britain and Ireland.
Area: 572 sq. km.
Climate: Cool summers and ▫mild winters.
Geography: Hills in north and south, valley in centre.
Population: 73,873.
Nationality: Manx (▫norse-celtic).
Languages: English, but the ancient Manx language is being revived.
Government: ▫British dependency with its own parliament called the Tynwald. Elections every 5 years.

C

Daily flights to the Scilly Isles

The Scilly Isles, with their subtropical climate and exotic flowers, are only 28 miles from Cornwall, and are the most southwesterly point of the British Isles. Enjoy the 20-minute flight from Penzance to St Mary's, the largest island, in one of our helicopters.

Why not make a day of it?

After exploring St Mary's, you could take a boat to visit the famous **tropical gardens** and ▫shipwreck museum on the island of Tresco.

Flight times	**Penzance–St Mary's: every half hour from 7.30 to 18.00** **St Mary's–Penzance: every half hour from 8.00 to 18.30**
▫Fares	**£80 adult, £60 child/▫OAP (day return)**

WORD BANK

British dependency ▫ a territory that has its own elections and government, but that is ruled by Britain
fare ▫ the price of a journey
mild ▫ warm and comfortable
norse ▫ from ancient Scandinavia
OAP ▫ old age pensioner
shipwreck ▫ the ruins of a ship that has been destroyed at sea
to slope ▫ to have an incline from a high point to a low point
unmissable ▫ something that you must definitely see

D

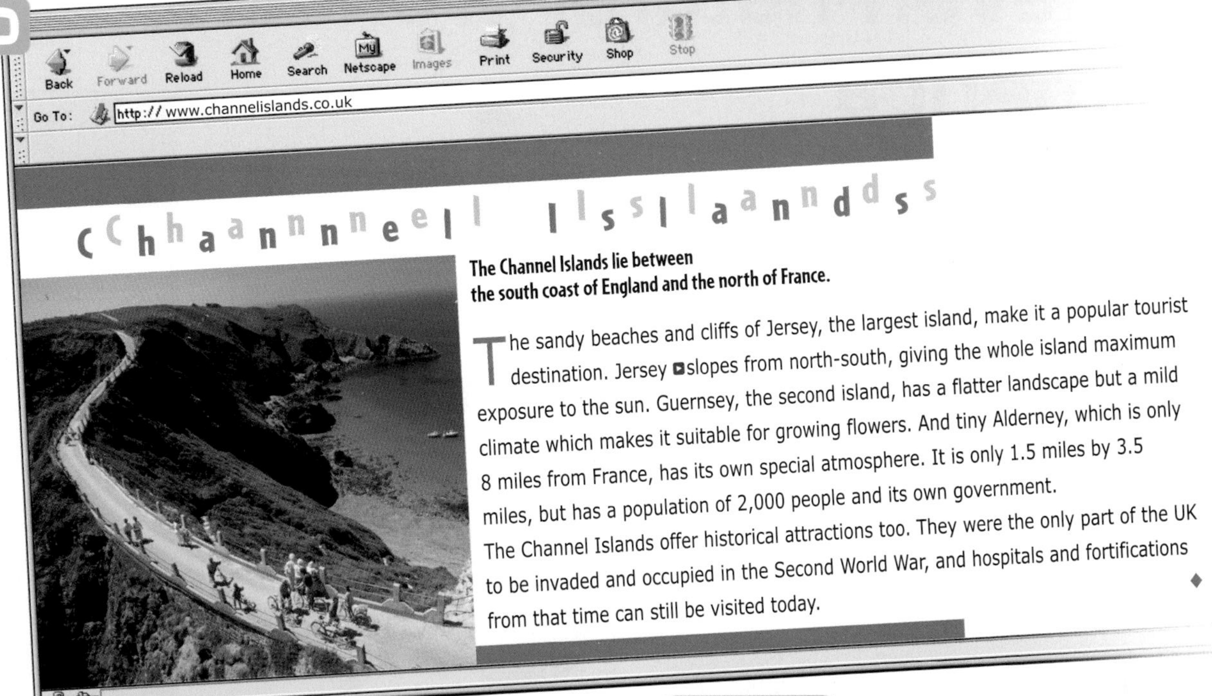

Channel Islands

The Channel Islands lie between the south coast of England and the north of France.

The sandy beaches and cliffs of Jersey, the largest island, make it a popular tourist destination. Jersey ▫slopes from north-south, giving the whole island maximum exposure to the sun. Guernsey, the second island, has a flatter landscape but a mild climate which makes it suitable for growing flowers. And tiny Alderney, which is only 8 miles from France, has its own special atmosphere. It is only 1.5 miles by 3.5 miles, but has a population of 2,000 people and its own government.

The Channel Islands offer historical attractions too. They were the only part of the UK to be invaded and occupied in the Second World War, and hospitals and fortifications from that time can still be visited today.

E

The Orkney Islands

Travel information: Be warned – the Orkney Islands, off the north-east coast of Scotland, are very remote!

Air: Flights operate from Glasgow (90 mins), Edinburgh (90 mins) or Aberdeen (45 mins). There are plenty of internal flights within the islands.

Sea: Ferries leave Aberdeen in the evening and arrive in Lerwick in the morning.

The geography of the Orkneys is flat and rather uninteresting, and the climate is wet, but the islands' ancient history make them an ▫unmissable destination. There are 1,000 prehistoric monuments here – the most in Europe. And rare birds and flowers are a popular attraction in spring and summer too.

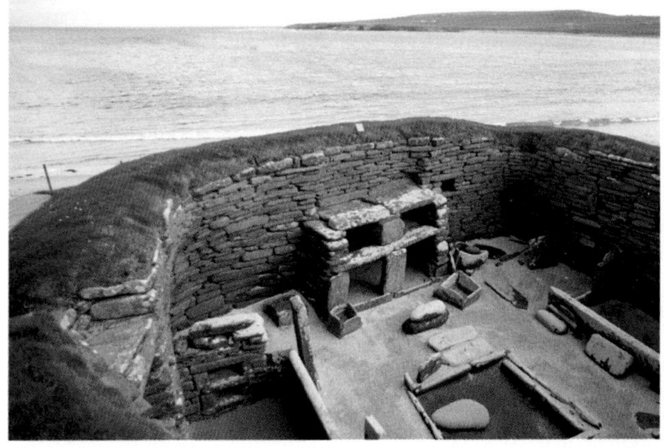

Vocabulary

1 Find these items in the photos.

beaches cliffs hills a prehistoric monument tropical plants a castle

Before you read

2 EP Look at the texts quickly. Which text has come from:

1. an encyclopedia?
2. an advertising leaflet?
3. a postcard?
4. a guidebook?
5. a website?

Reading

3 Read the texts. What are the names of the islands, or groups of islands, that have been enlarged on the map (1-5)?

4 EP Which texts mention:

1. the history of the islands?
2. the climate of the islands?
3. the wildlife of the islands?
4. transport to the islands?
5. the government of the islands?

5 EP Are these sentences true or false?

1. The helicopter flight from Penzance to the Scilly Isles is short.
2. Tresco is the biggest of the Scilly Isles.
3. The Isle of Man is to the east of Great Britain.
4. The Isle of Man has its own language and culture.
5. The Channel Islands are in Scotland.
6. Guernsey has a lot of mountains.
7. You can fly between the different Orkney Islands.
8. There are many ancient sites on the Orkneys.

Speaking

6 Which of the islands you would most like to visit and why? Which other places in Britain would you like to visit?

I'd like to go...
I'd also like to visit...

Writing

7 Write a postcard to an English-speaking friend from one of the islands you've read about, or from any other island that you know.

The seven natural wonders of America

2 Giant Redwood and Bristlecone Pine Trees (California)

General Sherman, a giant redwood tree in the Sequoia National Park measuring 84 metres tall, is the largest plant in the world. It is also 3,000 years old, but it isn't the oldest tree in the world! That's also in California. The bristlecone pine grows in the White Mountains, and it is the oldest living thing on earth. The most famous, named Methuselah, is over 4,000 years old.

1 Death Valley (California)

Death Valley is a 250 km valley between two Californian mountain ■ranges. It is the hottest and the lowest place in the USA, and at one famous point – Badwater Basin – you arrive at the lowest place in the western hemisphere (86 metres below sea level). Summer temperatures in Death Valley can reach 54 °C, and for several months of the year the average night-time temperature is over 27 °C.

3 The Grand Canyon (Arizona)

The Grand Canyon, eroded over thousands of years by the Colorado River and its ■tributaries, is 400 km long. It is 2,000 metres deep at its deepest point and 30 km wide at its widest point. It is one of the most important geological sites in the world (some of the rocks are over 1,800 million years old) and it is home to a great diversity of wildlife.

Before you read

1 Look at the photos. Do you recognise any of these places? Can you locate numbers 3, 5, 6 and 7 on the map?

Vocabulary

2 Put the adjectives into six pairs of opposites.

deep high large long low narrow shallow short short small tall wide

Reading

3 EP Read the texts quickly. Which of the natural wonders:

1. are partly in Canada?
2. are further north than Canada?
3. are in California?
4. consist entirely of water?

4 Read the texts again. Complete the tables with the correct statistics.

Length	
Death Valley:	....
Grand Canyon:	....

Depth	
Death Valley:	....
Grand Canyon:	....

Height	
General Sherman:	....
Old Faithful:	....
Niagara Falls:	....

Width	
Grand Canyon:	....

Age	
General Sherman:	....
Methuselah:	....
Oldest rocks in the Grand Canyon:	....

Size	
Lake Superior:	....

WORD BANK

to erupt ▫ to eject something violently
geyser ▫ a spring that ejects steam and hot water
glacier ▫ a large mass of ice
range ▫ a group of mountains
spring ▫ where water comes up from below the ground, forming the start of a river
tributary ▫ a small river that flows into a larger river
wilderness ▫ a wild, natural place

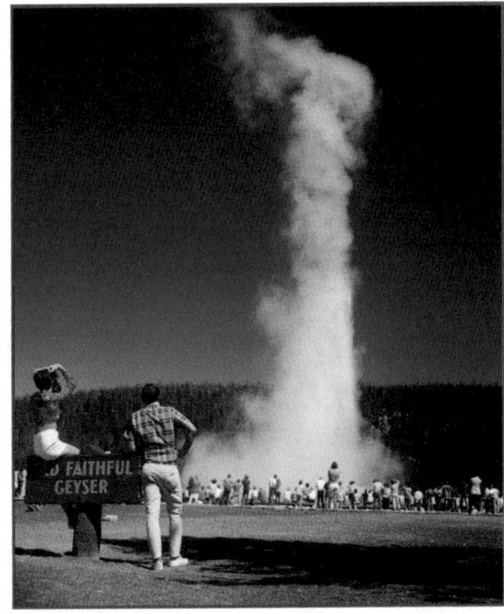

4 Old Faithful (Idaho)

Much of the Yellowstone National Park (which extends into Idaho, Montana and Wyoming) is volcanic rock, and there are over 10,000 ▫geysers and hot ▫springs in the park – the biggest concentration in the world. The most famous geyser, called Old Faithful, ▫erupts about every 75 minutes. The eruptions last for 1-5 minutes, and shoot hot water up to 50 metres in the air.

6 Glacier Bay (Alaska)

▫Glacier Bay is a ▫wilderness of mountains, glaciers, estuaries, beaches and lakes which was covered by ice only 200 years ago. The glaciers of Glacier Bay are still retreating, revealing new landscapes every few years. Glacier Bay is now a nature reserve and is used extensively for scientific research.

5 The Great Lakes (Michigan, Wisconsin, Minnesota and Ontario, Canada)

The Great Lakes (Lakes Superior, Michigan, Huron, Erie and Ontario) form the largest system of fresh water on earth, containing 18% of the world's supply. Lake Superior is the largest and the deepest. It has the largest surface area of any freshwater lake in the world (81,000 sq. km) and holds enough water to cover the entire continents of North and South America with a third of a metre of water.

7 Niagara Falls (New York State and Ontario, Canada)

The Niagara Falls are formed where the Niagara River flows between Lake Erie and Lake Ontario. There are two main waterfalls: the Horseshoe Falls in Canada and the American Falls in the USA. The falls are 55 metres high, and 160,000 cubic metres of water flows over them every minute.

Speaking

5 How can humans pose a danger to natural features such as the ones in this unit?

Listening

6 EP You are going to hear a ranger talking about the negative effects of tourism on the Grand Canyon. Guess which of the following environmental problems he will talk about, then listen and see if you were right.

- ☐ *litter*
- ☐ *fires*
- ☐ *danger to animals*
- ☐ *erosion of paths*
- ☐ *noise*
- ☐ *traffic*
- ☐ *vandalism*

7 Listen again and answer the questions.

1. How many people visit the Grand Canyon each year?
2. What two problems can pollution cause in the canyon?
3. Which two months does the ranger say are particularly hot and dry?
4. What are two ways in which visitors start fires?
5. Why should visitors not feed the animals in the canyon (two reasons)?

Speaking

8 Discuss in pairs. What are the most-visited attractions in your country (natural or man-made)? Are they being damaged by tourism? Is anything being done to preserve them?

Climate extremes

How does the weather affect your day-to-day life? Does it influence what clothes you put on? Whether you put an umbrella in your bag or not? In certain parts of the world, people's actual survival depends on the way that they adapt their lives to the extreme weather conditions of their environments.

Extreme heat

Temperatures in the Australian outback – the central desert area of Australia – can often exceed 50 °C for the summer months. New houses are sometimes specifically situated towards the east or west, to avoid the summer sun. Their roofs are insulated to stop heat getting in, and their wood is specially treated to resist the heat. Due to the strength of the sun over this part of the world, Australia has the highest rate of skin cancer in the world. Since 1981, there has been an official campaign by the Australian government to encourage Australians to protect their skin from the sun. Forest fires are another result of consistently high temperatures. These have become more and more common in the past few years, even happening around the city of Sydney.

Snow and extreme cold

Valdez in Northern Alaska is used to battling against the elements. The town was relocated in 1964 after an earthquake and tidal wave completely destroyed it, and it currently has the record snowfall for the whole continent of North America – 7.7 metres per year. Snow and ice are part of daily life for Alaskans. Many towns, including the state capital Juneau, are accessible only by sea or by air, as roads either don't exist or are blocked for most of the year. Some houses are built without excavating any foundations, and most have special strong roofs to support the snow, and features such as windows that only open inwards so that they aren't ripped off by the Arctic wind.

Global temperature rise due to greenhouse gas emissions

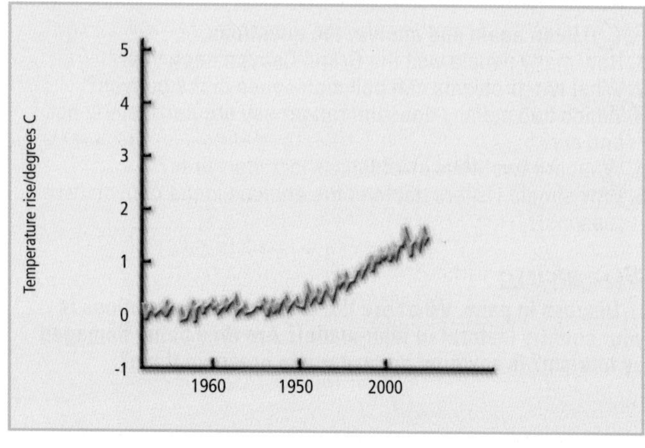

Change in sea level in Newlyn, Cornwall, UK

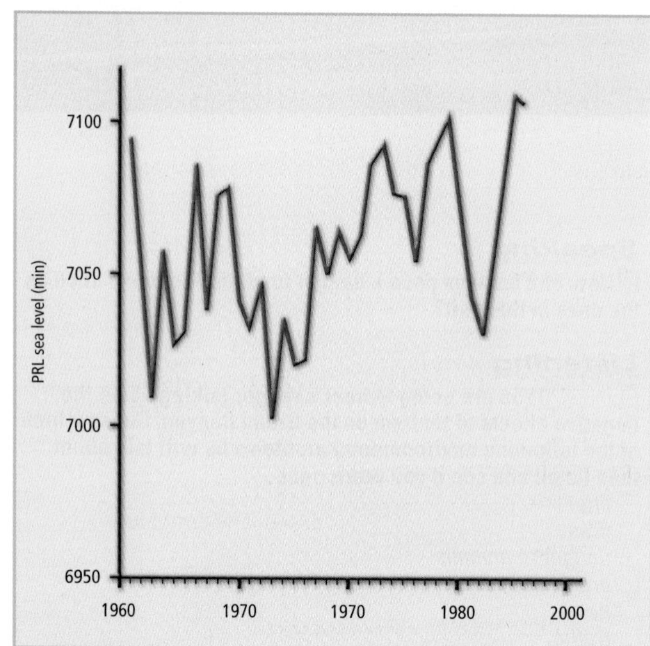

WORD BANK

- cellar ▫ underground room
- concrete ▫ cement + sand + water
- crust ▫ hard outer covering
- funnel ▫ a utensil with a wide mouth that gradually reduces to a small hole
- inwards ▫ towards the interior of something
- on average ▫ normally
- to pull down ▫ to destroy
- to rip ▫ to tear one thing violently from another
- to shelter ▫ to cover and protect yourself
- shutter ▫ a cover for a window
- to spin ▫ to turn quickly
- worth ▫ value

Hurricanes

Thanks to its coastal location and tropical climate, Florida is the American state most regularly hit by hurricanes. ▫On average a hurricane happens along the Florida coast every 3 years. Most cause some damage to buildings and vehicles but some, such as Hurricane Andrew in 1992, can cause devastation. Andrew was the worst hurricane in America's history and caused 65 deaths and $26 billion ▫worth of damage to property. Not surprisingly, Floridans spend a lot of money protecting their homes from hurricane damage. They prefer ▫concrete walls to wooden or metal constructions, and most windows and doors have hurricane ▫shutters. Some new houses are also being built with special reinforced rooms for ▫sheltering from hurricanes.

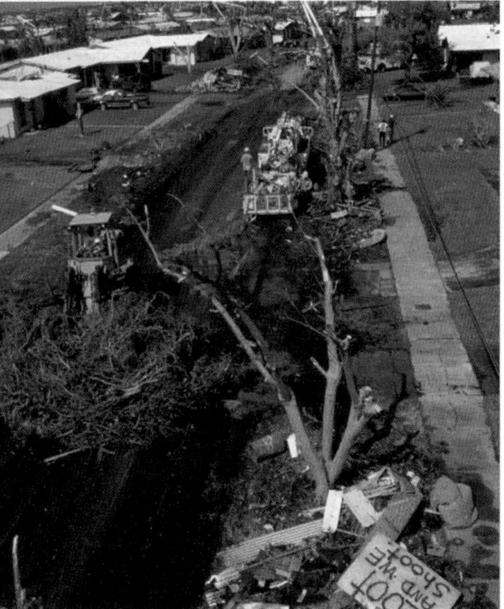

Tornadoes

Tornadoes happen during storms when warm air and strong winds begin to ▫spin upwards. These distinct ▫funnel-shaped winds can cause great damage along their paths. Central states such as Kansas and Oklahoma see the majority of the USA's tornadoes. In fact, there is a famous tornado 'route' through ten midwestern states which is known as 'Tornado Alley'. Homes in that area often have storm ▫cellars where families can shelter from the weather.

Earthquakes

The San Andreas Fault is a break in the Earth's ▫crust that lies underneath California, causing several small earthquakes every year. Most of the earthquakes are not even noticeable, and the last large one happened in 1994. However, a catastrophic earthquake nearly destroyed San Francisco in 1906. Scientists say that it is possible that another massive earthquake may happen in the future, but they predict that they will recognise the warning signs years before it happens. As a precaution against earthquakes, some older buildings in Californian cities are being ▫pulled down, and there is very little new building along the fault line itself.

Vocabulary

1 Match the natural disasters to their definitions.

1. earthquake
2. hurricane
3. tidal wave
4. tornado

a. a storm with severe winds, often in coastal areas
b. a storm where winds turn around a central point
c. movement of the surface of the earth, caused by activity below the surface
d. a gigantic sea wave

2 Read the text quickly and note down all the words that you can find connected to weather.

Reading

3 EP Read the text again and match the weather conditions to the geographical areas.

1. earthquakes
2. extreme heat and forest fires
3. hurricanes
4. snow and extreme cold
5. tornadoes

a. Australia
b. central USA
c. northern USA
d. southeastern coast of the USA
e. western coast of the USA

4 Answer the questions about the text.

1. What health problem does the sun cause in Australia?
2. Why was Valdez rebuilt in the 1960s?
3. Can you drive to the state capital of Alaska?
4. How often do hurricanes hit the Florida coast, on average?
5. Where do most of the USA's tornadoes happen?
6. When was the last serious earthquake in California?
7. Why do scientists say that people should not panic about a future major earthquake in California?

5 How are houses and house-building in certain areas of the USA and Australia influenced by the extreme weather conditions there?

Speaking

6 Look at the graphs showing climate change over the last 60 years and answer the questions.

1. Which graph shows information about the world, and which graph shows information about Britain only?
2. What do the horizontal axes of both graphs indicate?
3. What does the vertical axis of the first graph indicate?
4. What does the vertical axis of the second graph indicate?
5. What do you think might have caused these changes?

Writing

7 Write about the climate in your country. Which regions get which type of weather? Do any regions get extreme weather? Has the climate changed over the last 100 years?

Topic: Urban and rural lifestyles
Countries: UK
Vocabulary: The city
Links: 3a, 6b, 8c, 11b, 11c

Town...

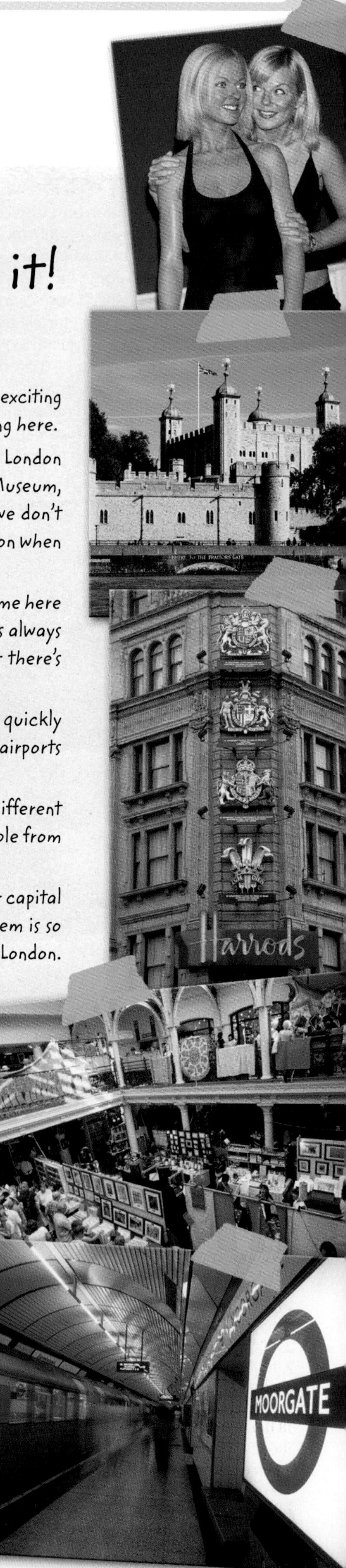

My home – love it or hate it!
by Ali Khazan

A I live in Blackheath in South London. London's one of the largest and most exciting cities in the world, and there are advantages and disadvantages to living here.

B The main advantage is that there's a lot to do and see. In the centre of London there are tourist attractions like Madam Tussaud's and the Science Museum, and there are all kinds of parks and historic buildings. I suppose that we don't always make the most of it. We only visit places like the Tower of London when one of our relatives comes to visit!

C Secondly, London is a great place for entertainment. All the new films come here first, and if we want to go to a pop concert or a big sports events, there's always something right on our doorstep. And of course the shopping is great – there's everything from department stores like Harrods to Camden Market.

D Another advantage of living in London is that you can travel easily and quickly across the city on the underground. And we've got railway stations and airports to take you anywhere in the world.

E Lastly, London is truly cosmopolitan. Kids at my school are from lots of different cultures, but that doesn't stop us being friends. It's good to mix with people from different backgrounds. It stops you from becoming narrowminded.

F But there are some major problems if you live in London. Like most other capital cities, it is noisy, polluted and congested with traffic. The traffic problem is so bad that they have recently introduced a congestion charge for central London. Drivers now have to pay if they want to take their cars to the city centre. Hopefully that will improve the situation.

G Secondly, things are very expensive here – apparently it's more expensive to live here than to live in any American city. For example, if you go to the cinema in the centre of London it can cost you £12. And to go just one stop on the underground can cost you nearly £1.

H But the worst problem about living in London is that, in general, people aren't very friendly. Nobody will talk to strangers or help people in the street if they are in trouble. They don't trust each other, and I think that's because they are scared of becoming victims of crime. London has the highest crime rate in the country.

I But in spite of these negative points, I still wouldn't want to live outside of London. It's my home – love it or hate it!

WORD BANK

background ▫ the type of home and family that someone has
charge ▫ demand for money
in spite of ▫ ignoring
make the most of something ▫ use something for your benefit
narrowminded ▫ conservative and prejudiced
on your doorstep ▫ very near to your home

...and country

Dear Leo
Thanks for your letter.
I thought you would like
a postcard from my home town,
Gladwell. As you can see,
it isn't exactly New York!
It's only a small village in
Yorkshire, in the north of England.
About 500 people live here.
We've got a village pub and a church
– that's all! But it's in a very
beautiful area, and I like village life.
I'll send you a long letter soon.
love,
Alice

Leo Donovan
Apt 3A
183, East 88th Street
New York
NY 32091
USA

Before you read

1 The places in the photos on page 30 are all in London. Can you identify any of them? Can you think of any other famous places in London?

Reading

2 EP Read Ali's essay. Match the paragraphs A-I with these topics.

.... Conclusion
.... Crime and People's Attitude
.... Environmental Problems
.... Introduction
.... Leisure Choices
.... Multicultural London
.... The Cost of Living
.... Famous Sights
.... Transport

3 Find the names of all the places in the photographs in Ali's essay.

4 EP Complete the summary of the essay. Use these words:

activities expense home multicultural principal shops unfriendliness variety

For Ali, the ....(1) advantage of living in London is the ....(2) of things that there are to see and do. He thinks that the ....(3), the choice of leisure ....(4) and the transport are good, and he likes the fact that London is a ....(5) city. The disadvantages for him are the traffic, the ....(6), people's ....(7) and the crime, but he doesn't want to leave his ....(8).

5 Read the postcard and find out:

1. the name of the village.
2. where it is.
3. how many people live there.
4. what facilities it has got.

Speaking

6 Is living in the country better than living in the city? What are the advantages and disadvantages of living in a small village?

Listening

7 Listen to Alice talking about her life in Gladwell. Find at least two advantages and two disadvantages of living there that she mentions.

8 Listen again and answer the questions.

1. Why did the village shop have to close?
2. What other facility in the village might close?
3. Does Alice think that everyone in the village is friendly?
4. What time does the last bus leave from the village?
5. How many buses are there on Sundays?

Writing

9 Write a paragraph about the contrast between rural and urban life in your country. What problems are there for people who live in the cities or in the country?

Topic ▪ Popular music styles
Countries ▪ USA, Jamaica, Ireland, South Africa
Vocabulary ▪ Types of music
Links ▪ 1f, 3f, 8e, 9f

Soundtrack
A world of music

Eminem
⏭ **Lose Yourself**

Urban USA ....

These styles of music evolved in the 1970s in New York and Los Angeles. Black youths started to mix rhythms and melodies from existing records and then add poetry about their lives on the streets. The lyrics of their records are often ▪confrontational and competitive, and most of them deal with modern social problems. Eminem is one of the few successful white artists in this type of music.

Shania Twain
⏭ **You're Still the One**

Rural USA

....

This type of music developed in the 1920s from the folk music of the midwestern states of the USA, and it has a distinct 'cowboy' feel to it. Nashville, Tennessee, is the official home of this type of music, and it is still growing in popularity today. Garth Brooks, one of its top artists, has sold over 100 million albums, and is the most popular solo artist of all time. In recent years Shania Twain has given this music a stylish modern look.

Bob Marley
⏭ **No Woman No Cry**

Jamaica ....

Popular music is a key part of everyday life in Jamaica, even forming a part of the island's Rastafarian religion. Its superstar was Bob Marley who came to world recognition in the 1970s and 80s, and today Jamaican music has evolved into 'dancehall', an electronic form of dance music.

No woman, no cry (*repeat 4 times*)

'Cause I remember when we used to sit
In the government yard in Trenchtown
Observing the hypocrites
As they would ▪mingle with the good people we meet
Good friends we have had, oh good friends we've lost
along the way
In this bright future you can't forget your past
So dry your tears I say

No woman, no cry
No woman, no cry
Little darlin' don't ▪shed no tears
No woman, no cry

Said, said, said I remember when we used to sit
In the government yard in Trenchtown
And then Georgie would make the fire light
▪Log wood burnin' through the night
Then we would cook ▪corn meal porridge
Of which I'll share with you

My feet is my only ▪carriage
So I've got to push on through
But while I'm gone...

Ev'rything's gonna be alright (*repeat 8 times*)

So, no woman, no cry
No, no woman, no woman, no cry
Oh, little darling, don't shed no tears
No woman, no cry

No woman, no woman, no woman, no cry
No woman, no cry
Oh, my little darlin' please don't shed no tears
No woman, no cry, yeah

WORD BANK

ballad ▫ a slow, romantic song
carriage ▫ horse-drawn transport
confrontational ▫ angrily opposing something
corn meal porridge ▫ flour made from corn, cooked with a liquid
log wood ▫ wood cut for a fire
to mingle ▫ to be mixed with
to rely on ▫ to depend on
to shed ▫ to release
unaccompanied ▫ without any musical instruments
whistle ▫ a simple cheap metal instrument, like a flute

Enya

⏭ Orinoco Flow

Ireland

Irish folk music has evolved over hundreds of years and ▫relies on the voice and traditional instruments such as the harp, violin, drum and ▫whistle. The two different sides to Irish music are energetic dance music and haunting ▫ballads with lyrics that tell a story. Enya, from County Donegal, came to fame in the 1990s. Her melodic vocals keep the traditional Irish feel to her songs, but she uses electronic synthesisers widely too.

Ladysmith Black Mambazo

⏭ Rain, Rain, Beautiful Rain

South Africa

Black South African miners, forced to work far away from home, developed a style of competitive, ▫unaccompanied singing to help pass their days. Ladysmith Black Mambazo, a choir who sing in this style and who took their name from their home town of Ladysmith, came to international notice in the 1980s. Their music maintains the traditional African singing style and uses lyrics with a religious theme, sometimes in their native Zulu language and sometimes in English.

Before you read

1 Who are your favourite singers? What countries do they come from?

Vocabulary

2 Look at the map. Which countries do you associate with the following types of music? Insert them in the correct text.
traditional Celtic music *rap* *traditional Zulu music* *reggae* *country and western* *hip-hop*

Reading

3 EP Read the texts. Match the events to the decades.
1920s *1970s* *1980s* *1990s*

1. Enya became popular.
2. Bob Marley was most famous.
3. Hip-hop music began.
4. Ladysmith Black Mambazo became world-famous.
5. Country and western music began.

4 Answer the questions about the texts.

1. Which town is the country and western capital of the USA?
2. Who is the biggest-selling solo recording artist of all time?
3. In which two American cities did hip-hop begin?
4. Why is Eminem's success unusual?
5. Which instruments are common in Celtic music?
6. In which industry did Ladysmith Black Mambazo's style of singing originate?
7. Which languages do Ladysmith Black Mambazo sing in?

Listening

5 Listen to the song *No Woman No Cry* by Bob Marley, then look at the lyrics. Say which of these features you think are important in a reggae song.

a. Romantic lyrics
b. Political or social message
c. Use of a lot of different instruments
d. Beat and rhythm

Speaking

6 Discuss in pairs. Does your country have a traditional form of music? Do you like it? What are the most popular forms of music in your country?

Grammar Comparative and superlative adjectives, prepositions of place
Skills Speaking: giving directions

Language & Culture

Old or new, big or small, Oxford's got it all!

The city of Oxford is situated 50 miles west of London. The Cotswold hills are just beyond Oxford where you can get some lovely views over the West Country from the higher points, and the River Thames starts its journey near the city. Oxford is famous for its University and its colleges.

One of the best ways to see the beautiful buildings and architecture is to do a walking tour around the centre. You can visit the university's largest college, Christ Church, and visit England's smallest cathedral there! Go to Merton Street where you can see some of Oxford's most beautiful architecture. Merton College is one of the three oldest colleges in Oxford with the oldest library in the country. If you want to see some bigger colleges, Balliol and Saint John's are further out of town, so taking a bus is a better idea. If it's more modern architecture you prefer then go to see the new Business School near the railway station.

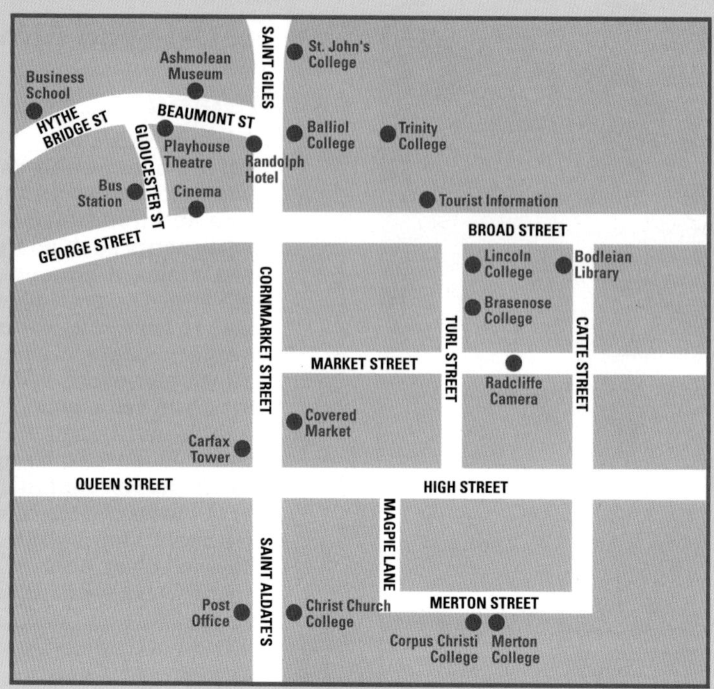

GRAMMAR

1 Read the description of Oxford and find the places that it mentions on the map.

2 Complete the table with words from the text.

Adjective	Comparative	Superlative
(1)	older	(2) ....
(3)	newer	newest
(4)	(5)	biggest
(6)	smaller	(7) ....
(8)	lovelier	loveliest
high	(9)	highest
(10)	more famous	most famous
good	(11)	best
large	larger	(12) ....
far	(13)	furthest
modern	(14)	most modern

3 Look at the map. Complete the sentences with the correct prepositions of place.

behind between in in front of near next to
on the left on the right opposite under

1. The main post office is .... Christ Church college.
2. Corpus Christi college is .... Merton College.
3. If you walk down Cornmarket Street, Carfax Tower is ....
4. The covered market is .... the High Street and Market Street.
5. From the High Street, Lincoln College is .... Brasenose College.
6. The cinema on George Street is .... the Playhouse Theatre.
7. The smallest cathedral in England is .... Christ Church college.
8. The river Cherwell passes .... Magdalen bridge.
9. From Saint Giles, Balliol College is .... Trinity College.
10. If you walk down Beaumont Street from Saint Giles, the Playhouse Theatre is ....

SKILLS

4 Someone is asking for directions at the Tourist Information Office. Complete the dialogue with the correct expressions. Use the map to help you.

Go straight across Thank you very much ~~Can you tell me~~
Keep on the right hand side turn left into
Walk straight down You can't miss it
Is it far from here? go past

Tourist: Excuse me. (1) *Can you tell me* where the nearest post office is?
Local: Yes, of course.
Tourist: (2) .... ?
Local: Well, not too far. You can walk there in about five minutes. We're in Broad Street just now. You need to walk to the crossroads with George Street and (3) .... Cornmarket Street. (4) .... Cornmarket Street, (5) .... all the shops until you come to the traffic lights at the bottom. (6) .... the traffic lights onto Saint Aldate's. (7) .... and after a short distance, about 50 metres down Saint Aldate's, you'll see the main post office. (8) ....
Tourist: (9) ....
Local: Good luck!

5 You're outside the main post office in Oxford. In pairs, use the map of the centre to ask for and give directions to these places:

1. The Randolph Hotel
2. The Playhouse Theatre
3. Christ Church College
4. The bus station
5. The cinema in George Street
6. The tourist information office

Module 3

Links with the past

IN THIS MODULE YOU WILL READ AND HEAR ABOUT:

- the history of Britain from the Roman occupation to Elizabeth I
- the story of British colonisation from Elizabethan to Victorian times
- ordinary British people's experience of the two World Wars
- the history of the USA from the 17th to the 19th century
- ways of reporting the news in the USA in the 20th century
- piracy and the slave trade in Jamaica
- the early history of Australia

1 Look at the photos on this page. Do you know any of the people? Can you put them in chronological order? What part did they play in British and American history?

2 Match these dates with the events in British and American history.

1066
1534
1776
1914
1929
1945
1969

a. The USA declares independence from Britain.
b. The Second World War ends.
c. The beginning of the Great Depression in the USA.
d. The Normans invade Britain.
e. An American man walks on the moon.
f. England breaks away from the Catholic church.
g. The First World War begins.

Topic ◘ English history
Countries ◘ England and Scotland
Vocabulary ◘ Historical events
Links ◘ 2a, 2e, 4b, 4e, 6d, 11a

England: a historical tour

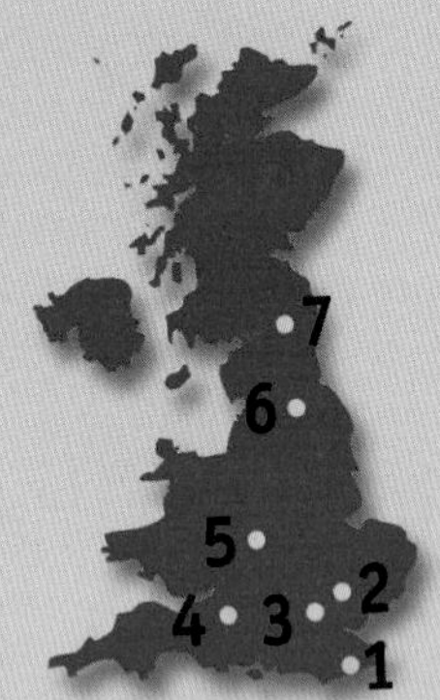

Heritage Holidays

Discover England's fascinating early history on our exclusive non-stop one-week tour.

DAY 1 ▼
Hastings, East Sussex

Our first stop is the beach at Hastings where William the Conqueror's armies arrived from Normandy in 1066, then we visit Battle Abbey, built by William to celebrate his victory, and watch actors in period costume ◘re-enact the battle and the death of the English King Harold.

DAY 2 ▼
Tilbury Fort, Essex

Elizabeth I's reign was a golden age of sea exploration, discovery and military victory.

DAY 2

On the second day of our tour we visit the exact spot where, in 1588, Elizabeth gave her famous speech to her troops on the day before they faced the much superior Spanish Armada – and defeated them!

DAY 3 ▼
The Tower of London

DAY 3

London's most famous ◘landmark was built by William the Conqueror in 1078, but its best-known historical connections are with the Tudor monarchs. Two of Henry VIII's six wives, Anne Boleyn and Catherine Howard, were ◘beheaded here at his command. After his death, his daughter Elizabeth was imprisoned here by her older sister Mary. But when Mary died in 1558, she was obliged to make Elizabeth her successor.

DAY 4 ▼
morning - **Stonehenge, Wiltshire**
afternoon - **Bath, Somerset**

On Day 4 we visit the West Country, stopping at mysterious Stonehenge, built by the native Celtic Britons around 2000 BC, and then spending the afternoon at Bath – once the Roman ◘spa town of Aquae Sulis ('the waters of the ◘goddess Sulis'). The tour includes a visit to the famous hot ◘springs and Roman baths.

DAY 4

Vocabulary

1 Write these words in the correct column of the table.

abbey army battle fort invasion kingdom monarch monastery navy occupation reign successor defeat troops victory

Kings and queens	Military action	Religion

Before you read

2 The people and places in the pictures are all important in English history. Can you identify any of them?

Reading

3 EP Complete the table with the missing dates and names from the text.

English history - key dates

Date	Event
....	Stonehenge built by native Britons
....	Roman invasion of Britain under Julius Caesar
....	Norman invasion of Britain under ....
1509-1547	Reign of King VIII
....	England breaks with Rome and forms the Church of England
1553-1558	Reign of Queen I
1558-1603	Reign of Queen I
....	Defeat of the Spanish Armada

WORD BANK

- to behead ▫ to kill someone by cutting their head off
- dissolution ▫ breaking up
- goddess ▫ a female god
- landmark ▫ a prominent feature in the landscape
- legion ▫ a division of the Roman army (consisting of about 5,000 men)
- to re-enact ▫ to re-create by using drama
- spa ▫ a town where there is a mineral spring
- spring ▫ where water comes up from under the ground
- tribe ▫ an ethnic group of people
- to wail ▫ to make a sound like a miserable cry

DAY 5 ▾
Stratford-on-Avon, Warwickshire

DAY 5

No tour of England is complete without a visit to Elizabethan Stratford-on-Avon, birthplace of the most famous writer of that age - William Shakespeare - and home to many historic buildings. In the evening we will see a play at the world-famous Royal Shakespeare Theatre.

DAY 6 ▾
Fountains Abbey, Yorkshire

On Day 6 we travel north and visit the majestic ruins of Fountains Abbey, perhaps the best example of the destruction caused by Henry VIII's ▫Dissolution of the Monasteries (1536-40) when Henry sold all the buildings and land that belonged to the Catholic monasteries. The King had broken away from the Catholic church in 1534 and made himself the Supreme Head of the Church of England.

DAY 6

DAY 7 ▾
Hadrian's Wall, Northumberland

On our final day we visit the most famous symbol of the Roman occupation of Britain - Hadrian's Wall. Although Julius Caesar led the first invasion of Britain in 55 BC, it was under the Emperor Hadrian that the Roman ▫legions reached the most northern point of their Empire and built a wall from coast-to-coast as protection against the Scottish ▫tribes.

DAY 7

Optional

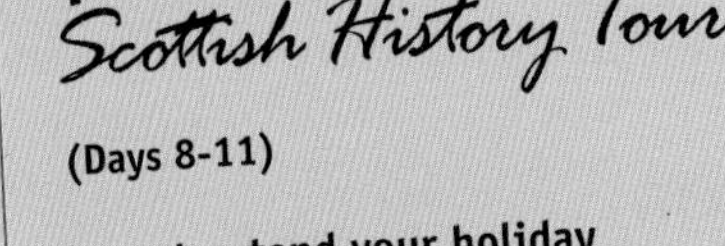

(Days 8-11)

Why not extend your holiday and take our optional four-day tour of Scotland too?

You'll learn all about the origins of these famous symbols of Scotland:

- **the haggis:** some say that this Scottish favourite (meat and cereal cooked inside a sheep's stomach) originally came from Scandinavia.
- **whisky:** was it made accidentally in medieval times, when wet cereal was left to ferment?
- **bagpipes:** used to frighten enemies with their terrible ▫wailing sound, perhaps these musical instruments were brought to Scotland by the Romans.
- **the kilt:** worn by Scottish tribes because it allowed them to move easily, it was warm, and it could also be used as a blanket.

Whisky and haggis

tartan and kilt

kilt and bagpipes

4 Answer the questions.

1. Why did the Romans build Hadrian's Wall?
2. What was the Roman name for the city of Bath?
3. What famous Roman site can you still visit there?
4. Who fought the Battle of Hastings, and who won?
5. Who built the Tower of London, and when?
6. Name three famous female prisoners at the Tower of London.
7. What happened to the Catholic monasteries during Henry VIII's reign?
8. Who was the monarch during Shakespeare's lifetime?

Vocabulary

5 Read the text about the Scottish tour. Name:

1. a Scottish musical instrument.
2. an article of Scottish clothing.
3. a Scottish drink.
4. a type of Scottish food.

6 EP Which of the things from exercise 5:

a. could be used to sleep in?
b. were used as protection from enemies?
c. might have originated without the help of humans?
d. gave freedom of movement?
e. might have come from a country outside Scotland?

Speaking

7 What was happening in your country during these periods of history? Who were the key people and which places are associated with them?

Writing

8 Write a table of key dates for your country, like the one in exercise 3.

Topic: British colonialism
Countries: Britain, Ireland, India, Singapore, Hong Kong, USA, West Africa, West Indies
Vocabulary: Wordbuilding
Links: 1d, 3d, 3f, 4c, 4e, 6c, 7a, 9f, 11d, 11e, 11l

Britain's colonial past

Food from the Colonies

How did the following everyday foods shape the history of Britain, Ireland and the USA?

Spices

In 1600 the East India Company was formed under Elizabeth I to compete with Dutch traders in the oriental spice trade. The company was given a monopoly on all goods imported to England from Asia. From the 1750s the company became more ambitious, starting to invade and conquer parts of India. It was now the biggest company in the world, and also an unofficial arm of the British government. When Queen Victoria came to the throne in 1837, the whole of India was under British rule, and she was made Empress of India. When she died in 1901, the British Empire had expanded so much that it included one fifth of the total population of the world.

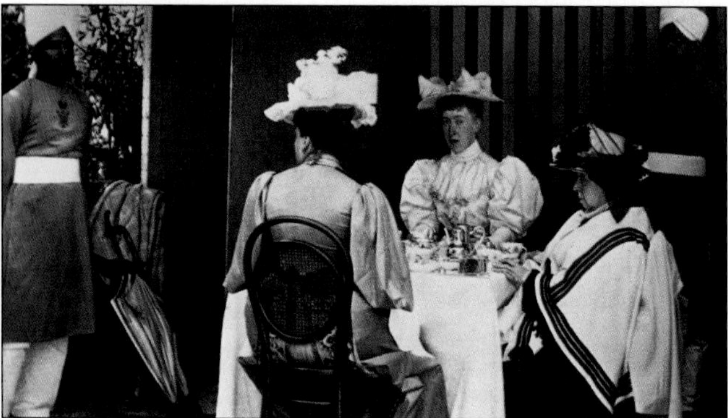

Queen Victoria with Indian servants.

Sugar

As tea and coffee grew in popularity in Britain in the 18th century, the demand for sugar to sweeten them also grew. Sugar plantations in the West Indies owned by European colonists needed more workers, so their owners imported slaves from West Africa. A circular trade developed and islands such as Jamaica and the Bahamas became British colonies. Ships from Britain carried cotton and metal goods to Africa, where they were traded for slaves, who were taken on a three-month voyage to the West Indies. They were traded with the plantation owners for sugar, and the sugar returned to Britain. Georgian Britain, especially the ports of Liverpool and Bristol, grew rich on the profits of the slave trade, turning a blind eye to the cruelty and the suffering involved.

The slave trade.

Healing the past

In recent years Bristol City Council has begun to publicly acknowledge the contribution that the slave trade made to the city's wealth. In 1999 a foot bridge named Pero's Bridge was opened, named after an African slave who was the servant to a rich Bristol family, and the plaque below can be seen on the wall of the city's Industrial Museum.

IN MEMORY OF THE COUNTLESS AFRICAN MEN, WOMEN AND CHILDREN WHOSE ENSLAVEMENT AND EXPLOITATION BROUGHT SO MUCH PROSPERITY TO BRISTOL THROUGH THE AFRICAN SLAVE TRADE

UNVEILED ON 12 DECEMBER 1997
DURING EUROPEAN YEAR AGAINST RACISM

BY IAN WHITE
MEMBER OF THE EUROPEAN PARLIAMENT FOR BRISTOL
AND PHILIPPA GREGORY
AUTHOR OF "A RESPECTABLE TRADE"

This letter appeared in the Bristol Evening Post about the possibility of building a new concert hall to replace the city's old one. The old concert hall is named after Edward Colston, a businessman who became rich from the slave trade in the 18th century.

Dear Sir,

I have been reading with interest the letter regarding the Colston Hall debate. I think it's a shame that we have to think about changing its name.

I am sure that most Bristol people feel the same way. As Bristol was heavily involved in the slave trade, why don't we rename Bristol?

I wonder if people who are against Colston drive Japanese or German cars. Do they have any Japanese or German electrical equipment? I bet they do.

We forgave the Germans for bombing our city – surely we can forgive Edward Colston for the things that he did. So, please, let Mr Colston rest in peace as we have made peace with people who have wronged us in the past.

WORD BANK

crop ▫ plants grown for human use
to forgive ▫ to pardon
the Georgian period ▫ the period 1714-1830 in Britain, when Georges I, II and III were the kings
goods ▫ things that are bought and sold
to sweeten ▫ to make sweet
to turn a blind eye ▫ to ignore something that you know is wrong
to wrong ▫ to hurt or offend
yield ▫ the amount produced in a crop

Tea

The East India Company also held a monopoly on the import of Chinese tea, which became popular and fashionable in the 18th century. Trading posts around China such as Singapore and Hong Kong soon became colonies. At the same time, people in America, which the British had colonised in Elizabethan times, were protesting about high taxes on the import of common goods from England. A revolutionary group called the Sons of Liberty began turning back British tea ships from American ports, and in 1773 they threw tea worth thousands of pounds into Boston Harbour. The 'Boston Tea Party' was the first of many acts of rebellion that quickly led to war with England and, in 1776, to American independence.

Americans throwing the Cargoes of the Tea Ships into the River, at Boston

The Boston Tea Party in 1773.

Potatoes

Potatoes, originally from Colombia, were introduced to England by Elizabethan explorers. Sir Walter Raleigh grew them on his land in Ireland, which in those days was under British rule. The Irish, poor and constantly at war internally or with the English, began to rely on this ▫crop, which was easy to grow and produced a good ▫yield. The poorest families ate nothing else. But in the 1840s a fungus infected the crops and more than one million people died of hunger. Another two million emigrated, mostly to North America, and a de-populated Ireland remained under British rule until 1922.

The Irish potato famine of the 1840s.

Before you read

1 Look quickly at the *English everywhere* units in this book. Which countries do they deal with? Why do you think that there are so many English-speaking countries in the world? How did the English language travel so far?

2 Look at the photos of the foods. How could these things have helped to spread British influence around the world?

Vocabulary

3 Complete the table with words from the texts.

verb	noun (the person)	noun (the place)
to colonise	....	....
to	....	settlement
to trade	....	....

Reading

4 EP Insert the names of the countries in the correct sentences.

America China Hong Kong India Ireland Jamaica Singapore

1. .... and .... became British colonies as a result of the tea trade in the 18th century.
2. .... became a British colony as a result of the sugar trade in the 18th century.
3. .... became a British colony as a result of the spice trade in the 18th century.
4. .... was a British colony from medieval times until 1922.
5. .... was a British colony from the 16th century until 1776.
6. .... was never a British colony.

5 Look at the texts about Bristol on page 38 and answer the questions.

1. Who was Pero?
2. What is significant about naming a bridge after him?
3. Why was 1997 an appropriate year to put up a plaque in memory of African slaves?
4. What position did Ian White have in 1997?
5. What do you think Philippa Gregory's book is about?
6. Who was Edward Colston?
7. What does the writer of the letter think about Edward Colston?

Speaking

6 Do you think that Britain should feel guilty about its involvement in the slave trade? Do gestures like the ones made by Bristol City Council help to heal the past? Discuss with the class.

Topic ◘ British history
Countries ◘ UK
Vocabulary ◘ Military words
Links ◘ 2b, 3e, 11a, 11h

The British at war

A

1917

April 2nd
Arrived at Roisel. Large town, only one house standing. After ◘clearing out explosives we occupy it. The streets are ◘beyond description. Beds, etc, mixed up with kitchen utensils all over the town. Rode back to tell the rest to follow on. It's a regular ◘blizzard, very cold. Had a look around several wine ◘cellars. Nothing left.

April 5th
They shell the roads every time any troops move. Kept us awake last night. Expected to get shelled any minute. All around us every evening the Infantry pass on their way to the front line, and the Medical Corps start to bring back the wounded. Hundreds pass here every day. The majority help each other down, poor devils.

April 7th
Our troops always pass by whistling or singing, but the papers lie regarding the coming back. The poor ◘fellows can hardly keep their eyes open or have enough strength to walk.

April 9th
Easter Day, but no holiday. All days are the same here. In fact, we ◘get mixed up what day it is sometimes or what date of the month it is.

April 11th
Rotten cold day, snowing. They've stopped the rum rations. Hard luck.

B

They have been teaching us bayonet fighting today and I can tell you it makes your arms ◘ache, when you ◘lunge out at an imaginary enemy with the rifle at arm's length. I think with this hard training they will either make a man of me or kill me. You ought to see me in my shrapnel helmet and gas mask, it would make you laugh, especially as the helmet ◘wobbles from side to side every time I walk.

Yes, I got my food alright ... and you can bet I always go for supper. I am taking your advice and eating all I can.

Yes, I did remember Dolly's birthday, and I have sent her a little badge of my Regiment which she asked for.

Hoping you are quite well.
From your loving son

Before you read

1 How was your country involved in the First and the Second World Wars? What dates do you give to those wars in your country?

2 EP Match these captions to the texts A-D.

1. British public information poster from World War II.
2. Extract from the diary of Thomas Howes, an English soldier who fought in World War I in France and Belgium.
3. Government leaflet delivered to every house in Britain in 1940.
4. Letter to his father from Ted Poole, who joined the British army in 1918 and was killed at the age of 18.

Vocabulary

3 Match the military words to their definitions.

1. shrapnel	a. exploding missile
2. Cavalry	b. the point on a battlefield where soldiers meet the enemy
3. shell	c. sharp point fixed to a gun
4. bayonet	d. soldiers on foot
5. Infantry	e. soldiers on horses
6. front line	f. pieces of metal – the results of an explosion

WORD BANK

A.R.P. warden ▫ member of the Air Raid Patrol who gave instructions to the public about bomb attacks from the air
to ache ▫ to hurt
beyond description ▫ impossible to describe
blizzard ▫ bad snowstorm
cellar ▫ underground room
to clear out ▫ to remove
fake ▫ non genuine
fellow ▫ man
to get mixed up ▫ to be confused
to keep watch ▫ to be observant
to lunge out ▫ to make a sudden forward movement
to stay put ▫ to not move
to wobble ▫ to move dangerously, as if going to fall

C

Issued by the Ministry of Information in co-operation with the War Office and the Ministry of Home Security

If the INVADER comes

WHAT TO DO – AND HOW TO DO IT

I

If the Germans come, by parachute, aeroplane or ship, you must remain where you are. The order is ▫'Stay put'.

II

Do not believe rumours and do not spread them. When you receive an order, make quite sure that it is a true order and not a ▫fake order. Most of you know your policemen and your ▫A.R.P. wardens by sight. You can trust them.

III

▫Keep watch. If you see anything suspicious, note it carefully and go at once to the nearest police officer or station, or to the nearest military officer.

IV

Do not give any German anything. Do not tell him anything. Hide your food and your bicycles. Hide your maps. See that the enemy gets no petrol.

V

Be ready to help the military in any way, but do not block roads until ordered to do so by the military authorities.

VI

In factories and shops, all managers and workmen should organise some system for resisting a sudden attack.

VII

Think before you act, but think always of your country before you think of yourself.

D

Come and help with the
VICTORY HARVEST
You are needed in the fields!
APPLY TO NEAREST EMPLOYMENT EXCHANGE FOR LEAFLET & ENROLMENT FORM OR WRITE DIRECT TO THE DEPARTMENT OF AGRICULTURE FOR SCOTLAND 15 GROSVENOR STREET, EDINBURGH.

Part of London in ruins.

Reading

4 Answer the questions about the two First World War texts.

1. What was the weather like near the front line in France in April 1917?
2. What reference does Thomas Howes make to newspaper reports of the war?
3. What did Ted Poole think about his military training?
4. What two questions do you think his father had asked him in an earlier letter?

5 EP Match these commands to the instructions I-VII in the Second World War leaflet.

a. Be observant.
b. Hide things that the invader needs.
c. Make a plan for your place of work.
d. Don't move.
e. Put the needs of your country first.
f. Don't follow false orders.
g. Wait for commands before you act.

6 What is the intention of the poster?

Before you listen

7 Were any members of your family directly involved in the First or Second World War? Do you know anyone who remembers the Second World War?

Listening

8 Listen to Betty remembering what it was like to be a teenager in England during the Second World War and answer the questions.

1. How old was Betty during the war?
2. What does she remember about the day that Britain entered the war?
3. What was her father's job? Did he go to war?
4. What happened to her home town during the war?
5. What did she do in 1945?
6. What are her feelings about the war now?

Speaking

9 Does the British experience of the First and Second World Wars seem similar or different to people's experience in your country?

History at the movies

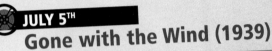

AMERICA: Revolution and War

Through the summer, the Arts Cinema presents a season of films based on American history in the 17th, 18th and 19th centuries.

JULY 5TH

Gone with the Wind (1939)

We open our season with this popular classic. Set in Georgia during the south's war against the northern states, *Gone with the Wind* tells the story of how Scarlett O'Hara sees her traditional way of life destroyed, and how she rebuilds a life for herself and her family.

JULY 12TH

How the West was Won (1962)

A classic western starring some of American cinema's biggest names, including John Wayne, Henry Fonda and James Stewart. This epic story shows us three generations of a 19th-century family as they travel from the east coast to establish a new community in the west.

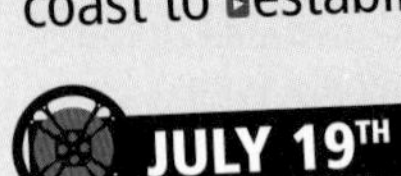

JULY 19TH

The Last of the Mohicans (1992)

Based on Cooper's classic book, Daniel Day Lewis plays Hawkeye, a white man raised by the native Mohicans, who fights on the side of the British against the French in their colonisation of North America and Canada.

JULY 27TH

The Scarlet Letter (1995)

Set in a community of early settlers in east-coast New England, the film stars Demi Moore as Hester Prynne, whose husband is in England and who has a baby that cannot be his. Hester is punished by the villagers, but her story shows the hypocrisy of the religious community she lives in.

AUGUST 3RD

Amistad (1997)

Steven Spielberg's *Amistad* reveals the terrible treatment that slaves received during their transportation by ship to America. It concentrates on the real-life trial of a group of African slaves who, in 1839, revolted on ship and killed their masters.

AUGUST 10TH

The Patriot (2000)

Mel Gibson stars in this story of America's fight for independence from British rule. Gibson plays a plantation owner who is at first reluctant to fight against the British, but who gradually realises that his country's freedom and future depend on it.

WORD BANK

to ban ▫ to make illegal
to establish ▫ to build from nothing
hypocrisy ▫ telling people what to do, but not doing it yourself
to raise (a person) ▫ to help and look after someone as they grow
reluctant ▫ not wanting to
to set (a story) ▫ to locate in time or place
settlers ▫ the first people to build a community somewhere
to surrender ▫ to stop fighting and agree to lose
trial ▫ a legal process of judgement

Landmarks in American history

A European Settlement and the French Wars

In the 17th century, settlers from England and from Holland started to make their home in America. Many of them were from small religious groups who suffered persecution in Europe. In the 18th century, France fought England for control of Canada and the northern border. Both sides used the help of Native Americans, but England won the war in 1763.

B The War of Independence

After the French Wars, some US states began to rebel against control and taxation by England and its king, George III. In 1776, thirteen states declared independence from England. A war between the English army and the Americans lasted until 1781, when the United States of America became an independent country.

C The Civil War

In the 19th century, states were created in the west, where settlers took land from the Native Americans and farmed it. The southern states used many slaves from Africa and the Caribbean on their plantations, but the northern states wanted to ▫ban slavery. In 1861, eleven southern states left the USA and set up their own Confederacy. A civil war lasted until 1865, when the southern states ▫surrendered and their slaves were freed.

Left: Declaration of Independence, 4 July 1776, by John Trumbull.
Right: Artillery unit on parade at their camp during the American Civil War.

Before you read

1 **Do you know any of the films in the photos on page 42? Do you know who the stars are or what the films are about?**

Reading

2 **EP** **Read the paragraphs about American history and the stories of the films. Which period of history (A, B or C) does each of the films deal with?**

3 **EP** **Complete the table with the missing dates and the names of the films.**

Date	Event	Film
17th century	English Puritan settlers move to America	....
17th - 19th century	The use of slavery in the south	....
.... century	The French Wars	....
17	The Declaration of Independence	....
.... century	Settlement in the western states	....
18 .... - 18	The American Civil War	....

4 **Answer the questions about paragraphs A, B and C. Who:**

1. won the French Wars?
2. won the War of Independence?
3. won the American Civil War?
4. was King of England in 1776?
5. helped the Europeans in the French Wars?
6. were forced to work on American plantations?

Listening

5 **EP** **Listen to someone giving his opinion about *The Patriot*. Circle his general opinion of the following things.**

The main character	The story	The dialogue	The camerawork	The historical accuracy
☺	☺	☺	☺	☺
😐	😐	😐	😐	😐
☹	☹	☹	☹	☹

6 **Listen again and note down the reasons for his opinions.**

Speaking

7 **If you have seen any of these films, tell the class your opinion of them. Talk about: the characters, the story, the camerawork, the music.**

Topic ▫ American history
Countries ▫ USA
Vocabulary ▫ Historical events
Links ▫ 3c, 9a, 11j

The USA: making the news in the 20th century

In 1999 the Newseum, a museum of journalism in Virginia, USA, asked journalists and historians to select the top 100 news stories of the 20th century. Here are their top 10.

1	Atomic bomb dropped on Hiroshima, Nagasaki	1945
2	First man walks on the moon	....
3	Japan bombs Pearl Harbor. USA enters World War II	....
4	The Wright brothers fly the first powered aeroplane	....
5	Women in the USA given the right to vote	....
6	President John F. Kennedy assassinated in Dallas	....
7	Nazi concentration camps exposed	....
8	World War I begins in Europe	....
9	The end of racial segregation in US schools	....
10	The US ▫stock market crashes. Beginning of the Great Depression	....

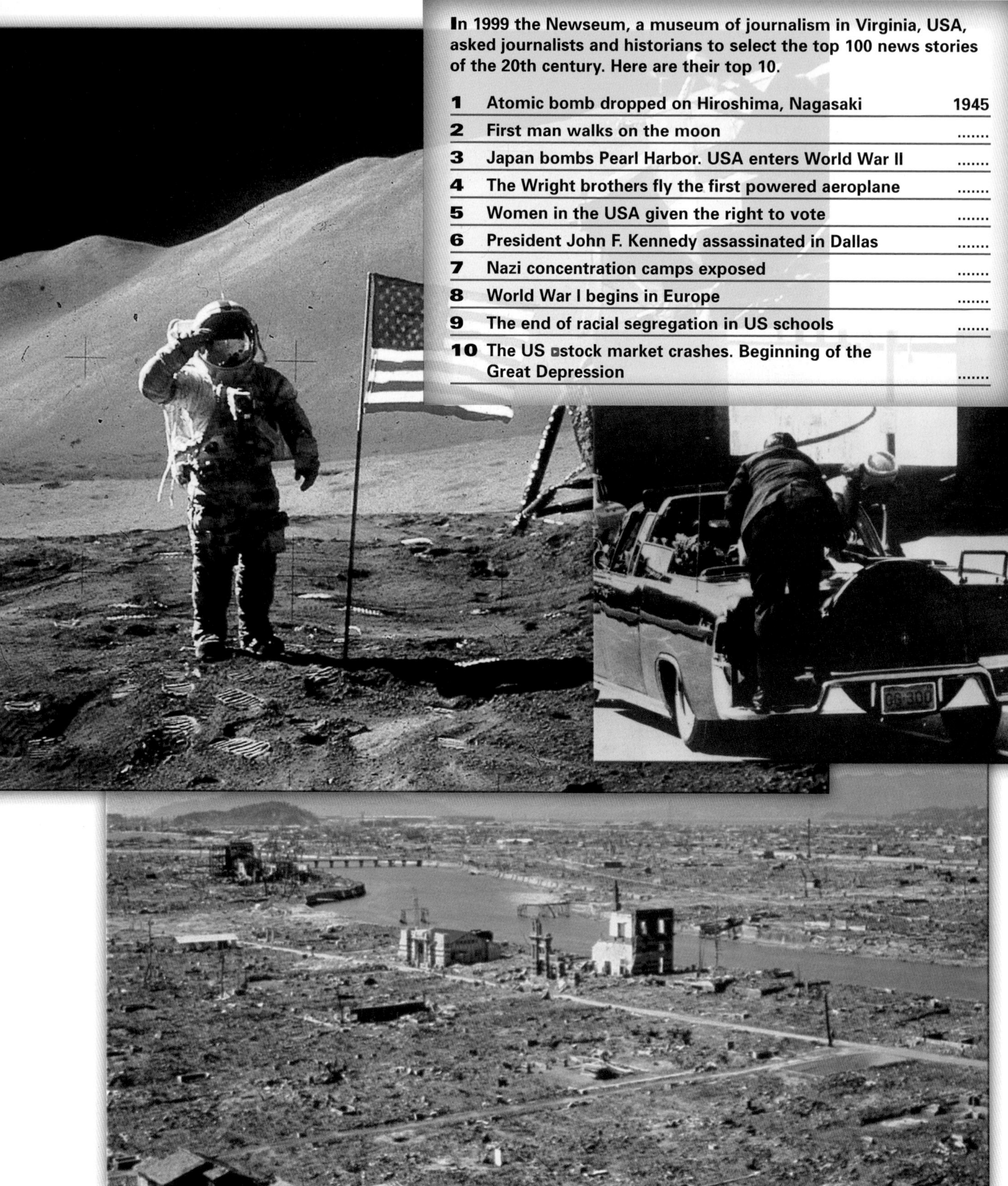

WORD BANK

broadcast ▫ a transmission by radio or television
coverage ▫ amount of reporting of an event
slant ▫ inclination in a certain direction
stock market ▫ where shares in companies are bought and sold
to update ▫ to make more current
viewer ▫ member of a TV audience

Reporting the century

During the Great Depression of the 1930s, when the USA suffered financial crisis, poverty and hunger, President Franklin D. Roosevelt began a series of radio ▫broadcasts in which he addressed the American people in a friendly, informal way. These fifteen-minute talks, broadcast in the evenings, became known as his 'fireside chats'. They made a great impression on the people, helping to sustain their morale through difficult times. On December 8th, 1941, the day after the Japanese attack on the US navy at Pearl Harbor, 90 million Americans listened to Roosevelt refer to December 7th as 'a date which will live in infamy' and ask Congress to declare war on Japan. The declaration happened the same day, and Roosevelt's fireside chats continued throughout the war.

Although radio was the most popular form of mass media during the Second World War, around 100 million Americans also watched images of the war's events at their local cinemas each week. Short news films, called 'newsreels', were made by film companies such as Fox and Paramount, often with a propaganda ▫slant, and shown before every main film. They were ▫updated twice a week so that audiences could be informed of important events of the war, such as the dropping of the atomic bomb and the death of the president in 1945.

The USA was the world's first 'TV society', with 90% of American homes owning a TV by 1960. In 1969, when 600 million people watched the first moon landings on TV, over a third of the audience was American. It was the biggest TV audience in the medium's history, even though the pictures, received by a satellite station in Australia, were black and white and indistinct. The American networks showed continuous ▫coverage of Apollo 11's three-day journey from Florida to the moon. When Neil Armstrong, Buzz Aldrin and Michael Collins entered the moon's orbit it was the middle of the night. There were no video recorders in those days, so the networks told ▫viewers to go to sleep with the TV sound turned down low, and promised to wake them with a loud alarm just before the spacecraft landed.

Before you listen

1 Which of the events in the top ten list are illustrated by the photos on page 44?

2 Can you put the events from the top ten list into chronological order? Do you know the exact years of any of them?

Listening

3 Listen and check your answers. Complete the missing years in the top ten list.

Speaking

4 What different ways of reporting the news can you think of? Which of these forms of communication existed before the 1970s?

Reading

5 Read the text. Which form of media is covered in each paragraph? Which form of media isn't covered?

6 Answer the questions about the text.

1. Who was the President of the USA during the Great Depression and the Second World War?
2. What were his 'fireside chats'?
3. On which date did the USA declare war on Japan?
4. What were newsreels?
5. How often was a new newsreel shown to the public in US cinemas?
6. How many people watched the first moon landings on TV in 1969?
7. What were the names of the three astronauts?
8. Where on earth were the pictures received from space?

Speaking

7 Discuss. Is the list on page 44 a fair summary of world events of the 20th century, or is it too 'American'? What were the important 20th century events for your country?

Writing

8 Write your own list of top ten 20th century events, either for the world or for your own country.

Topic ▪ Jamaican history
Countries ▪ Jamaica
Vocabulary ▪ Wordbuilding
Links ▪ 2f, 3b, 3d, 7a, 11e

English everywhere
Jamaica

MONTEGO BAY
SPANISH TOWN
KINGSTON

In 1655, Jamaica, a Spanish colony, was taken by the British and became notorious as a base for piracy. The unofficial capital, Port Royal, was the biggest port in the English colonies at that time, populated by pirates, slave traders, runaway slaves and criminals.

A large 18th century colonial building.

A historical print of Captain Kidd and his pirates.

WELCOME TO
PORT ROYAL

Once called "the richest and wickedest city in the world", Port Royal was also the virtual capital of Jamaica. To it came men of all races, treasures of silks, dubloons and gold from Spanish ship, looted on the high seas by the notorious "Brethren of the Coast" as the pirates were called. From here sailed the fleets of Henry Morgan, later lieutenant-governor of Jamaica, for the sacking of Camaguey, Maracaibo and Panama, and died here despite the ministrations of his Jamaican folk doctor. Admirals Lord Nelson and Benbow, the chilling Edward "Blackbeard" Teach were among its inhabitants. The town flourished for 32 years until at 20 minutes to noon, June 7, 1692, it was partially buried in the sea by an earthquake.

Jamaica National Heritage Trust

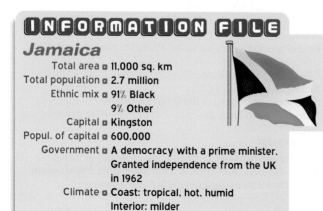

A typical market selling tropical fruit.

INFORMATION FILE

Jamaica

Total area ▪ 11,000 sq. km
Total population ▪ 2.7 million
Ethnic mix ▪ 91% Black
9% Other
Capital ▪ Kingston
Popul. of capital ▪ 600,000
Government ▪ A democracy with a prime minister. Granted independence from the UK in 1962
Climate ▪ Coast: tropical, hot, humid
Interior: milder

Before you read

1 Do you know anything about Jamaica? Can you name any Jamaican towns or any famous Jamaicans? What type of music is the country famous for?

Reading

2 Look at the map and read the Information File on Jamaica. Answer the questions.

1. Does Jamaica share a border with any other countries?
2. Where in the country is its capital city?
3. How many people live in the capital city?
4. When did Jamaica become an independent state?
5. Is it hotter on the coast or inside the country?

WORD BANK

brethren ▫ brothers
chilling ▫ very frightening
dubloon ▫ gold coin
fleet ▫ group of ships
to flourish ▫ to be rich and successful
to loot ▫ to steal
ministrations ▫ care
piracy ▫ robbery at sea
sacking ▫ destruction and robbery
strike ▫ when workers protest by refusing to work
wicked ▫ evil, morally bad

Montego Bay

Walking Tours

Begin your tour at Sam Sharpe Square, named after the slave who led the Christmas Rebellion of 1831. In the 18th century, Jamaica was the largest producer of sugar in the world and British plantation owners imported 700,000 slaves from West Africa. Although the slave trade was officially abolished by the British government in 1807, Jamaican plantation owners refused to give up their slaves. Sam Sharpe was an educated slave and a Baptist preacher who lived in Montego Bay. By reading newspapers, he learned about the abolition movement and he spread the word among his fellow slaves. He organised a peaceful ▫strike for the 28th of December, just after the Christmas holiday, when he knew that the sugar cane was ready and needed to be cut quickly, but other slaves grew violent and the government sent soldiers to end the rebellion. 300 slaves were executed for their part in the protest, including Sharpe, who was hanged in this square in 1832.
Take a look at 'The Cage' in the northwest corner of the square – a prison built in 1806 for runaway slaves and drunk British sailors. Its bell was rung at 2pm every afternoon to warn slaves from the country that they had an hour in which to leave the town.

A British plantation owner in a 19th century print.

3 Read the plaque about Port Royal and answer the questions.
1. What did people call Port Royal in the 17th century?
2. The plaque mentions four men: Morgan, Nelson, Benbow and Teach. Which two do you think were pirates and which two do you think were officers in the navy?
3. How was the town destroyed?

4 EP Read the extract from the tourist guide. Are the following statements true or false?
1. Sam Sharpe was a free man.
2. He knew about the abolition of slavery in Britain.
3. He wanted to make a violent protest against slavery.
4. He wanted to protest at the end of December because it was an important time for sugar-growing.
5. He was killed during the rebellion.
6. Slaves from the country had to leave Montego Bay at 3pm every day.

Vocabulary

5 EP Complete the sentences with new nouns formed from the words in brackets. All the missing nouns can be found in this unit.
1. The main business of Port Royal was .... (pirate)
2. Slaves were imported to work on British .... (plant)
3. Slaves were the property of their .... (own)
4. During a ...., slaves attacked their masters. (rebel)
5. The .... of .... in Jamaica didn't happen until 1838. (abolish/slave)
6. Jamaica celebrates .... Day on the first Monday in August. (independent)
7. Jamaica now has 2.7 million .... (inhabit)

Speaking

6 Do you think that Jamaica sounds like an interesting place to visit? If you went there, would you be more interested in its history, or in its hot weather and beaches?

Grammar ▫ Past tense review (past simple, past continuous, past perfect)
Skills ▫ Writing a summary

Language & Culture

A short history of Australia

1 Australia's first people were the Aborigines. They have occupied the continent for at least 50,000 years, and before the Europeans arrived in 1788 their population was probably between 300,000 and 750,000. They occupied a lot of the northern territory.

Captain Cook landing at Van Diemen's Land, now Tasmania, in 1777.

2 Although Captain James Cook had sailed the length of the east coast in 1770 the British did not settle in Australia until 1788. The first ships arrived and brought 1,000 ▫convicts from England. They called the area where they landed New South Wales.

3 Historians still argue today about why the British settled in Australia. Some say that Britain was trying to find new places to send convicts because British prisons were too crowded. Others say that the British wanted to use Australia's natural resources or that they were attempting to stop other Europeans from claiming Australia.

4 Australia's white population grew slowly after 1788. Most of the people were either convicts or former convicts who had finished their ▫sentences.

5 In the 1830s, more migrants arrived in Australia from Britain looking for a new life. Sheep farming had already developed and many people found jobs on farms. New colonies appeared called Victoria, Western Australia, Tasmania and Queensland. They later became the States of the Commonwealth of Australia.

convicts ▫ people found guilty of a crime
sentence ▫ the punishment given to someone who has committed a crime

GRAMMAR

1 Read the text *A short history of Australia* quickly and find out why the British first settled in Australia.

2 Look at the verbs highlighted in the text. Write them in the correct column in the table. Then say why each tense is used each time.

Past simple	Past continuous	Past perfect
were	....	....
....	....	....
....		....
....		
....		
....		

3 Complete the text below with the correct form of the verb in brackets (past simple, past continuous or past perfect).

The Aborigines (1) *were* (be) the first Australians. There are fewer aborigines now than when the European settlers (2) .... (arrive) because a lot of Aborigines (3) .... (die) from diseases brought by the settlers. In 1921, there (4) .... (be) only 61,000 Aborigines in Australia. By 1991, this number (5) .... (increase) to 270,000, which is approximately 1.5% of the Australian population. After the European settlement in Australia in 1788, almost 5 million people from 200 different countries (6) .... (immigrate) to Australia. They (7) .... (look) for new lives away from problems in their own countries and they (8) .... (hope) to start new lives. They (9) .... (find) new lives in Australia and (10) .... (make) it their home. If the British (11) .... (not invade) Australia in 1788 it could have been very different.

SKILLS

4 Read the text again and match the paragraphs (1-5) with the topics below.

a. Why the British settled in Australia.
b. Growth of the white population.
c. Development of the States of the Commonwealth.
d. Australia's first people.
e. The British settlement of Australia.

5 Read the text again. Delete any sentences which you think repeat information or give non-essential information.

6 Now look at the remaining sentences. Can you rewrite any of them so that they give the same information but using fewer words?

7 Now write a summary in 90 words. Use linkers (*and, but, then,* etc.) to join the sentences that you selected and shortened so that the summary reads smoothly.

Module 4

States and systems

IN THIS MODULE YOU WILL READ AND HEAR ABOUT:

- the British parliament and recent changes in the system
- how the British monarchy has faced crises and survived
- the US constitution
- the US legal system
- national days in Britain, the USA and Ireland
- pop music as a form of political protest
- the US government

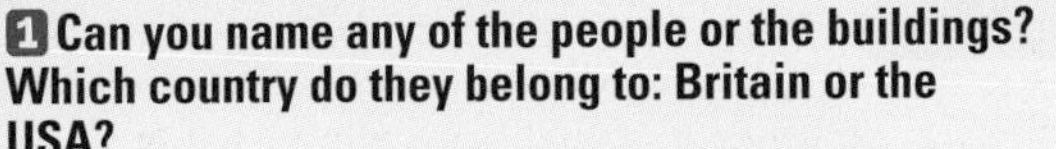

1 Can you name any of the people or the buildings? Which country do they belong to: Britain or the USA?

2 Match the people in the photos (A-D) to the buildings (1-4).

UK parliament: tradition...

In the 14th century, the British parliament split into two divisions, the House of Lords, which included the ▫bishops and the aristocracy (or 'peers'), and the House of Commons, which included representatives of the ordinary people. The two Houses still exist today, but over the centuries the elected House of Commons has become the more powerful. The Lords, whose members are not elected and who traditionally inherited their seat in the House from their fathers, no longer have the automatic right to block new laws. The British parliament is one of the oldest parliamentary systems in the world, and foreigners are often ▫puzzled by some of its ancient customs. During debates in the House of Commons, for example, members are not permitted to refer to each other by name, but must use the title "The Honourable Member". The Lord Chancellor, who controls debates in the House of Lords, must sit on the 'woolsack', a seat filled with wool that originated in the 14th century when wool was a symbol of Britain's prosperity. The position of the Lord Chancellor will soon be abolished. This is just one of the radical changes that have been imposed on the 700-year-old parliament in recent years, including the creation of a separate Scottish Parliament and Welsh and Northern Irish Assemblies.

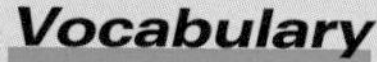

Vocabulary

1 Match the political words to their definitions.

1. candidate
2. to stand
3. to elect
4. seat
5. debate
6. Act

a. to ask for people's votes
b. a position in parliament
c. a formal, controlled argument
d. to give someone the most votes
e. a law that parliament passes
f. a person who wants your vote

Before you read

2 Do you know what the photos on this page represent? What is an English Lord?

Reading

3 Read the text on this page and answer the questions.

1. Which has the most political power – the House of Lords or the House of Commons?
2. Which House has members who used to inherit their places in parliament?
3. What must members of the House of Commons call each other during debates?
4. Who sits on 'the woolsack'?
5. What is its symbolic meaning?

WORD BANK

to back ▫ to support
to be tried ▫ to be legally judged
Bill ▫ a proposal for a new law
bishop ▫ a high rank of priest
by-election ▫ an election for a single seat in parliament that happens when someone dies or resigns
to launch ▫ to start
puzzled ▫ confused
turnout ▫ the number of voters that vote in an election

...and change

LORD'S PROPOSAL FOR A LOWER VOTING AGE

Conservative peer Lord Lucas of Crudwell and Dingwall has proposed a new voting age of 16, and a campaign supporting his ▫Bill has ▫been launched at the Houses of Parliament. The Votes at 16 Campaign is ▫backed by a wide range of political and youth groups, and the reformers have a strong case. At sixteen, they argue, young people can leave school, marry (without parental consent in Scotland), be company directors, ▫be tried in a Crown Court and join some sections of the armed forces.

British voter ▫turnout in recent elections

General (national) elections	
1997	2001
72%	*59%*
Local (council) elections	
1998	2003
29%	*35%*
European elections	
1994	1999
36%	*23%*

THE GUARDIAN

March 24th 2003

Peers stand in Lords by-election

The son of a war hero and the grandson of a prime minister are among the 81 candidates standing in a House of Lords ▫by-election tomorrow, following the death in January of hereditary peer Viscount Oxfuird. Lord Oxfuird was one of 92 peers with inherited titles allowed to stay in parliament after the passing of the House of Lords Act in November 1999, when more than 600 dukes, marquesses, earls, viscounts and barons lost their hereditary right to a seat in the House.

The 92 hereditaries were allowed to stay as a concession to the opposition and the government agreed that any of the 92 who died would be replaced in a by-election.

4 EP Read the two texts on this page and choose the correct alternatives.

1. Lord Lucas wants people to be able to
   a. marry
   b. join the army
   c. vote
   when they are 16.
2. His supporters think that 16-year-olds are old enough for this because:
   a. they already understand a lot about politics.
   b. they already have a lot of responsibilities.
   c. people in other countries can vote at that age.
3. In 1999, the government took away seats in parliament from
   a. 92 hereditary peers.
   b. nearly all hereditary peers.
   c. members of the House of Commons.
4. When a hereditary peer now dies,
   a. an election takes place.
   b. their son inherits their position in parliament.
   c. their position in parliament disappears.

Before you listen

5 Look at the statistics about voter turnout in British elections. Why do you think the statistics are like this? How often, roughly, do the British have elections?

Listening

6 Listen to two young British people talking about politics. For each person, answer these questions.

1. How old are they?
2. Are they interested in politics?
3. Have they ever voted?
4. Are they going to vote in the local elections?
5. Would they like the voting age to be lowered to 16?
6. Why (not)?

Speaking

7 Discuss in pairs. How often do you have elections in your country? Do you think that more or fewer people vote than in Britain? What is the attitude of young people in your country to politics?

Writing

8 Research the answers to the following questions, then write a paragraph about the way your country is governed.

> Is the parliament divided into different houses, like the UK parliament?
> How many members of parliament are there?
> How often are they elected?
> What are the main political parties?
> What is the leader of the government called?
> How is he/she chosen?
> What party does the current leader belong to?

The ups and downs of the British monarchy

The British people have had a monarchy for over a thousand years. The relationship between the monarch and the people has suffered some serious crises in the country's history, but the monarchy always seems to recover.

Revolution: Charles I

The biggest crisis in the monarchy's history came in 1649 when the king was actually condemned to death by parliament. Charles I wanted the monarchy to have more power, and in 1629 he dismissed the parliament and ruled for 11 years without it.
In 1642 a Civil War broke out between the Royalists and the supporters of parliament, the Roundheads under Oliver Cromwell. The Roundheads won, Charles was beheaded and the monarchy abolished. England was, in effect, a republic for 11 years, governed by a Lord Protector (first Cromwell and then his son). But in 1660 the age of the Restoration began when Charles's son, Charles II, was made king.

King Charles I.

Queen Victoria celebrating her Diamond Jubilee in 1901.

Retirement: Victoria

When Queen Victoria's husband, Prince Albert, died in 1861, the Queen suffered a terrible depression. She ◘withdrew from public life and spent more time at her palaces in Scotland and on the Isle of Wight than she did in London. For over 20 years she ◘performed no national duties. People became critical of the monarchy and, in a time of huge industrial and scientific progress, members of parliament began to talk about republicanism. But Victoria recovered and in 1897 her Diamond Jubilee, celebrating a record 60 years on the throne, was a great public relations success with huge processions, ceremonies and public celebrations.

Before you read

1 Can you identify any of the royal people in the photos? Can you name any members of the current British royal family?

Vocabulary

2 Complete these 'royal' words. Find them in the texts if you are not sure.

1. The son of a monarch is a p....... .
2. The daughter of a monarch is a p....... .
3. The special chair which a monarch sits on is a th....... .
4. The ceremony where a monarch is created is a c....... .
5. The person who will become the next monarch is the current monarch's h....... .
6. A royal residence is a p....... .

Reading

3 Complete the table with the correct dates from the text.

....	The English Civil War begins
....	The execution of Charles I
....	The Restoration of the monarchy
....	Death of Prince Albert
....	Victoria celebrates 60 years on the throne
....	Edward VIII becomes king
....	Edward VIII abdicates
....	Elizabeth II becomes queen
....	Prince Charles marries Princess Diana
....	Prince Charles and Princess Diana divorce
....	Princess Diana dies
....	Elizabeth II celebrates 50 years on the throne

4 EP Which British king or queen:

1. became less popular immediately after the death of Princess Diana?
2. became very private when her husband died?
3. came to the throne because his brother abandoned it?
4. couldn't get married and become monarch?
5. had a coronation in 1660?
6. wanted to take power away from parliament?

5 Read the newspaper article on page 53 and answer the questions.

1. Find:
   a. the name of the Queen's husband.
   b. the name of the Queen's residence in London.
   c. the name of the street in front of her residence.
   d. the titles of two patriotic songs.
2. How many members of the public, according to the writer, sang to the Queen on her jubilee day?
3. Why do you think the crowd was 'red, white and blue'?
4. What impression do you get of the success of the jubilee celebrations?

Before you listen

6 Can you name any of Queen Elizabeth's children or grandchildren?

Listen

7 Listen to Gary, Emma and Linda giving their views on the monarchy. Who supports the monarchy, who opposes it and who has no strong feelings about it?

WORD BANK

boost – an improvement	outdated – old-fashioned
cheer – when people shout to show their appreciation	to perform – to do
to crown – to be the climax of	rendition – performance
to discharge – to do a duty	to threaten – to promise danger
drop – reduction	thunderous – as loud as thunder
low-key – not very visible	to withdraw – to retire from other people's company

Abdication: Edward VIII

When George V died in January 1936, his heir Edward was in love with a twice-divorced American woman, Wallis Simpson. His family and the government disapproved of Mrs Simpson, but Edward wanted to marry her. In the end he was forced to choose between his love and the throne, and he chose to abandon the throne. In December of that year, five months before his planned coronation and with war threatening the world, Edward VIII addressed the nation by radio and told them that "I have found it impossible to carry on the heavy burden of responsibility and to discharge the duties of king ... without the help and support of the woman I love". His brother George VI took his place at the coronation, and proved to be a strong monarch. When George's daughter, Princess Elizabeth, came to the throne in 1952 the monarchy was once again extremely popular.

Edward VIII and Mrs Simpson.

A sea of flowers for Princess Diana.

Tragedy: Princess Diana

In modern times, people began to see the monarchy as outdated, but the royal family was given a tremendous boost in 1981, when Prince Charles married the popular Princess Diana. Diana became an international superstar, more popular than her husband from whom she divorced in 1996.

When she died in a car crash in 1997 many people accused the royal family of treating her badly during her marriage and abandoning her after her divorce.

The Queen and Prince Charles suffered a huge drop in popularity, and they were advised to modernise and become less formal and distant. Celebrations for the Queen's Golden Jubilee in 2002 were deliberately kept low-key, as the organisers feared that the public would not be interested.

8 EP Listen again and complete the sentences in the most appropriate way.

1. Gary has a good opinion of:
   a. the Queen and all her children.
   b. the Queen and one of her children.
   c. the Queen's children, but not the Queen.
2. Emma wants the royal family:
   a. to pay for themselves.
   b. to be abolished.
   c. to be more modern.
3. Linda thinks the monarchy will survive because:
   a. the young generation are very popular.
   b. the Queen works very hard.
   c. they never have any problems.

Speaking

9 Which other countries still have a monarchy? Do you think there is any place for kings and queens in the 21st century?

THE DAILY TELEGRAPH June 5th, 2002

A jubilee sea of red, white and blue

BY CAROLINE DAVIES

Three balcony appearances and more than a million voices raised in a thunderous rendition of the National Anthem crowned the Queen's Golden Jubilee celebrations yesterday.

On the day that the Queen spoke of her 'gratitude, respect and pride' in the nation, the nation responded with cheers, applause and enough flag-waving to transform the Mall into a patriotic sea of red, white and blue.

Three times the crowd brought the Queen and Prince Philip to the balcony of Buckingham Palace and three times they were repaid in song, as the huge mass of spectators sang Land of Hope and Glory and God Save the Queen.

The land of the free

The American Declaration of Independence

This is part of the original American Declaration of Independence, written by Thomas Jefferson to challenge the British government on July 4th 1776.

The unanimous declaration of the thirteen United States of America
... We ▫hold these truths to be self-evident, that all men are created equal, that they are ▫endowed by their Creator with certain ▫unalienable Rights, that among these are Life, Liberty and the ▫pursuit of Happiness.

The American Constitution

This is the introduction to the American Constitution, written by members of the newly-independent US government in 1787.

We the People of the United States, in Order to form a more perfect Union, establish Justice, insure domestic Tranquillity, provide for the common defense, promote the general Welfare, and secure the Blessings of Liberty to ourselves and our Posterity, do ordain and establish this Constitution for the United States of America.

The Amendments

These are some of the 27 amendments added to the Constitution by different governments over the years.

Amendment I 1791

Congress shall make no law respecting an establishment of religion, or prohibiting ▫the free exercise thereof, of ▫abridging the freedom of speech, or of the press, or the right of the people peaceably to assemble, and to ▫petition the Government for a ▫redress of grievances.

Amendment II 1791

A well regulated militia being necessary to the security of a free State, the right of the people to keep and bear Arms shall not be ▫infringed.

Amendment XIII 1865

Neither slavery nor ▫involuntary servitude... shall exist within the United States, or any place subject to their jurisdiction.

Amendment XIX 1920

The right of citizens of the United States to vote shall not be denied or abridged by the United States or by any state on account of sex.

Amendment XXV 1967

In case of the removal of the President from office or of his death or resignation, the Vice President shall become President.

Amendment XXVI 1971

The right of citizens of the United States, who are 18 years of age or older, to vote, shall not be denied or abridged by the United States or any state on account of age.

Before you read

1 When and why did America become an independent nation? What is a nation's 'constitution'?

Reading

2 Read the extract from the Declaration of Independence. What is its main message?

a. The USA will be a more religious nation than Britain.
b. God intended all people to have the same rights and freedoms.
c. The USA will make all its people happy.

3 Read the introduction to the American Constitution. Which of the underlined phrases mean the same as the following?

1. Defend the people.
2. Make sure that there is peace in the country.
3. Make sure that we and the people that come after us are free.
4. Make sure that the people are treated in a fair way.
5. Look after the people's needs.

4 EP Read the Amendments to the Constitution. Match them to these descriptions.

a. The abolition of slavery.
b. The lowering of the voting age from 21 to 18.
c. The right of the vice president to take command if the president is killed.
d. The right of women to vote.
e. The right of the people to carry guns.
f. The right of the people to free speech and religion, including political protest.

WORD BANK

to abridge ▪ to cut, make smaller
appeal ▪ when someone challenges a legal decision
to be sworn in ▪ to accept an official position in a formal ceremony
to craft ▪ to create
to deem ▪ to believe
to endow ▪ to provide
founders ▪ the people who wrote the original Constitution
to head ▪ to go in a specific direction
to hold ▪ to believe
in the event Bush should be incapacitated ▪ in case Bush is unable to function
to infringe ▪ to violate
involuntary servitude ▪ being someone's servant when you don't want to be
neat ▪ fantastic
to petition ▪ to ask for something
pursuit ▪ attempt to get
redress of grievances ▪ making right something that is not fair
to roll back ▪ to reverse
tarmac ▪ the piece of ground where aeroplanes land and take off
the free exercise thereof ▪ the freedom to practise it (religion)
unalienable ▪ that cannot be taken away
undisclosed ▪ secret
worrisome ▪ frightening

The Constitution's 27 Amendments: the ways we embrace their spirit every day

FIRST AMENDMENT (1791)

Bill Gazzo, 81, of Hampton, was furious when he got his new property tax assessment in 2000. After an appeal, Allegheny County cut his assessment.
Then, for the next year, it rose again. That's when he picked up a sign and headed Downtown to the City-County Building with a few dozen others. Gazzo had never taken part in a demonstration before. "It was OK. It was a little noisy, cold. There were a lot of others." His assessment has since been rolled back to the 2001 level and he just got a letter from Allegheny County saying it will stay at that level until 2005.

SECOND AMENDMENT (1791)

When she took up arms herself a few years back, Catherine Montest of Coraopolis "was scared to death" at the idea of carrying a gun. Her job in industrial sales sometimes took her to places she found worrisome. Her husband encouraged her to get training and now, on some travels, she takes along a handgun. "I've got these two really neat kids that I would like to come home to," she explains today. Like many in the midst of the debate over handguns, Montest believes the founders intended the Second Amendment as a guarantor of individual liberties. "You look at these amendments and they all speak to individual rights."

25TH AMENDMENT (1967)

On Nov. 22, 1963, President John F. Kennedy lay lifeless at Parkland Hospital in Dallas. The uncertainty about who was in charge of the nation led his vice president, Lyndon B. Johnson, to be sworn in on an airplane on the tarmac at a Dallas airport. Searching for a way to end ambiguity about who was in power in moments of crisis, Congress crafted a new amendment. It allowed for the vice president to temporarily assume the duties of chief executive if the president deemed himself, or was determined by the vice president and a majority of the cabinet, unable to fulfill the duties of office.

After the terrorist attacks on New York and Washington, presidential succession became so important that Cheney and Bush are rarely seen in the same place. Since that time, Cheney has spent numerous days secured in what officials will only call "an undisclosed location" assuring a continuity of leadership in the event Bush should be incapacitated.

5 EP Read the texts on this page and match them with the correct amendment from exercise 4.

6 Answer the questions.

1. Why did Bill Gazzo demonstrate against his local government?
2. Has his situation improved since he protested?
3. Why did Catherine Montest start to carry a gun?
4. What reason does she give to justify her decision?
5. What crisis forced the creation of the 25th Amendment?
6. What security measures did George Bush and his vice president take in 2001?

Speaking/Writing

7 There is a lot of discussion about the Second Amendment these days. Do you think it is relevant now, 200 years after it was written? Write a letter to a newspaper explaining your opinion.

US law: show business...

In the USA, law is a prestigious, high-profile business that can make a lot of money both for lawyers and for plaintiffs. American TV series and films about crime and the law are popular with audiences all around the world, and some real-life American legal cases and trials could almost have been written by Hollywood scriptwriters, particularly those dealing with extreme compensation claims.

NYPD Blue, which began in 1993, brought a new realism to the TV cop show. Concentrating on the detectives of the Police Department's 15th precinct, it depicts the chaotic nature of the police officers' work and private lives as much as the dangers of the New York streets.

In **The Silence of the Lambs** (1991), Clarice Starling from the Federal Bureau of Investigation (the government's investigation agency) is assigned to a murder case. She specialises in psychiatry and, as part of her investigations, she has to interview the notorious serial killer Hannibal "The Cannibal" Lecter.

Dead Man Walking (1995) tells the real-life story of a nun, Sister Prejean, who works with prisoners on death row. In the film she forms a relationship with Louisiana murderer Matthew Poncelet, who killed two teenagers. Although she is disgusted by his crime, she does not sympathise with his harsh punishment.

CSI started in 2000 and depicts the often horrific investigations of the Crime Scene Investigation Unit in Las Vegas. The unit's forensic scientists interpret clues in each episode in order to solve crimes in a way similar to Sherlock Holmes.

LA Law, made between 1986 and 1994, follows the various attorneys, including the deputy District Attorney, of a Los Angeles law firm. The lawyers take on a variety of cases, but the series also concentrates on their personal relationships.

Number of executions in the US in 2002

Texas	33	Ohio	3
Oklahoma	7	Alabama	2
Missouri	6	North Carolina	2
Georgia	4	Mississippi	2
Virginia	4	California	1
Florida	3	Louisiana	1
South Carolina	3		

There are 38 states that still have the death penalty. Since 1995, all executions have taken the form of an injection of lethal drugs, although other methods, such as the electric chair, are still legal in some states.

WORD BANK

to allege ▪ to state as a true fact
to dismiss ▪ to reject
to file ▪ to record publicly
firm ▪ company
harsh ▪ strict, hard
lawsuit ▪ legal case
to mislead ▪ to deliberately confuse
notorious ▪ famous for bad reasons
plaintiff ▪ someone who initiate legal action aganist another person
precinct ▪ a district of a US city
to take on ▪ to accept

...and big business

WORLDNEWS

McDonalds targeted in obesity ▪lawsuit

> "I had always believed McDonald's was healthy for my son"
>
> **Mother of plaintiff**

The US fast food industry and health campaigners are watching closely a lawsuit ▪filed on behalf of several obese teenagers who claim the fast-food company McDonald's is responsible for making them fat.

The lawsuit, filed by lawyer Samuel Hirsch in a Manhattan federal court, ▪alleges that McDonald's deliberately ▪misled consumers into thinking their cheeseburgers and other products were healthy and nutritious.

It says the company did not adequately provide information on the health risks associated with fast food, and the children developed health problems such as diabetes, high blood pressure and obesity from eating its products.

If Hirsch is successful, fast-food companies fear that it could start a series of further suits and huge payments to victims – potentially running into billions of dollars – similar to those that have severely damaged the tobacco industry.

The mother of one of the children, who at the age of 15 weighs more than 180 kilos, said in papers filed before the court that "I had always believed McDonald's was healthy for my son".

McDonald's has asked the court to ▪dismiss the case.

Before you read

1 Do you recognise any of the TV programmes or films on page 56? What are they about?

2 These abbreviations are all connected with the US legal system. Do you know what they stand for? You can find them all in the texts on page 56.

CSI .... FBI ....
DA .... NYPD ....

Vocabulary

3 Find these words in the text.

1. A slang word for a police officer.
2. A police officer who investigates a crime.
3. Someone who analyses physical clues, and dead bodies, from a crime.
4. A lawyer who can represent people in court.
5. A problem that needs to be solved legally.
6. A murderer who has killed several times.
7. Part of a prison where prisoners are waiting for execution.

Reading

4 EP Which film or TV series deals with:

1. lawyers who work in court?
2. a prisoner who is waiting to be executed?
3. a government agent and a murderer?
4. ordinary police officers at work in the streets?
5. scientists who investigate crimes?

5 Read the facts about the death penalty and answer the questions.

1. How many US states have the death penalty?
2. Which is the usual method of execution today?
3. How many states executed prisoners in 2002?
4. Which state was responsible for nearly half of all executions in 2002?

6 Read the news report on this page and answer the questions.

1. What is the teenagers' official reason for taking McDonald's to court?
2. Why does their lawyer think that they have a good case?
3. What will McDonald's have to do if the teenagers win their case?
4. How much could cases like this one cost the fast food industry?
5. What other industry has had to make large payments to its 'victims'?
6. Who do you think took that industry to court?

Speaking

7 Discuss these questions.

1. Can you think of any other films or TV series that deal with crime and law? Describe the plots of some of them.
2. What's your opinion of the families that took McDonalds to court? Do you think McDonalds are guilty? What reasons could the families have for bringing a lawsuit against them?
3. Does your country still have the death penalty? If not, when was it abolished? What is your opinion of it?

National celebrations

A time to celebrate

England has no official national holiday, but with Scotland and Wales achieving more political independence recently, there is a growing group of patriotic English people who want to persuade the government to create one. Some people would like to create an extra ◘bank holiday. England has only eight official holidays per year, the lowest number in Europe, and there are no holidays between the last Monday in August and Christmas Day. One suggestion for a new autumn bank holiday is Trafalgar Day, on October 21st, which commemorates a famous English naval victory.

Other people are trying to establish St George's Day (April 23rd) as England's official day of celebration, because St George is England's national saint. A new phenomenon is starting to appear in shops at the start of April – decorations and greetings cards for St George's Day.

On St. George's Day

This precious stone set in the silver sea
Which serves it ◘in the office of a wall,
Or as a ◘moat defensive to a house,
Against the envy of less happier lands,
This blessed ◘plot, this earth, this ◘realm, this England

(from Shakespeare's 'Richard II')

WORD BANK

bank holiday ▪ national public holiday
ceilidh /ˈkeɪli/ ▪ a traditional Irish or Scottish party with dancing
in the office of ▪ in the same way as
moat ▪ water around a castle
neeps ▪ swedes (a yellow root vegetable)
plot ▪ piece of earth
range ▪ selection
realm ▪ kingdom
tatties ▪ potatoes
toast ▪ when you give someone a tribute by drinking to them

1

You are invited
to a traditional
Burns Night Supper

at the Caledonian Hotel
on Burns Night
(January 25th)
to celebrate the birthday
of Scotland's national poet,
Robert Burns.

7pm Drinks

Entrance of the haggis, accompanied by bagpipes

Recital of Burns' "Address to a Haggis"

Cutting of the haggis

▪Toast to the haggis with whisky

Dinner: roast beef, haggis, ▪neeps, ▪tatties

Toast to the ladies

Reply from the ladies

Toast to The Immortal Memory of Robert Burns

Traditional Scottish dancing

Singing of Burns' "Auld Lang Syne"

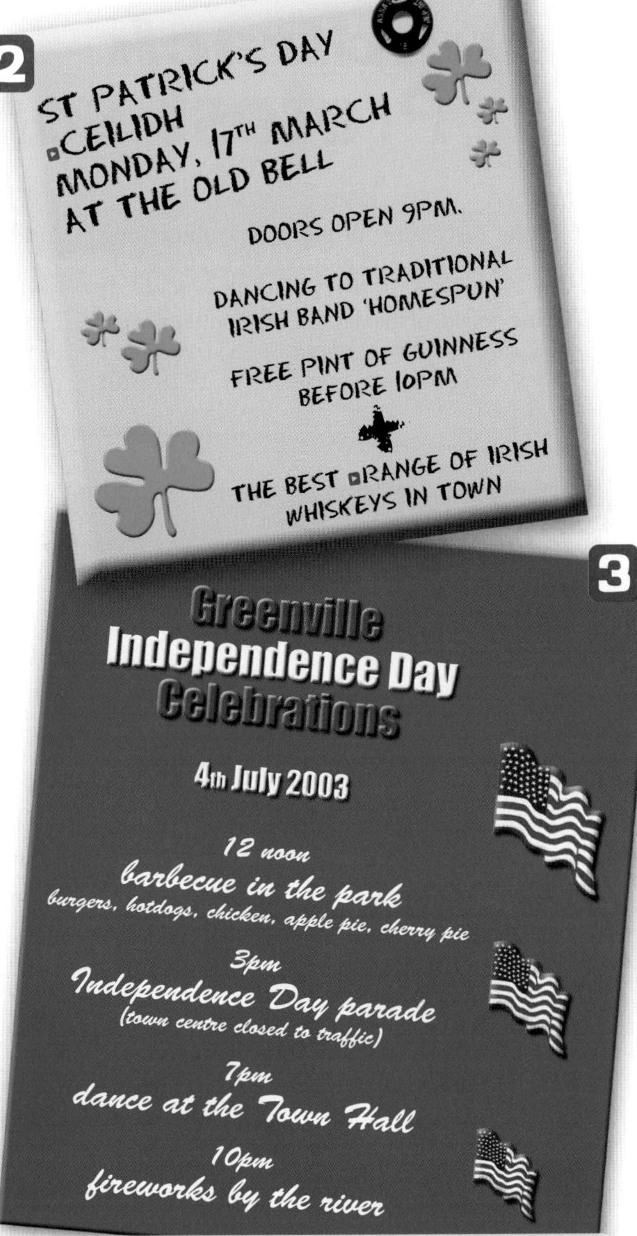

2
ST PATRICK'S DAY
▪CEILIDH
MONDAY, 17TH MARCH
AT THE OLD BELL
DOORS OPEN 9PM.
DANCING TO TRADITIONAL IRISH BAND 'HOMESPUN'
FREE PINT OF GUINNESS BEFORE 10PM
THE BEST ▪RANGE OF IRISH WHISKEYS IN TOWN
3
Greenville
Independence Day
Celebrations
4th July 2003
12 noon
barbecue in the park
burgers, hotdogs, chicken, apple pie, cherry pie
3pm
Independence Day parade
(town centre closed to traffic)
7pm
dance at the Town Hall
10pm
fireworks by the river

Before you read

1 Which nationalities do you think the people in the photos are? Do you know what festivals they are celebrating? When is England's national day?

Reading

2 Match the photos (A-C) with the texts (1-3).

3 Complete the table with details about the festivals.

Festival	Country	Date	Traditional food/drink
Burns Night	....	....	....
....	....	17th March	....
....	USA	....	....

4 Answer the questions about the festivals.

1. What does Burns Night celebrate?
2. Find the names of two of Burns' poems.
3. What three toasts are given on Burns night?
4. When can you get a free pint of Guinness at the Old Bell?
5. What four activities are planned in Greenville for 4th July?

5 EP Read the text *A time to celebrate*. Are the statements true or false?

1. England doesn't have a national day.
2. The last Monday in August is a bank holiday in England.
3. Some English people want an extra bank holiday in the autumn.
4. Trafalgar Day is already a bank holiday.
5. St George is Scotland's national saint.

Speaking

6 Does your country have a national song or anthem? What are the words and music like? Is the song popular in the whole country?

Writing

7 Write a paragraph about your country's national day(s). Explain:

> when it is.
> what its historical origins are.
> what happens on that day.
> what people eat and drink.

Soundtrack
Protest songs

During the early years of pop music, most song lyrics were about love and romance, but in the 1960s, political songwriters started to use their lyrics to criticise the politics of the day. The first protest singers were folk singers such as America's Bob Dylan, and the protest song reached a peak in the 1970s with America's unpopular involvement in the Vietnam War. British pop protest songs did not really appear until the 1980s, when Britain's traditional industries began to disappear, and many young people found themselves unemployed and opposed to the policies of the Prime Minister, Margaret Thatcher.

WORD BANK

buddy ▫ friend
for dear life ▫ (slang) to save our lives
to get filled in ▫ (slang) to be attacked
hiring man ▫ man who decides which people to employ
jam ▫ trouble
Khe Sahn ▫ a battle of the Vietnam War
next of kin ▫ your closest relative (the person who is informed of your death)
rumour ▫ something people say without knowing if it is true
shipyard ▫ where ships are built
to take someone to task ▫ to put someone under pressure (also a play on the term 'task force' - a group of soldiers)
up to me ▫ my decision
V.A. man ▫ representative of the Vietnam Veterans Association
with all the will in the world ▫ with good intentions

Born in the USA

Bruce Springsteen, 1984

Bruce Springsteen is one of the USA's most enduring rock artists, having a string of world-wide hits in the 1970s and the 1980s. His songs often deal with the frustrations of the ordinary working-class man, and this song reveals the bitterness of a Vietnam War veteran.

Born down in a dead man's town
The first kick I took was when I hit the ground
You end up like a dog that's been beat too much
'Til you spend half your life just covering up

[chorus]

Born in the USA
Born in the USA
Born in the USA
Born in the USA

I got in a little hometown ▫jam
And so they put a rifle in my hands
Sent me off to Vietnam
To go and kill the yellow man

[chorus]

Come back home to the refinery
▫Hiring man says "Son, if it was ▫up to me"
I go down to see the ▫V.A. man
He said "Son, don't you understand?"

[chorus]

I had a ▫buddy at ▫Khe Sahn
Fighting off the Viet Cong
They're still there, he's all gone
He had a little girl in Saigon
I got a picture of him in her arms

Down in the shadow of the penitentiary
Out by the gas fires of the refinery
I'm ten years down the road
Nowhere to run, ain't got nowhere to go

I'm a long gone Daddy in the USA
Born in the USA
I'm a cool rocking Daddy in the USA
Born in the USA

Shipbuilding

Elvis Costello, 1982

Elvis Costello first became famous during the British punk music era of the late 1970s. His hits of the 1980s were known for their lyrics and often had a political message. This song is set in a British industrial town during the Falklands War against Argentina.

Is it worth it?
A new winter coat and shoes for the wife
And a bicycle on the kid's birthday
It's just a ▫rumour that was spread around town
By the women and children
Soon we'll be shipbuilding
Well, I ask you
The boy said "Dad they're going ▫to take me to task, but I'll be back by Christmas"
It's just a rumour that was spread around town
Somebody said that someone ▫got filled in
For saying that people get killed in
The result of this shipbuilding
▫With all the will in the world
Diving ▫for dear life
When we could be diving for pearls
It's just a rumour that was spread around town
A telegram or a picture postcard
Within weeks they'll be reopening the ▫shipyards
And notifying the ▫next of kin
Once again
It's all we're skilled in
We will be shipbuilding
With all the will in the world
Diving for dear life
When we could be diving for pearls

Before you read

1 Do you know what events are shown in the photos on page 60? What are the people protesting about?

Reading

2 Read the text on page 60. Find out:

1. what a protest song is.
2. when pop lyrics started to become political.
3. the name of a famous protest singer.
4. an event that inspired a lot of protest songs.
5. a person who inspired a lot of protest songs.

Reading/Listening

3 Listen to the Bruce Springsteen song and answer the questions.

1. Why did the singer go to the Vietnam War?
2. What happened to his friend there?
3. What difficulties did he have when he came home?
4. What does he feel about his future now?

4 EP Read and listen to the Elvis Costello song. Choose the correct answer to the questions.

1. What happened to the shipyards in the town?
   a. They were closed down.
   b. They were bombed in a war.
2. What is the 'rumour that was spread around town'?
   a. That there would soon be a war.
   b. That people had been killed.
3. What effect would a war have on the people of the town?
   a. They would be in danger.
   b. They would find jobs again.
4. What is the significance of the things in lines 2 and 3? They are things that
   a. people couldn't afford during a war.
   b. people would be able to buy because of their new jobs.
5. How does the singer feel about this attitude?
   a. He doesn't approve of people earning money through war.
   b. He is pleased that the people will be employed again.

Speaking

5 How effective do you think these songs are as protest songs? Can you think of any pop singers today who have a political message?

Language & Culture

The US government

The part of the US government which makes and passes laws is known as the Congress of the United States of America. It was created in 1789 by Article 1 of The Constitution of the United States.

Congress is made up of two houses: the Senate and the House of Representatives. The Senate consists of two Senators from each state. When a senator has been elected they serve a six-year term. Until 1913 senators were elected by state law makers but since that year senators have been chosen by the people's vote. The House of Representatives consists of 435 members. Representatives are elected from congressional districts and serve two-year terms.

The two main parties in US politics are the Democrats and the Republicans. When a president is elected he or she serves in government for a period of four years. After four years elections are held. If the president (and vice president) win, they stay in government for another four years. However, a president can only ever serve for two terms (eight years in total).

There has never been a female president of the USA, but perhaps in the future a woman will be elected.

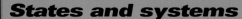

ABRAHAM LINCOLN

a) Became president 1861-65 (during the American Civil War)
b) Born: Kentucky, 1809
Parents = poor country people. Educated himself
c) 1865 - assassinated by John Wilkes Booth (at the theatre)
d) Lincoln Memorial = huge statue in Washington DC (opened in 1922).
National Memorial Day (inspired by Lincoln's 'Gettysburg Address' speech 1863), remembering Americans who have died in wars
e) Wanted to keep the USA united.
Opposed to slavery. 1863 The Emancipation Proclamation - freed all US slaves

GRAMMAR

1 Read the text *The US government* quickly and find out how long a US president can remain in power.

2 Read the text again and underline all the examples of the passive tense. Then write them in the correct column in the table.

Present simple	Past simple	Present perfect	Future
is known	....	....	....
....	....	....	
....			
....			
....			

3 Complete the sentences with the verbs in brackets in the passive.

1. In Britain, members of the House of Lords *are not elected* (not elect).
2. Slavery ...... (abolish) in the USA in 1865.
3. When senators in the US ...... (elect), they serve a six-year term.
4. The American Declaration of Independence ...... (write) by Thomas Jefferson.
5. An election ...... (hold) every four years in the USA.
6. A new law ...... (just pass) in parliament.
7. ...... a woman president ...... (elect) in the future?
8. Two changes ...... (make) to the America Constitution in 1791.

SKILLS

4 Read the notes (a-e) about a famous US president. Put them in a logical order for an oral presentation by matching them to the topics (1-5).

1. Lincoln's childhood.
2. His term as president.
3. His politics.
4. His death.
5. How he is remembered today.

5 Look at the sentences below. Choose a sentence to introduce the presentation and a sentence to close it.

1. Lincoln was president for only four years.
2. I'm going to talk about Abraham Lincoln, one of the USA's most famous and respected presidents.
3. Even today, Lincoln remains an inspiration to other presidents and to ordinary Americans.
4. I'm going to talk about how Abraham Lincoln was assassinated.

6 Now write the whole presentation, then read it aloud. Remember to use the opening and closing sentences you chose in exercise 5.

7 Now choose a famous politician or leader from your country. Write notes about him/her, then put the notes in order. Add an introductory and a concluding sentence and read your presentations aloud to the class.

Module 5

Education

IN THIS MODULE YOU WILL READ AND HEAR ABOUT:

- a British school that encourages very young children to study
- college students in the UK
- American high school culture
- virtual high schools on the Internet
- specialist music and drama schools in the UK and USA
- bilingual education in Canada and Wales
- a UK student trying to decide what to do after leaving school

Most popular exam subjects for British 16-year-olds (2002)

Subject	Candidates (in 1,000s)
Maths	569
English	560
Science	559
English Literature	501
Design & Technology	409
French	312
Geography	208
History	194
Art & Design	182
German	125

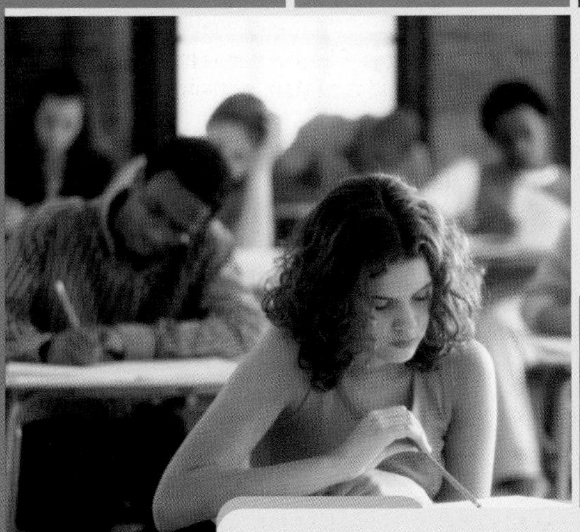

What causes stress for American high school students?

Pressure to get good grades	44%
Pressure to get into college	32%
Pressure to fit in socially	29%
Pressure to use drugs or alcohol	19%
Pressure to have a boyfriend/girlfriend	13%

1 What are the school pupils in the photos doing? Which countries do you think they are from? Do the schools look like your school?

2 Read the statistics about exams and stress. Would the statistics be roughly the same in your country?

Too much too young?

Hothouse

It's 10am on a bright Saturday morning, but, in a classroom in Hertfordshire, a group of four-year-olds are starting what is, for them, a school day like any other. They start to ▫ tap at their keyboards, producing a database of all their toys. Half an hour later they write up the theory that they have just put into practice. Welcome to Ryde College, the place where you are never too young to start.

Children compiling a database of their toys.

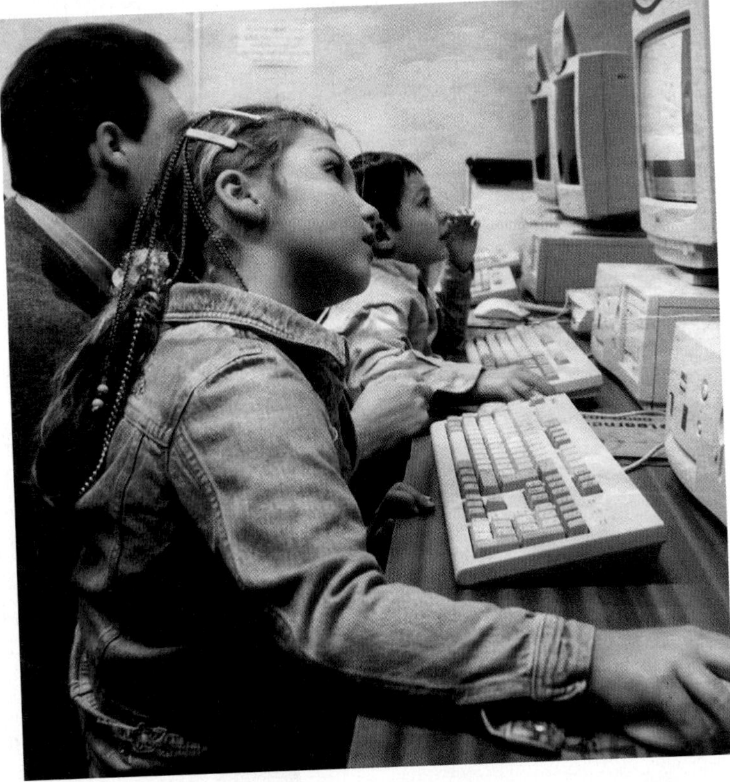

Ryde College opened in 1982 and has become famous for the precocious success of its students. Most of its pupils attend regular state primary or secondary schools during the day, and then have classes at Ryde in the evening and on Saturdays. Pupils come here to ▫get ahead of the rest. You can put a child into a 'technology for ▫toddlers' class before it has reached its second birthday, or enter your seven-year-old for a GCSE.

100 per cent of Ryde GCSE students pass their exams, even though they cover the courses in nine months. Most secondary schools cover the same syllabus in two years. Last year the college's successes included a six-year-old who passed a GCSE in Information Technology, and a 10-year-

Before you read

1 At what age do children start school in your country? When do they take major exams? Do you think those ages are appropriate?

Reading

2 Read the text and answer the questions.

1. What is the difference between Ryde College and most other British schools?
   - **a.** Ryde College has better teachers.
   - **b.** Ryde College students study earlier and more quickly.
   - **c.** Ryde College takes only the best students.
2. Find the names of two English school exams.
3. Find the English word for a university qualification.

3 Complete the table about the usual education system in England. You can find the information in the text.

The state system	Age
Begin primary school	.... or ....
Begin secondary school	11
Start studying for GCSE exams	14
Take GCSE exams	.... (students can leave school at this age)
Take .... exams	18
School hours: Monday to ...., approximately 9am - 3.30pm	

WORD BANK

ethos ◘ fundamental principles
to get ahead of ◘ to be better than
gifted ◘ extremely talented
hothousing ◘ to intensely educate young children (as a plant in a hothouse gets intense heat)
to lessen ◘ to diminish
OAP ◘ Old Age Pensioner
to tap ◘ to hit with the finger
toddler ◘ a child aged approximately 18 months-3 years
well-off ◘ rich
well-rounded ◘ complete and varied

flowers

old who passed an A-level in computing. Dr Ryde, the college's 71-year-old founder, believes that the ◘ethos of the college is the right one:
'When a child is young, their brains are like sponges, they absorb everything you give them,' he says. 'By the time they are in their late teens, their ability to learn ◘has lessened. They are the ◘OAPs of the academic world.'

Dr Ryde calls his methods 'accelerated learning'. Others call it ◘hothousing. Call it what you like, but it is a growing trend in British education. These days the competition to get a child into a good school is so intense that parents are increasingly using private tutors to help their child survive the education system. Some ◘well-off parents even employ private tutors for their three-year-olds.

Hothousing is also a phenomenon of the state system these days. Whereas children used to start formal education at five, some now start at four, and increasing numbers of state pupils are taking GCSEs before they reach secondary school.
In a Ryde world, all children would be able to take exams when they were ready, even to start degrees at 11. Some argue that such children are being deprived of their childhood and become less ◘well-rounded adults as a result. Dr Ryde dismisses such criticism. 'If you have a child that is ◘gifted in ice-skating or singing, then no-one comments if those children get extra training at a young age,' he says. 'So why is it wrong to give children who have a passion for learning extra education when they are ready for it?'

by Lucy Elkins

Parents waiting for their children in the hall where the college's successes are displayed on the noticeboard.

4 What is the youngest age for a student at Ryde College to:
1. start a technology class?
2. pass a GCSE exam?
3. pass an A-level exam?

5 EP Match the beginnings and the ends of the sentences.
1. Most Ryde students
2. GCSE students at Ryde
3. According to Dr Ryde, young children
4. Some rich English people
5. Critics of Ryde
6. Dr Ryde

a. give their three-year-olds private tutors.
b. learn better than teenagers.
c. thinks that children who love studying should have extra education.
d. only study for 9 months.
e. go to state school too.
f. think that the pupils don't have a real childhood.

Writing

6 Write a table like the one in exercise 3 for your country's education system.

Speaking

7 What are the advantages and disadvantages of encouraging very young children to study and be successful? Think about:
> making the most of your abilities.
> getting good qualifications.
> getting a good job.
> being different from other children.
> free time.
> stress.

Topic ▪ Higher education   Vocabulary ▪ Education and exams
Countries ▪ UK   Links ▪ 7e, 10a

Students at home...

At 18, British school-leavers with A-levels can apply for a degree course at university. Most of these courses last for three years, and students must pay all of their own accommodation and living costs, and some of their tuition fees. Since 1990, the government has offered student loans to help the situation. The loans are between £3,000 and £5,000 per year depending on whether students live with their parents or away from home, and also whether or not they live in London.

Students have to pay back their loans when they leave university, but not until their income reaches £10,000 per year. The interest rates are low and there is no deadline for repayment. However, most students find that the loans do not fully meet their needs, so many have to stay in the family home to avoid accommodation costs, or take part-time jobs while they are studying.

Amanda Jenkins, 20, is a student at the University of Cardiff, her home town, in Wales.

Monday 15th March

Had a big row with mum and dad today. They still treat me like I'm at school even though I'm 20 now. It's not my fault that I have to live at home.
I would have loved to have gone to university in Scotland – Glasgow or St Andrew's – but there's no way we could have afforded it.

Tuesday 16th March

Went to the job centre today to look for a part-time job. I have to start saving some money for my future – after all, I'll have a £12,000 loan to pay off when I graduate. I've got interviews with McDonald's and a pub, so I can work after my lectures are finished. And then I can do more studying when I finish work.

Wednesday 17th March

Went into the uni library to study, then went to see Kate and Ali in their flat. They're really lucky – I'm really jealous of my friends who have their own accommodation. But their rent's £120 a week!

Thursday 18th March

Another row with mum. To be honest, I think she resents me being here. She thinks that I'm too old to be living at home. It was OK when she was a student in the 70s. She got a grant from the government, so she had more freedom to choose her university and her accommodation. Anyway, I've got my interview at McDonald's tomorrow. Perhaps something will come of that.

WORD BANK

to afford ▫ to have enough money for
to apply for ▫ to ask for
deadline ▫ time limit
grant ▫ money given to you by an official body that you don't have to pay back
income ▫ the amount of money you earn
row ▫ disagreement

...and abroad

It is common these days for 18-year-old school leavers to take a 'gap year'. Instead of going to university immediately after their A-levels, they go travelling for a year or do charity work abroad, often in exotic locations. Popular destinations for British gap year students are Australia, India and South Africa.

Speaking

1 **What do you want to do when you leave school? Do you want to get a job or do you want to continue studying?**

Reading

2 **EP** **Read the text about British university students. Choose the correct answers to the questions.**

1. British degree courses are usually
   a. five years long.
   b. three years long.
   c. two years long.
2. The British government gives loans to help students pay for
   a. their education.
   b. their living expenses.
   c. both.
3. a. Every student receives / b. Some students receive / c. No student receives } loans of £4,000 per year.
4. Students have to pay back their loans as soon as
   a. they finish their degree.
   b. they get a job.
   c. they start earning a certain sum.
5. a. There is always / b. There is sometimes / c. There isn't } a time limit on the repayment of student loans.

3 **Read Amanda's diary and answer the questions.**

1. What accommodation does she live in?
2. How much money will she owe the government when she leaves university?
3. How much is the rent on her friends' flat?
4. How was the situation different when her mum was at university?

Vocabulary

4 **Find words in the texts that mean:**

1. money that you must pay a university for teaching you.
2. students who have just taken their A-levels.
3. to leave university with a degree.
4. talks given by a university tutor to a large number of students.
5. a slang abbreviation for 'university'.

Before you listen

5 **Read this page and answer the questions.**

1. What is a gap year student?
2. What is the name of the company?
3. What work opportunity are they offering?
4. How many different areas of the world do they operate in?
5. Who do you think this advert is principally aimed at?

Listening

6 **Listen to Mark and Rachel discussing the Greenforce advertisement. Answer the questions.**

1. What does Mark think of the advertisement? Why?
2. What does Rachel think of it? Why?
3. What does Mark want to do with his gap year?
4. What does Rachel want to do?

Speaking

7 **How is the British higher education system different to the system in your country? Do you think students in the UK are in a better or worse position than students in your country? If you could take a gap year, where would you go and what would you do?**

High school culture

Great adaptations

The world of the American high school has inspired numerous books, TV series and films. These popular films are all set in high school, but their plots are adapted from classic works of European literature.

Clueless (1995)

Cher, one of the most popular girls in her school, 'adopts' Tai, a new and unfashionable student, and tries to make her more popular. But Tai falls in love with Cher's stepbrother, Josh, who Cher loves without realising it.

10 Things I Hate about You (1999)

Bianca Stratford, a beautiful student at Padua High, is not allowed to date boys until her sarcastic and unfriendly older sister Katarina has a boyfriend. Bianca's admirers pay Patrick, a new student at the school, to date Kat.

She's All That (1999)

Zach, the class president, agrees to try to transform plain and shy Laney into the star of the end-of-term dance. He succeeds, and the couple start to grow close, but Laney then discovers that Zach's original motivation was a ◘bet with his friends.

Cruel Intentions (1999)

Kathryn, a ◘spoilt, rich teenager, bets her corrupt stepbrother, Sebastian, that he cannot ruin the reputation of Annette, their headmaster's innocent daughter. Sebastian accepts the bet with pleasure, but soon finds that he is falling in love with Annette's honourable character.

1. The Taming of the Shrew *by William Shakespeare*

Petruchio marries Katherine, a bad-tempered woman who loves to argue, for money and to prove that he can tame her. But in the end they genuinely fall in love.

2. Dangerous Liaisons *by Choderlos de Laclos*

The bored and manipulative aristocrats the Marquise de Merteuil and the Vicomte de Valmont plot to destroy the lives of innocent girls for fun.

3. Emma *by Jane Austen*

Emma Woodhouse tries to arrange marriages for everyone she knows, and decides to socially improve her poorer friend Harriet Smith. But her plans never succeed because the wrong people always fall in love.

4. Pygmalion *by G.B. Shaw*

Higgins, a professor of linguistics, accepts a bet to take flower-seller Eliza Doolittle from the street, to teach her to speak and act like a lady, and to convince everyone at a ball that she is a genuine aristocrat.

WORD BANK

- bet ▫ money placed on the possibility of something happening
- clique ▫ small exclusive group
- goths ▫ students who like independent music and dress in black
- jocks ▫ good-looking boys who are good at sports
- metal-heads ▫ students who like heavy metal music
- peers ▫ people who are the same age as you
- preppies ▫ rich students who wear smart, classic clothes
- prestige ▫ high status
- skaters ▫ students who are obsessed with skateboarding
- spoilt ▫ indulged by other people, having everything you want
- to stick out ▫ to draw attention to yourself

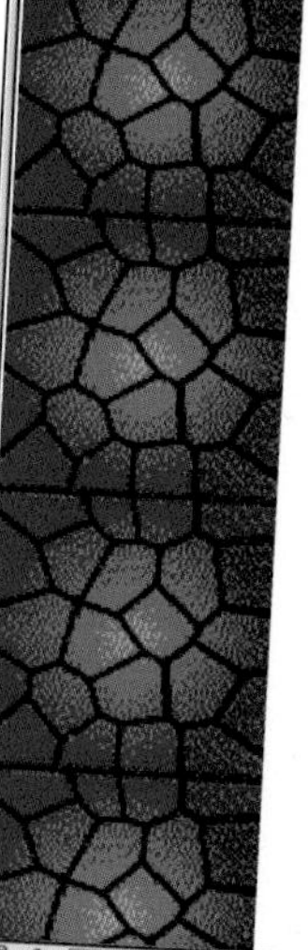

christianweek

Parents must challenge high school culture

Recent tragedies remind us of how dark and terrible a place high school can be to some of our children if they are made to believe that they do not fit in. The high school years coincide with the tremendous physical and social changes of adolescence. Changes to one's voice and body and shape that cause powerful feelings of self-consciousness and self-doubt.

In order to cope with these anxieties, teens are quick to form sub-cultures that assure them they are not alone. These little groups then adopt behavior, speech patterns and tastes in clothes and music that they use as criteria by which to judge who is 'in' and who is 'out'. These ▫cliques are both the cause and the cure of teenage insecurity.

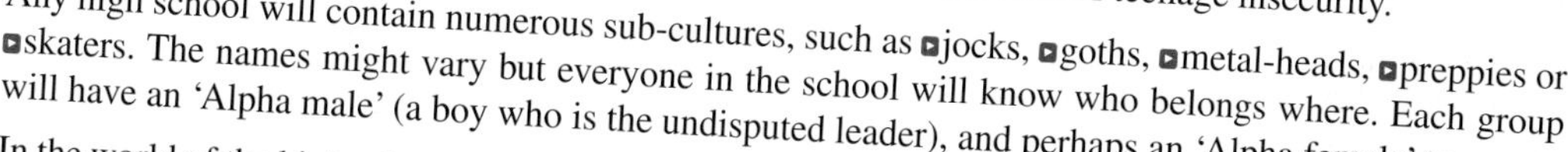

Any high school will contain numerous sub-cultures, such as ▫jocks, ▫goths, ▫metal-heads, ▫preppies or ▫skaters. The names might vary but everyone in the school will know who belongs where. Each group will have an 'Alpha male' (a boy who is the undisputed leader), and perhaps an 'Alpha female' too.

In the world of the high school there will be those who are respected and those who are widely hated, and most kids will learn it is best not to ▫stick out. Athletic skill gives ▫prestige to male students, the library club does not. Conventional physical beauty and a good fashion sense are prize qualities for females. Girls are allowed by their ▫peers to get good marks, but being an intelligent boy can be a disadvantage. A strong anti-intellectual current exists in most high schools.

Gerry Bowler

Before you read

1 Have you seen any of the films depicted on page 68? Where do you think the stories all take place?

Reading

2 Read the texts about the films. What aspects of plot and character seem to be repeated in each film?

3 EP Match the synopses of the classics books (1-4) on page 68 to the correct films.

Speaking

4 Why do you think that all these works of literature can be successfully updated into the world of the American high school?

Reading

5 EP Read the web page. Match these summaries to the four paragraphs.

1. Belonging to a fashionable group helps teenagers feel secure.
2. There are particular qualities that help teenagers to be admired at high school.
3. Students go to high school at a difficult time in their personal development.
4. High school cliques and their leaders are easy to identify.

Vocabulary

6 These words are all part of high school culture. Do you know what any of them mean?

sophomore cheerleader homecoming prom yearbook

Listening

7 Listen and note down what the words mean.

Speaking

8 How far does the description of school culture in the magazine text resemble your own school?

Cyber High

It is estimated that around 1 million American children are educated at home. Since the mid-1990s, those children have been able to access a variety of on-line schools, many of which offer high school diploma courses. Students receive lessons through the Internet and email their homework and tests to teachers.

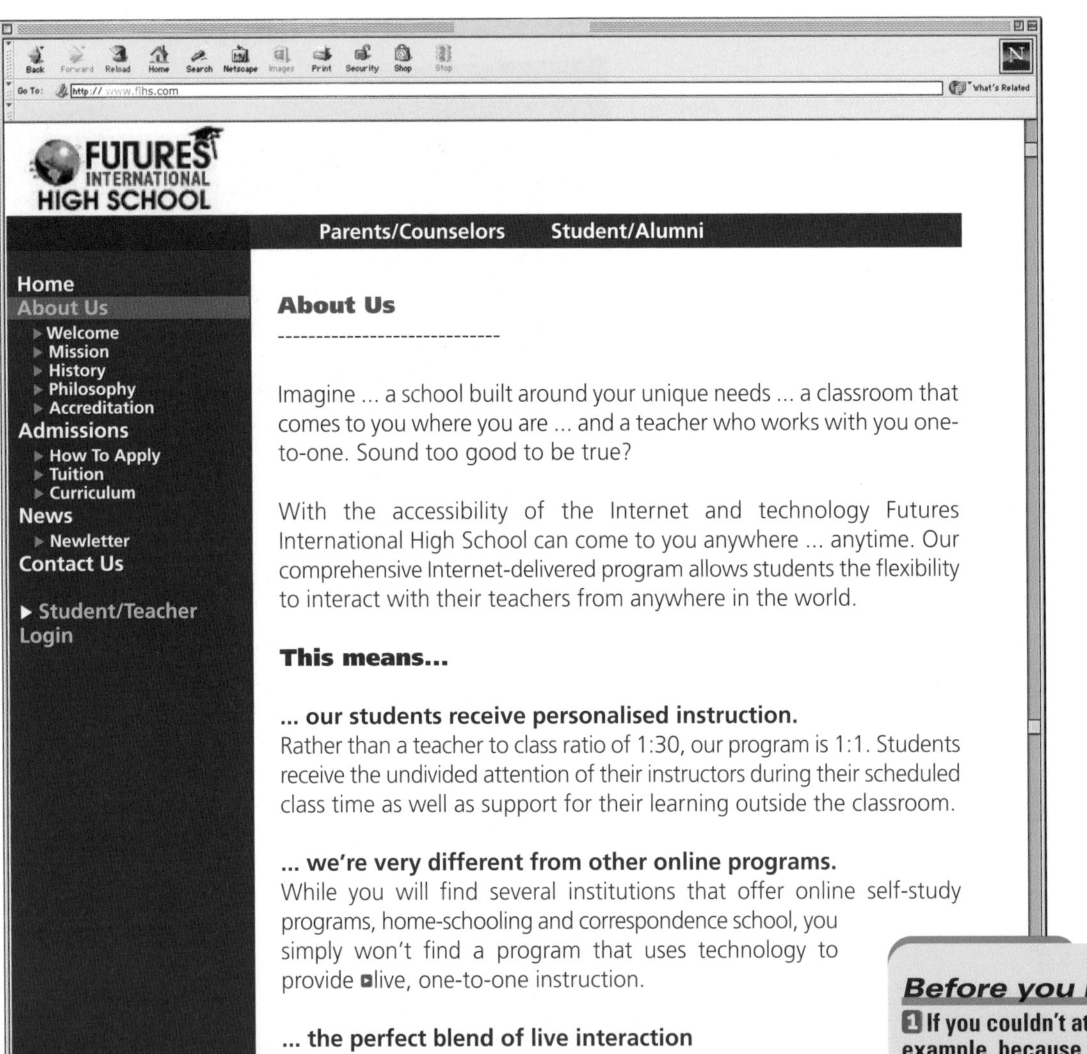

FUTURES INTERNATIONAL HIGH SCHOOL

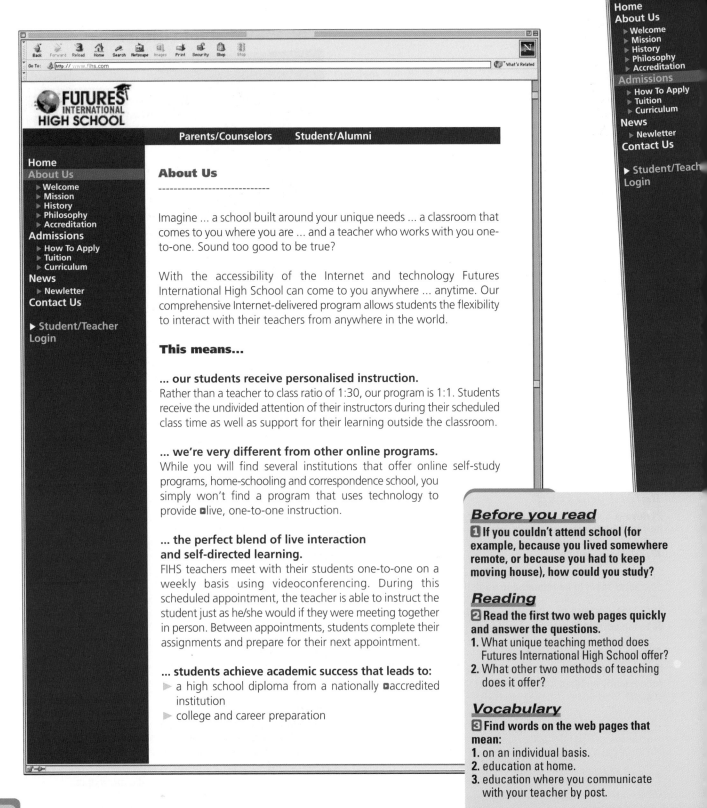

Parents/Counselors Student/Alumni

Home
About Us
- Welcome
- Mission
- History
- Philosophy
- Accreditation

Admissions
- How To Apply
- Tuition
- Curriculum

News
- Newletter

Contact Us

▶ Student/Teacher Login

About Us

Imagine ... a school built around your unique needs ... a classroom that comes to you where you are ... and a teacher who works with you one-to-one. Sound too good to be true?

With the accessibility of the Internet and technology Futures International High School can come to you anywhere ... anytime. Our comprehensive Internet-delivered program allows students the flexibility to interact with their teachers from anywhere in the world.

This means...

... our students receive personalised instruction.
Rather than a teacher to class ratio of 1:30, our program is 1:1. Students receive the undivided attention of their instructors during their scheduled class time as well as support for their learning outside the classroom.

... we're very different from other online programs.
While you will find several institutions that offer online self-study programs, home-schooling and correspondence school, you simply won't find a program that uses technology to provide ◘live, one-to-one instruction.

... the perfect blend of live interaction and self-directed learning.
FIHS teachers meet with their students one-to-one on a weekly basis using videoconferencing. During this scheduled appointment, the teacher is able to instruct the student just as he/she would if they were meeting together in person. Between appointments, students complete their assignments and prepare for their next appointment.

... students achieve academic success that leads to:
- a high school diploma from a nationally ◘accredited institution
- college and career preparation

Before you read

1 If you couldn't attend school (for example, because you lived somewhere remote, or because you had to keep moving house), how could you study?

Reading

2 Read the first two web pages quickly and answer the questions.
1. What unique teaching method does Futures International High School offer?
2. What other two methods of teaching does it offer?

Vocabulary

3 Find words on the web pages that mean:
1. on an individual basis.
2. education at home.
3. education where you communicate with your teacher by post.

WORD BANK

to accredit ▫ officially recognised
to catch up with ▫ to do something that is late
chat rooms ▫ places on the Internet where users can email each other in real time
fast-track ▫ intensive
live ▫ happening now, in real time

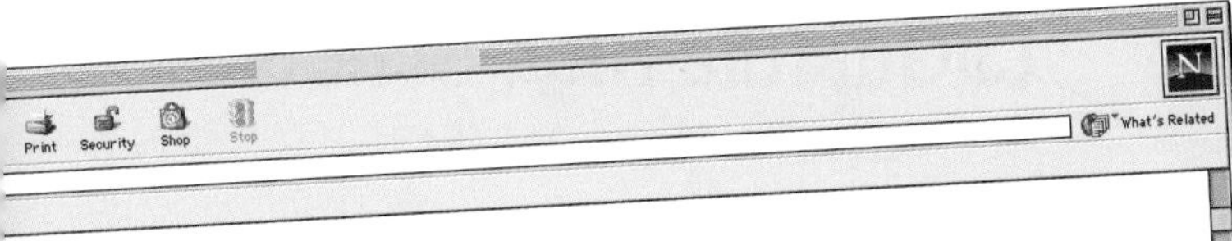

Parents/Counselors Student/Alumni

Admissions

With each course you receive:

- up to 17 private instruction appointments
- 45 minutes of instruction each week through videoconferencing
- teachers qualified in their subject area
- group interaction with students throughout the world
- supervised assessment
- a personalized program
- computer and software assistance
- an introduction to on-line instruction

Program options include:

PRIVATE
One-to-one direct instruction with 2-way videoconferencing
Teacher/Student Ratio is 1:1
$900 per semester course

SEMINAR
Small group instruction with 1-way video and 2-way audio
Teacher/Student Ratio is from 1:3 to 1:6
$600 per semester course

ASSISTED
Assisted E-mail instruction
$300 per semester course

Why attend Futures?
Students come to us because Futures offers:
A scheduling flexibility and encouragement to athletes, artists and other career-focussed students.
B consistent learning environment for students who move and/or travel frequently.
C support to international students with aspirations to attend an American university.

Kelly

I'm from Perth, in Australia. I want to go to college in America. I'm interested in business, and I think that American business schools are the best in the world. That's why I want to get an American high school diploma – it'll get me into an American college. I'm doing a ▫fast-track program.

Leonie

I do a lot of acting work. I've got a regular job on a TV series, so I spend a lot of time at the studios. And sometimes I have to go away to different locations, so I can't really attend a regular high school. That's why it's great being able to study over the Internet. I can do work while I'm waiting around on set or ▫catch up with lessons in the evening.

Jack

My dad's in the US Navy, so we live in special navy accommodation, and we have to move around a lot. Sometimes we only live in one place for a year, and then we move again. My mom thinks it would be too disruptive for me to keep changing school, so that's why I learn at home over the Internet. There are ▫chat rooms where you can talk to other people on your course, so you don't feel too isolated.

4. a written task that a teacher gives you.
5. a school term (a division of the school year into different blocks of time).
6. a small study group.

Reading

4 Choose the correct alternatives to complete the statements about Futures International High School.

1. Futures takes *only American students/students from any country.*
2. Teachers give *live/recorded* lessons to the students.
3. Students 'meet' their teachers online *once/twice* a week.
4. Each online lesson lasts for *an hour/three quarters of an hour.*
5. Students *have to/don't have to* do homework between the lessons.
6. At the end of the course, students will have *a college/high school* qualification.
7. Futures can help you solve any problems with your *computer/library.*
8. The largest number of students in a seminar group is *three/six.*

5 EP Read the three student profiles. Match them to the reasons for choosing Futures (A, B and C).

Writing

6 Write an email to Futures International High School asking for more information about the school. Ask about:

- students' age.
- courses offered.
- teachers (who?).
- semester dates.
- time of weekly interactive lessons.
- length of time needed to complete the high school diploma.

Speaking

7 Do children have to go to school in your country, or are other methods, like homeschooling, permitted? What are the advantages and disadvantages of homeschooling?

Star pupils

Chetham's School of Music

Chetham's School of Music is a unique school taking pupils from many different backgrounds, from all over the UK and abroad. With over 280 pupils, Chetham's is housed in and around a historic fifteenth century college building, and is ▫at the forefront of music education in Britain and Europe.

Pupils, who are admitted solely on the basis of musical audition, develop a specialist interest to the highest level, which may be in an orchestral instrument, guitar, keyboard, voice, electronic music, jazz or composition, and all sing in choirs.

Since 1980, the government has provided grants for pupils at Chetham's. The school is open to all, ▫irrespective of financial or social background, and 80% of our pupils come from state schools.

LaGuardia High School of Music & Art and Performing Arts

Dance department

In 1948 the School of Performing Arts opened in the heart of New York's theater district to provide professionally trained talent for NYC's important theatrical industry. Now part of a larger school, and with a new name, LaGuardia continues to give aspiring performers the training, encouragement and support needed to ▫launch their careers in the arts.

In the dance entrance exam, students are grouped in units of 20-25 and are given a ballet class followed by a modern dance class. Students are then evaluated by a group of 4-7 instructors, and may also be asked to perform a solo work. ▫Applicants are then given a grade from 1 to 100. No-one with a grade under 80 is considered.

Judgement ▫criteria include body alignment, dance technique and performance skills.

Speaking

1 Look at the photos. What are the students studying? Do you know anyone who is very talented in music, dance or drama? How are they encouraged in their talent?

Reading

2 EP Read the school prospectuses quickly. Which school(s):

1. is in the USA?
2. is in the UK?
3. was formed specifically to provide performers for theatres?
4. allows students to work professionally at the same time as they study?
5. receives money from the UK government?

WORD BANK

applicant ▫ someone who asks for something officially
at the forefront of ▫ among the best
to benefit ▫ to help, improve
chaperone ▫ someone who accompanies you somewhere to make sure you are safe
criteria ▫ standards by which you judge something
to equip ▫ to provide with
irrespective of ▫ ignoring
to keep your feet firmly on the ground ▫ to have a lot of common sense
to launch ▫ to begin
to nurture ▫ to take care of and help to grow
to secure engagements ▫ to get jobs
sound ▫ solid

Redroofs Theatre School

At Redroofs we aim to provide a ▫sound academic education and, within a caring environment, to ▫nurture the individual artistic talents of the child or young adult to the highest professional standard of which they may be capable, ▫equipping them for a career in theatre and the related arts.

The school has its own Theatrical Employment Agency. From time to time, pupils may be permitted to audition for, and to accept, TV, film, radio and theatre work that may ▫benefit their careers and build confidence and knowledge of the way the industry operates. For those who are lucky enough to ▫secure engagements, we are careful to ▫keep their feet firmly on the ground.

We try to arrange auditions to take place after school so as to disrupt the school day as little as possible. Most auditions take place in central London, and pupils will be accompanied to and from their destination by a licensed ▫chaperone.

Daily life at Redroofs

Pupils at Redroofs are aged between (1) .... and (2) .... Classes begin each day at (3).......... . Mornings are dedicated to (4) .... classes, and afternoons are spent studying performing arts such as speech, (5) ...., (6) ...., (7) ...., modern dance, (8) .... dance and (9) .... dance. Pupils are taken on regular visits to (10) ...., (11) .... and other places of interest to support their studies. The school has its own practical exams every summer, which pupils do at the school's (12) ...., and pupils must also take the Royal Academy of (13) .... exams. Senior students study for (14) .... exams.

Vocabulary

3 Find these words in the texts:

1. when you sing, dance, act or play an instrument so that people can judge your ability.
2. a general term for musical instruments like a piano or an organ.
3. two styles of music.
4. the skill of writing music.
5. a large group of people who sing together.
6. a general term for music, singing, dancing and acting.
7. classical dance.
8. a performance given by one person alone.

Reading

4 Answer the questions about the texts.

1. How many pupils are there at Chetham's?
2. When was the college building at Chetham's built?
3. Do you need a lot of money to study there?
4. When did the New York School of Performing Arts open?
5. What do applicants have to do at an audition for the dance department?
6. What grade do they have to get from the instructors to be successful?
7. What type of professional work might Redroofs students do?
8. When and where do most Redroofs students do professional auditions?

Before you listen

5 Read the paragraph about daily life at Redroofs School and predict what the missing words will be.

Listening

6 EP Listen to Natasha answering questions about her life as a pupil at Redroofs and check your answers to exercise 5.

Speaking

7 Do specialist schools like these exist in your country? Do you think that they are a good idea? Which of the performing arts would you like to be good at?

English everywhere
Canada and Wales

Quebec – French by force

In the 1960s, the French speakers of the Quebec region of Canada gained political power there. Since then, they have passed many laws designed to protect the French language. In 1977, Bill 101 made French the official language of Quebec, imposed French language tests for admission to many professions and ruled that most businesses with more than fifty employees must operate in French. It also prohibited the use of English on commercial signs, although this was modified in 1993, when it was decided that English could appear on outdoor signs as long as the French words were more prominent. There is still, however, an official 'language police', the Office Quebecois de la Langue Française, who constantly check that these language laws are not broken.

Most controversially, Bill 101 made it obligatory for almost all students, particularly those moving to Quebec from outside the region, to attend French-only schools until they reach college age. In 2002, on the 25th anniversary of Bill 101, a new law even closed the ◘loophole that had allowed children who had been previously educated at ◘anglophone schools, or those in private education, to continue to attend English-speaking schools. Although all pupils at ◘francophone schools in Quebec have English lessons, they do not start them until the fifth grade. Critics of the system say that this puts them at a serious disadvantage if they want to study or try to get a job outside of Quebec when they leave school.

INFORMATION FILE

Canada

Total area	10,000,000 sq. km
Total population	32 million
Ethnic mix	59% White (English-speaking) 23% White (French-speaking) 2% Native American 16% Other
Capital	Ottawa
Popul. of capital	1 million
Government	A democracy with a prime minister. Canada was a British colony until 1867. Canada is independent, but the British monarch is still head of state.
Climate	South: moderate North: subarctic and arctic

WORD BANK

anglophone ▫ English-speaking
backward ▫ not well-developed
to carve ▫ to cut into wood
fine ▫ money that you must pay as a penalty
francophone ▫ French-speaking
loophole ▫ an omission in a law that allows people to legally ignore the law
plaque ▫ a flat shape, like a plate
tide ▫ the movement of the sea as it grows and recedes

Welsh – a lesson in survival

Welsh, the native Celtic language of Wales, is one of the oldest languages in Europe. In spite of a variety of pressures over the centuries, the language has survived into the present day.

One of the worst times for the Welsh language was the 19th century. Reforming Victorian educators reported that the Welsh people were ▫backward, and that Welsh-speaking children were uneducated. English-only schools were established in Wales, especially near the border with England, and English teachers were specially imported.

Children speaking Welsh in school received severe punishments. They were made to stand in a corner of the classroom for hours, to pay ▫fines to the teacher or, most notoriously of all, forced to wear the "Welsh Not" or carry the "Welsh Stick", a ▫plaque or a stick ▫carved with Welsh Not or W.N. This was passed to the next child who spoke Welsh in the classroom, and the child who had it at the end of the lesson received a punishment.

However, after the Second World War the ▫tide started to turn, and Welsh-only schools began to be built. These days, about 25% of children in Wales go to Welsh-only schools. The 1967 and 1993 Welsh Language Acts in parliament stated that Welsh must have equal status with English in Wales, and the 1988 Education Reform Act made Welsh language an obligatory subject for all children aged 5 to 16, whether they go to English-speaking or Welsh-speaking schools.

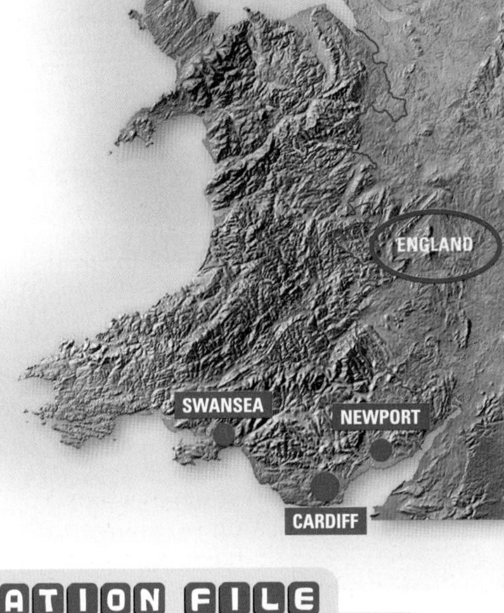

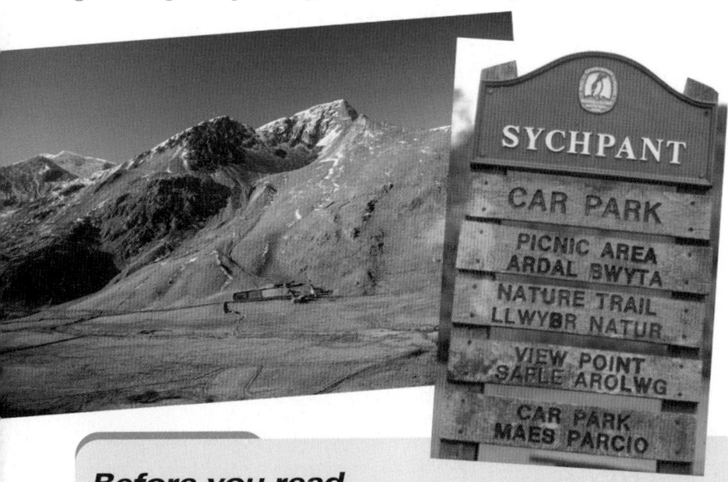

INFORMATION FILE

Wales

Total area ▫ 21,000 sq. km
Total population ▫ 2.9 million
Ethnic mix ▫ 76% White (English-speaking)
20% White (Welsh-speaking)
4% Other
Capital ▫ Cardiff
Popul. of capital ▫ 320,000
Government ▫ Part of the UK, but has its own National Assembly and First Minister
Climate ▫ Mild, wet

Before you read

1 What are the two languages other than English that you can see in the photos? What countries do Canada and Wales share a border with?

Reading

2 Look at the maps and read the Information Files on Canada and Wales. Answer the questions.

1. What percentage of the Canadian population speak French as their first language?
2. Is Canada governed by the British government?
3. What is the coldest part of Canada?
4. What percentage of the Welsh population speak Welsh as their first language?
5. What title does the leader of the Welsh National Assembly have?

3 Read the text *Quebec – French by force* and answer the questions.

1. Find five ways that Bill 101 affected day-to-day life in Quebec.
2. What modification to the Bill was made in 1993?
3. What do the Office Quebecois de la Langue Française do?
4. What modification to the Bill was made in 2002?
5. Do children at French-speaking schools in Quebec study English?
6. Why could children at French-speaking schools be at a disadvantage?

4 EP Read the text on Welsh education. Are the following statements true or false?

1. The Welsh language is still alive today.
2. In the 19th century, the Welsh language was promoted in schools.
3. Children were given the "Welsh Not" if they forgot to speak Welsh.
4. About a quarter of Welsh pupils today have teachers who teach in Welsh.
5. All 17-year-olds in Wales have to study Welsh.
6. Children at English-speaking schools in Wales have to study Welsh.

Speaking

5 What differences are there in the two different governments' attitude to bilingual education?

Speaking

6 Is there more than one language in your country? Are there local dialects? If so, do people make a special effort to preserve those languages? How are they dealt with at school? Should we make an effort to stop minority languages dying out?

Language & Culture

Essay

Choices, choices...

1 I am a student at a sixth-form college in Cambridge. I've just finished my AS level exams in Geography, Biology, English and French but I haven't received the results yet. I still haven't finished my studies because I have to do my A level exams next summer. I haven't decided yet what to do after A levels: go to university, get a job or do a gap year and then go to university after that.

2 On the one hand, I could go to university immediately after my A levels. I could continue my studies and then find a well-paid job. The main advantage of a well-paid job is that I could pay back my loan quickly. However, I've heard that lots of students end up borrowing even more money. One of the disadvantages of going to university is that I couldn't afford to leave home so I'd end up having to stay at home for another three years with my parents.

3 On the other hand I could get a job straight after my A levels. There are two main advantages to this. The first is that I could earn my own salary and be independent very quickly. The second is that I could save up and buy a flat. I've seen flats for £50,000 in the centre of town. However, there are also disadvantages to getting a job straight away. The main one is that I'd miss my friends. Since my friend Matthew started work last month, I've only seen him about three times. He's stuck in an office from 9.00am until 6.00pm every day.

4 Then again, I could wait for a year before going to university and do a gap year. One big advantage is that it would be a good experience to see a different country and its lifestyle. I've never been abroad before and I could even learn another language. I've searched the Internet recently and found a lot of good organisations. On the other hand, if I do this I would need money to pay for the trip. This would mean getting a part-time job while studying for A levels.

5 In conclusion, I think that I might wait and see what results I get in my exams next summer and I think I'll probably go to university straight after school. I'm not keen to get a job straight away and miss out on my youth and I don't think a gap year is a good option because I'm not sure I could work and study at the same time.

GRAMMAR

1 Read the text *Choices, choices...* quickly and find out what John thinks he will do after he leaves school.

2 Look at the verbs highlighted in the text. Which tense are they? Can you say why this tense is used in each case?

3 Read the paragraph and put the verbs in the correct tense: present simple, past simple or present perfect.

I (1) *study* (study) at a school in Manchester. There (2) ...... (be) 25 students in my class and we (3) ...... (just take) our GCSE exams. We (4) ...... (not receive) the results yet. They usually (5) ...... (arrive) some time in August. Last year I (6) ...... (study) eight subjects altogether and now I (7) ...... (have to) choose three of those subjects to study for A levels. I (8) ...... (still not decide) which four subjects to choose for AS levels. I (9) ...... (never have) good results in Maths so I don't think I'll chose Maths. However, I (10) ...... (have) a great teacher last year for Physics, and I (11) ...... (enjoy) Art since I was little, so I (12) ...... (think) I might study those subjects next year.

SKILLS

4 Match the subjects below with the paragraphs (1-5) in the essay above.

a. The advantages and disadvantages of a gap year.
b. The advantages and disadvantages of going to university.
c. The advantages and disadvantages of getting a job.
d. Conclusion.
e. Introduction.

5 Read the text again and underline the phrases used to introduce the paragraphs, to make comparisons and to introduce advantages and disadvantages.

6 Think about the education system in your country and what you are going to do in the next few years. Write an essay similar to the one on this page. Include some of the phrases you identified in exercise 5.

Module 6

Global markets

IN THIS MODULE YOU WILL READ AND HEAR ABOUT:

- working life for nurses in the UK and the USA
- people who swap stressful jobs for life in the country
- supermarket culture in the USA, and how some European supermarkets employ African labour
- crisis in the tourism industry in the UK and USA
- the UK's relationship with the rest of the EU
- the UK's pop industry
- business letters in the UK and the USA

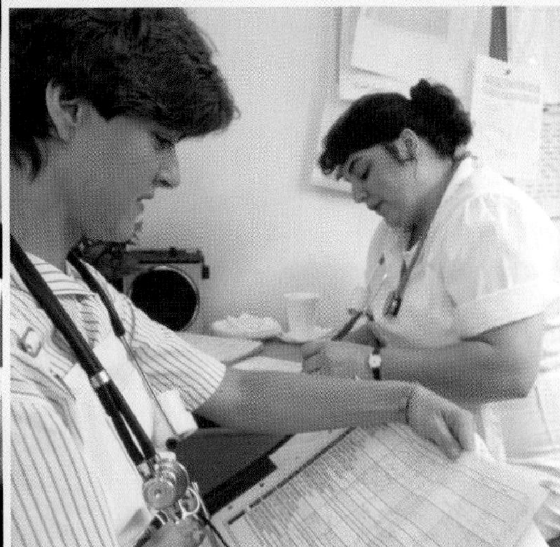

1 What jobs do you think that the people in the photographs do? Which of the people do you think are: American? British? European? African?

2 Which eight countries form the G8 group, which consists of the world's richest industrial nations?

Topic ▫ Working life in hospitals
Countries ▫ UK and USA
Vocabulary ▫ Employment/Hospitals
Links ▫ 1a, 6b, 10d

Overworked and underpaid

Britain's National Health Service (the NHS) is ▫funded by the government, and is the biggest employer in Europe, with 1.2 million employees. But nursing recruitment in the UK is at its worst level for 25 years, and 40% of new nurses come from overseas, often from South East Asia. In 2001, the Royal College of Nursing published the results of a survey of its members. These are some of the key results.

- Most nurses work both day and night shifts.
- three fifths of NHS nurses work an average 6.5 hours overtime per week. One third do this for no extra pay.
- 90% think that they are poorly paid.
- A quarter have a second job to supplement their salary.
- The biggest age group is 35–44. Only 1 in 8 nurses is under 30.
- 31% would leave nursing if they could.

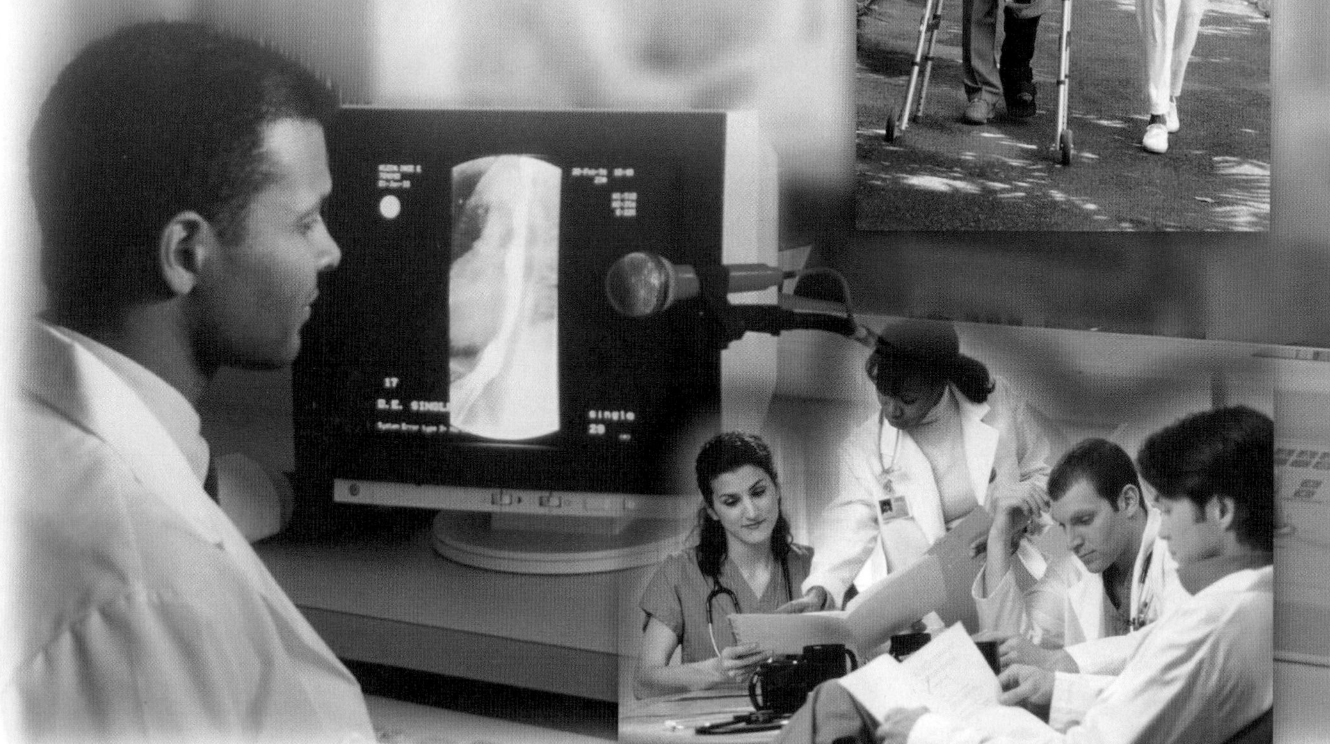

Before you read

1 What job is depicted in the photos? Do you know anyone who does this job? How do they feel about it?

Vocabulary

2 Read the text on this page. Find words that mean:

1. someone who gives someone a job.
2. people who do a job for someone else.
3. bringing new people into a profession.
4. blocks of time that you work.
5. extra work outside of your normal hours.
6. the money that you earn from your job.

Reading

3 Find the right statistics.

1. How many people work for Britain's NHS?
2. What percentage of new nurses are from outside the UK?
3. What is the average length of nurses' overtime per week?
4. What percentage of nurses think that they are well-paid?
5. What percentage of nurses have another job?
6. What age are 7/8 of nurses?

4 EP Look at the newspaper article. Place the sentences A-D in the correct gap.

5 EP Complete the table about Katie Morgan's life.

	18 months ago	Now
Address	Torbay, England	....
Job	....	....
Type of house	....	....
Car(s)	....	....
Typical salary	£............	$............
Any limit on her pay?	.....	.....
Holidays	..... weeks per year	..... weeks per year

WORD BANK

to cap ▫ to put an upper limit on
council house ▫ house built, owned, and rented out by the local council
cramped ▫ with very little space
to entice ▫ to try to persuade
exodus ▫ a mass movement out of a place
to fund ▫ to pay for
green card ▫ US immigration permit
midwifery ▫ the study of pregnancy and childbirth
to rust ▫ when metal turns brown and decays

GuardianUnlimited

Nurses desert NHS for good life

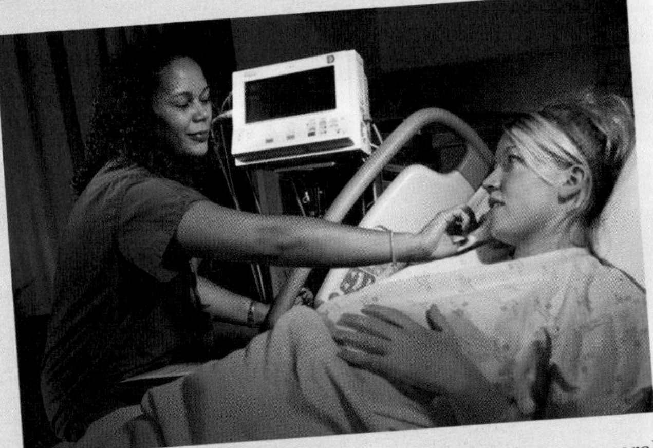

Eighteen months ago, Katie Morgan was living in a ▫cramped former ▫council house in Torbay and travelling to work at the local hospital in a ▫rusting car that often refused to start. Now she lives in a large house – with swimming pool – in Phoenix, Arizona, and has two new cars. **1** ....

Figures to be released next month from the UK Central Council for Nursing and ▫Midwifery will show that 5,500 nurses emigrated last year.

Morgan, 26, earned £14,000 a year at Torbay Hospital's cardiology department, but instantly doubled her salary in the United States. 'Once you are here for a while, it is possible to increase your pay almost without limit – it's not ▫capped like in the UK,' she said. '**2** .... But here you are seen as a professional and paid a professional salary.'

Trade magazines such as the Nursing Times carry several pages of advertisements ▫enticing nurses to leave the UK. Nurses going to work in the US – which also has a nursing shortage – have their flights paid and receive ▫green cards for their families. **3** ....

The only disadvantage is two weeks' holiday a year, compared with seven in Britain. '**4** ....,' said Morgan. 'I'm never going to go back, not in a million years.'

A But I couldn't afford to go anywhere on holiday, so I just sat at home – there was no point to it.

B I feel really sorry for my friends back home. They work so hard and don't get rewarded for it.

C She is part of a growing ▫exodus of nurses deserting terrible NHS pay and conditions for a better life overseas.

D They get starting salaries of up to $56,000 – almost £ 40,000.

Vocabulary

6 Match the words with their definitions.

1. ward
2. admission
3. patient
4. intensive care
5. records
6. consultant

a. a senior, specialist doctor
b. a hospital department for seriously ill people
c. papers showing someone's medical history
d. a room full of beds in a hospital
e. someone who is being looked after in hospital
f. someone who has just entered hospital

Listening

7 Listen to Jenny, a senior nurse, talking about her typical working day in hospital and answer the questions.

1. What type of ward does she work on?
2. How is the shift system organised?
3. How many beds do they have?
4. What time do the doctors see the patients on the ward?
5. What does she do in the afternoons?
6. What is the last thing she does before going home?

Speaking

8 Does the government pay for health care in your country, as in the UK, or do patients have to pay, as in the US? What are the advantages and disadvantages of each system? Discuss with the class.

6b Global markets

Topic: Escaping from a stressful lifestyle
Countries: UK
Vocabulary: Words connected with breadmaking
Links: 1d, 2b, 2e, 6a

Downshifting

downshifting /ˈdaʊnˌʃɪftɪŋ/: *n.* abandoning a well-paid but stressful lifestyle for a simpler, often rural, way of life.

Bread of Heaven

On the Isles of Scilly, the seas are azure, puffins fly in for the summer, you can picnic on rocks accompanied only by seals, and you go about not by bus but by boat. It's a long way from the traffic-choked streets of London, and it's not difficult to see why Toby Tobin-Dougan swapped one for the other. Now when he's working he looks out on a field of flowers rather than a road full of taxis. Toby and his wife Louise live on one of the larger islands, St Martin's, and run a bakery of the same name, supplying bread to their own island and delivering by boat to their neighbours on the other inhabited islands of Tresco, Bryher, St Agnes and St Mary's.

It sounds idyllic, and in many ways it is. But it's also hard work, although Toby and Louise are now helped by a night baker who produces most of the basic breads overnight. They bake on Mondays, Wednesdays and Fridays in the winter, and every day including Sunday during the summer. On baking days they have to be up at four in the morning to make the dough. They shape all their loaves by hand, finishing the baking by mid-morning, when they prepare the deliveries and work in the shop, where the queues often stretch out of the door.

BOOK OF THE WEEK

Escape from the Rat Race: Downshifting to a Richer Life

Nicholas Corder
(Right Way Plus)
Our price: £7.19

What is the point of spending long, stressful hours working, or travelling to work, if it makes you too tired to enjoy your leisure time? Or earning high wages if you are too stressed to enjoy the material benefits that your money can bring?

Nicholas Corder has chosen an alternative to the rat race – downshifting. A lifestyle choice that more and more people are beginning to make, and one that is available to you too. Corder shows the reader how to make that life-changing decision, and explains how a simpler life is usually a happier one.

Before you read

1 What are the advantages and disadvantages of having a very highly-paid job in a city? What do you think would be an ideal job?

Vocabulary

2 Complete the table. Look in the text *Bread of Heaven* for any words that you don't know.

1. To make bread:	to bake
2. A person who makes bread:	b ....
3. A shop where bread is made and sold:	b ....
4. Uncooked bread mixture:	d ....
5. Separate pieces of bread:	l ....

Reading

3 EP Read the *Bread of Heaven* text. Put these events in the correct chronological order.

a. Toby and Louise started offering courses in baking.
b. Toby and Louise made bread and sold it at a campsite.
c. Toby and Louise married.
d. Toby and Louise opened their own bakery.
e. Toby first came to the Scilly Isles on holiday.

WORD BANK

affinity ▫ feeling of belonging
azure ▫ bright blue
to choke ▫ to be unable to breathe
deli ▫ (= delicatessen) speciality food shop
to be drawn to ▫ to be attracted by
falcon ▫ fast predatory bird
idyllic ▫ ideal, heavenly
puffin ▫ large migratory sea bird
rat race ▫ the stress of business, especially in the city
seal ▫ large sea mammal
trial and error ▫ experimentation

So what inspired them to leave the ▫rat race and move to one of the mildest climates and most beautiful environments in Britain? Toby, 44, first visited St Martin's in the early 1980s and was irresistibly ▫drawn to the island. At the time he was living in Brighton but working in London, running a photographic laboratory.

He finally sold the business in 1992, packed his bags and moved to St Martin's. He found accommodation with a local fisherman and worked on boats and in the St Martin's Hotel. Louise, 34, from Bristol, also fell in love with the island during a holiday and found a job in the same hotel.

They have been married for five years and both knew that they wanted to start their own business. Breadmaking happened almost by chance – the learning process was very much ▫trial and error. "We taught ourselves to bake in our own kitchen," Toby remembers. "We sold our loaves at the campsite nearby for campers to buy – just 25 or 30 a day." The business expanded rapidly. The bakery opened four years ago and this year it will be extended into the old fire station next door.

The shop is becoming more like a ▫deli, offering picnic food for holidaymakers to take to the beach. Toby and Louise now grow their own organic fruit and vegetables and keep ducks, chickens and a pig. They have also started running baking classes in the quieter months of the year.

The point of all their work, Toby says, isn't money. They both earn less than they would have if they'd stayed in hotel work. The satisfaction comes from providing a useful service – and living in a place for which they have a real 'love and ▫affinity'. Is there anything they miss from their pre-Scillies life? As their two dogs wander happily around and a ▫falcon flies overhead in the fresh wind off the sea, there is a long silence.

f. Toby sold his photography business.
g. Toby started a photography business in London.
h. Toby started working in the St Martin's Hotel.

4 EP Choose the correct answer to the questions.

1. What do you think the name of the bakery is?
   a. Toby and Louise's Bakery.
   b. The St Martin's Bakery.
   c. The Scillies Bakery.
2. How many islands does the bakery sell bread to?
   a. One.
   b. Four.
   c. Five.
3. How many days a week do Toby and Louise work in August?
   a. One.
   b. Three.
   c. Seven.
4. What is going to happen next year?
   a. The bakery is going to get bigger.
   b. They are going to start giving classes in baking.
   c. They are going to sell the bakery and buy a fire station.
5. Why do they enjoy their work?
   a. Because it is very well-paid.
   b. Because it's useful to the community.
   c. Because it's easy work.

5 Read the book review on page 80 and answer the questions.

1. What is the book's title, author, publisher and price?
2. Which phrase from the *Bread of Heaven* article does the review also use to describe the competitive world of business?
3. What play on words is there in the book's subtitle (*Downshifting to a Richer Life*)? Read the dictionary definition too.
4. Why does the book's author think that trying to earn lots of money is a waste of time?

Speaking

6 What practical advice do you think that the book offers?

Writing

7 Write a paragraph about what your ideal way of life would be. Write about where you would live and what work you would do. Write about a realistic way of life – not something that could only happen if you won the lottery!

Topic ▫ Supermarkets as businesses
Countries ▫ USA, UK and Kenya
Vocabulary ▫ Business
Links ▫ 1d, 3b, 10c, 11j

The global supermarket

Since the Second World War, the retail sector (supermarkets in particular) has become one of the biggest sectors in international business. But are the people who supply this industry always treated fairly?

COMPANY PROFILE: WAL-MART

Business: low-price supermarkets
Country of origin: USA

Company history:

1962: first store opened in Arkansas by brothers Sam and Bud Walton
1970: becomes a public company on the New York stock exchange
1977: makes its first acquisition (Mohr-Value Stores)
1990: becomes the biggest retailer in the USA
1991: first international store opens (Mexico City)
1997: becomes the biggest employer in the USA
1999: enters the UK. Becomes the most successful retailer and the biggest employer in the world. Has given millions of dollars to charity since its formation.

Number of countries: 10
Number of employees: 1.3 million
Sales 2002-3: $244.5 billion

SOME ASPECTS OF WAL-MART CULTURE

The Wal-Mart ▫ Cheer
Shouted by employees at the start of every working day:

"Give me a W!
Give me an A!
Give me an L!
Give me a ▫ squiggly!
Give me an M!
Give me an A!
Give me an R!
Give me a T!
What's that spell?
Wal-Mart!
Who's number one?
The customer! Always!"

The Sundown Rule
Wal-Mart employees are expected to fulfil every request, whether made by a customer or another store, by sundown on the day they receive it.

The ▫ Ten Foot Rule
If a Wal-Mart employee comes within 10 feet of a customer, they should look them in the eye, greet them and ask if they can help them.

Before you read

1 **Does most of your family's food come from a supermarket, or from smaller shops? Which countries do the fruit and vegetables that you eat come from?**

Vocabulary

2 **Read the company profile of Wal-Mart and find words that mean:**
1. a business that anyone can buy shares in.
2. the 'place' where you can buy and sell shares in American companies.
3. when one business buys another.
4. a business that specialises in shops and selling things.

Reading

3 **Answer the questions.**
1. What type of shops are Wal-Mart stores?
2. Where was the first Wal-Mart store outside the USA?
3. When did the company make acquisitions in Britain?
4. Why is Wal-Mart a record-breaking company?
5. How many people work for Wal-Mart?

4 **Why should a Wal-Mart employee never do these things?**
1. Tell a customer that the product that they want won't be available until Monday.
2. Pass a customer without speaking.
3. Think that their first loyalty is to the company.
4. Try to make more profit by raising the price of a product.

WORD BANK

black market ▫ an illegal system of buying and selling, without regulations
capricious ▫ unpredictable
cheer ▫ shout of encouragement
fancy ▫ specialised, refined
hovel ▫ very poor and dirty home
lingering ▫ remaining
motto ▫ a phrase that sums up your philosophy
proponent ▫ supporter
to quintuple ▫ to increase five times
sporadic ▫ occasional
squiggly ▫ (= squiggle) a small, curving line
ten foot/feet ▫ about 3 metres

Supermarkets are responsible for the sale of around 70% of fruit and vegetables in Britain. In the search for cheap and cosmetically perfect produce, British supermarkets often import everyday fruit and vegetables that could just as easily be grown at home: apples from the USA, carrots from South Africa and beans from Kenya are just a few examples.

THE NEW YORK TIMES

Beside Blossoming Fields, Where Poverty Grows

NAIVASHA, Kenya – The shores of the broad lake that spreads across Africa's Rift Valley ...

In the past 20 years, the lake shores have exchanged any ▫lingering memories of the past for a booming industry in the cultivation and sale of out-of-season vegetables like snow peas and trimmed beans, and cut flowers like roses and carnations - virtually all of them exported to distant markets in Europe. Paradoxically, the huge expansion of ▫fancy food for export has come in a land that, because of ▫sporadic drought and not-so-sporadic economic mismanagement, cannot grow enough of its own staple, corn.

As the flower and vegetable farms have expanded, ... the population living within three miles of the lake shore has ▫quintupled from 50,000 to 250,000. Most of the newcomers are women who have been drawn by cash wages from traditional agriculture in villages elsewhere.

...

A bouquet of spray carnations grown here costs around $3.20 in a British supermarket, while even the best-paid of manual workers earns a daily rate of $2.10, working a 46-hour week. While some workers live in compounds provided by employers, others live in ▫hovels. And while big companies pay twice the government-approved minimum wage, other growers pay the official minimum just over a dollar a day to cover housing, food and bare bones survival.

...

So, are Africa's flower workers, indeed, trapped in a cycle of poverty from which history offers no prospect of relief?

▫Proponents of globalization say the answer is no. ... "Done properly, corporations create a better environment for the future and for the lives of the people than does a sort of ▫black market ... that doesn't have controls," said Mr. Jones, the British executive.

But the counterargument is that no land can develop itself by supplying the ▫capricious demands of distant foreigners while its own people are simply too poor to provide the demand for goods needed to develop their own economy.

Vocabulary

5 Match these words connected with food cultivation to their meanings.

1. to blossom	**a.** enclosed accommodation for workers
2. compound	**b.** to cut
3. drought	**c.** basic food
4. snow peas	**d.** to produce flowers
5. staple	**e.** lack of water
6. to trim	**f.** very small vegetables that are eaten in their shells

Reading

6 EP Read the introduction to the newspaper article and the article itself. Are the following statements true or false?

1. Most fruit and vegetables in Britain are bought from supermarkets.
2. British supermarkets only import fruit and vegetables that can't be grown in Britain.
3. Fruit and vegetables are only imported from countries near to Britain.
4. It is difficult for Kenyans to grow corn in their country.
5. The European farms have attracted many Kenyan workers.
6. A typical worker on the European farms is a man from a poor village.
7. Farm workers earn between $1 and $2.10 a day.
8. Some people criticise this way of supplying supermarkets.

Speaking

7 Most supermarkets want to sell food at the lowest possible prices. Talk about the advantages and disadvantages of this. Think about these factors:

- buying from local/foreign producers.
- buying from small/large producers.
- transporting produce long distances.
- buying organic/non-organic/genetically-modified produce.

Topic ▫ Crisis in the tourism industry
Countries ▫ UK and USA
Vocabulary ▫ Tourist attractions
Links ▫ 3a, 7e, 11a

When the tourists stayed away

▫Stricken cities want tourism as national economic priority

ATLANTA – Mayors and tourism officials, ▫shaken by the loss of more than 500,000 travel and tourism jobs since the Sept. 11 terrorist attacks, are meeting here today to seek federal help.

It's not just New York and other big cities that haven't ▫bounced back. The drop in international tourism has cost US cities more than $12.5 billion, according to the US Conference of Mayors.

Tourism-related jobs in Nashville, for example, have dropped 14% since the attacks. Chicago lost 36,000 such jobs, Los Angeles 33,600 and Atlanta 28,600.

Alarmed by these numbers and seeing no immediate relief, the mayors of 17 cities are holding a summit to draw attention to the importance of tourism to the nation's economic health.

As in many other cities, Atlanta's economic well-being is tied to tourism. "It's people's jobs," Mayor Shirley Franklin says. "If hotel ▫occupancy is low, they don't have jobs for people. For cities like Atlanta, Las Vegas, Honolulu, San Francisco and New Orleans, the economic impact is tremendous."

Tourism officials say the USA has fallen to third place as an international tourist destination, behind France and Spain. Before the terrorist attacks, it came second only to France.

by Larry Copeland

VISTA TRAVEL

Client information
Name: ....
Address: ....
Date of birth: ....
Nationality: ....

Destination
Country: ....
Preferred location: ....
2nd preference: ....

Number of people
Adults: ....
Children: ....

Length of stay
Depart on: ....
Return on: ....

Type of accommodation
5★ Hotel/4★ Hotel/3★ Hotel/2★ Hotel/1★ Hotel/
Bed and Breakfast/Self-catering house/
Self-catering apartment/Campsite

Special requirements
....
....
....
....

WORD BANK

blow ▫ unexpected unlucky event
to bounce back ▫ recover quickly
foot-and-mouth ▫ very infectious disease of farm animals
high season ▫ most popular time of year for tourists
occupancy ▫ level of occupation
off-peak ▫ least popular time of year for tourists
shaken ▫ shocked
stricken ▫ desperate

Double ▫blow to UK's tourist industry

The British Tourist Authority has predicted that the combined effect of the ▫foot-and-mouth epidemic and the terrorist attacks in the US will cost the UK tourism industry £2.5 billion in lost business this year.

Stratford-upon-Avon is one of the tourist destinations that has been hit hard by overseas tourists staying away from the UK. Although the county was free of foot-and-mouth, some tourist attractions such as Shakespeare's birthplace were closed as a precautionary measure. Many accommodation bookings have been cancelled, particularly after the Ryder Cup Golf Tournament, due to be held elsewhere in Warwickshire, was postponed until next year.

According to Warwickshire's tourist authority, four out of five visitors to Stratford come from the UK, but overseas visitors spend much more money there. The largest number of overseas vistors to Stratford come from the USA, and spend an average of £25 million per year. Most importantly, Americans are prepared to come at ▫off-peak times as well as ▫high season.

Before you read

1 Can you identify any of the places in the photos? If not, find their names in the two texts.

Reading

2 Read both texts quickly and find out:

1. what crisis badly affected the US tourist industry in 2001.
2. what two crises affected the UK tourist industry in the same year.
3. how much money each country lost as a result of these events.

3 Answer the questions about the American news article.

1. Which American cities suffered a large drop in tourism after September 11th 2001?
2. How many city mayors met in Atlanta?
3. What was the reason for their conference?
4. Which country is the most popular tourist destination in the world?
5. Before September 11th, where was the USA in the list of top tourist destinations?

4 Read the British news article and find out:

1. the most famous tourist attraction in Stratford.
2. a famous sports event that took place in that region.
3. the name of the county in England where Stratford-upon-Avon is situated.
4. what percentage of the region's tourists come from the UK.
5. how much money American tourists spend there each year.

Speaking

5 If you had booked a holiday abroad, would you cancel the holiday if there were terrorist attacks or disease there? Would you be worried about visiting the USA or the UK today?

Listening

6 EP Listen to someone booking a holiday and complete the form on page 84 with their details.

Writing

7 Imagine you are booking a holiday in the UK or the USA. Complete the form for yourself.

Topic ◘ The UK's relationship with the EU
Countries ◘ UK
Vocabulary ◘ Metric and imperial measurements
Links ◘ 2a, 4a, 10c

UK + EU = OK?

Measuring up to Europe

Despite being a member of the European Union since 1973, other countries are often puzzled by the UK's apparent reluctance to integrate with the rest of Europe.

Many British people feared that the opening of the Channel Tunnel in 1994 would mean an end to Britain's unique island status, but it seems as if Britain's reputation for 'splendid isolation' has never been stronger. Britons still talk about going 'to Europe' or 'to the continent' when they cross the Channel, and foreign visitors to a British pub today are still served beer in pints, and still have to pay for those pints in pounds sterling.

The metric system has been taught in British schools since 1974 and today's teenagers use it without thinking, but most Britons over 40 still ◘cling on to imperial measurements. Since 2000, all food retailers have been obliged by law to price and weigh their food in metric measurements, but they are also allowed to show the imperial equivalents. This double-labelling, which will have to end in 2010, has led to a number of compromises. Milk and butter are still produced in their standard, recognised 1-pint cartons or 8-ounce packages, but proudly display the odd metric equivalents, and market traders often advertise the imperial prices of their fruit and vegetables much more clearly than the metric prices.

Feelings run high on this issue, with many people resenting the 'interference' of Brussels in the traditional British way of life.

WORD BANK
to cling on ▫ to hold something tightly and refuse to let go
fuss ▫ trouble, complaint
martyr ▫ someone who dies for what they believe in
spokesman ▫ representative

In 2002, five 'metric ▫martyrs', all market traders, were taken to court for not displaying metric prices on their goods. Their ▫spokesman, Neil Herron, said that their defeat meant "the death of democracy", but the five received huge support from the public, who raised £250,000 to help pay their legal costs. Britain has also constantly delayed adopting the euro, which other major European countries such as Germany, France and Italy accepted as their currency without ▫fuss in 2002. The British government has promised to hold a referendum on the subject and let the British people decide if they want the new currency or not, but with an estimated 65% of voters currently opposed to joining the euro, it is very uncertain when this will take place.

FROM THE MARKET
4 PTS ORGANIC MILK
2 LBS CHEESE
6 OZ OLIVES
3 YDS CURTAIN MATERIAL
4 FT RIBBON (1.5 IN. WIDE)

CONVERSION TABLE

Imperial	Metric
Length	
1 inch (in)	2.54 centimetres
1 foot (ft)	0.31 metre
1 yard (yd)	0.91 metre
Weight	
1 ounce (oz)	28.35 grams
1 pound (lb)	0.45 kilos
Liquid	
1 pint (pt)	0.57 litres

Before you read

1 What currency does your country use? How long have you had it?

Reading

2 Complete the table with the correct dates from the text.

Year	Event
......	UK joins the EU
......	Metric system introduced in British schools
......	Channel Tunnel opened
......	Obligatory pricing of food in metric measurements
......	Major European countries adopt the euro
......	Pricing of food in imperial measurements must end

3 EP Choose the correct alternatives to complete this summary of the text.

Britain *is/isn't* a member of the EU, but a lot of British people feel that their country is quite *separate from/similar to* the rest of Europe. The metric system of *currency/measurement* has been used in Britain since the 1970s, but many Britons, especially *older/younger* people, prefer to use the old imperial system. Food sold in Britain is usually priced using both types of measurement, but it is *legal/illegal* to price products using imperial measurements only. Britain uses the *euro/pound sterling* as its currency, *like/unlike* all of the other countries in the EU. A date for a referendum in the UK on the euro *has already/hasn't yet* been fixed.

Before you listen

4 Use a calculator and the conversion table to convert the shopping list above into metric measurements.

Listening

5 EP Listen to the conversations and tick the correct picture each time.

1. A☐ B☐ C☐ D☐
2. A☐ B☐ C☐ D☐
3. A☐ B☐ C☐ D☐
4. A☐ B☐ C☐ D☐

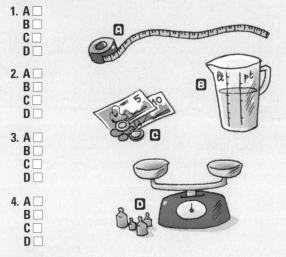

Speaking

6 Why do you think that Britain feels such a strong sense of independence from the rest of Europe? What is the stereotypical image of a British person? Do you think that national stereotypes have any truth in them?

Topic ▫ The UK pop industry
Countries ▫ UK
Vocabulary ▫ Words connected to the pop industry
Links ▫ 7d

Soundtrack
The music business

Hear Today, Gone Tomorrow

Pop groups manufactured by the music industry have existed since the days of the Motown 'factory' in 1960s America, but few groups can have appeared (and disappeared) quite as rapidly as the UK's Hear'Say.

In 2000, the UK's TV audience were ▫gripped by the first series of *Popstars*, where 3,000 hopeful young singers competed for the opportunity to be part of a pop group that would guarantee them fame and fortune. Public interest in the five winners, Danny, Noel, Myleene, Kym and Suzanne, was so high that they were hidden at a secret location until they had recorded their first songs. When they came out of seclusion in February 2000, they had a new image and a new name. Their first single, *Pure and Simple*, sold over 1 million copies and went straight to number 1 in the charts – making it the best-selling debut single of all time. Their first album, *Popstars*, also went to number one and they had another four top-ten singles.

Hear'Say were deliberately 'sold' to the under–14s market. As well as the usual

Before you read

1 Can you name the pop stars in the pictures? How much money do they have?

Reading

2 Read the text *The UK music industry* and answer the questions.

1. What age group are most of the singers on the 'richest pop stars' list?
2. What percentage of the world's music revenue comes from the UK?
3. How much money does the UK's music industry make each year?

3 EP Read the magazine article. Match these topics to the paragraphs.

a. The marketing of Hear'Say.
b. Some young people's desire for fame.
c. The group's downfall.
d. The long history of manufactured pop groups.
e. Hear'Say's formation and early success.

Vocabulary

4 Find words in the text that mean:

1. to put a song onto a disc or tape.
2. one song released for sale.
3. the weekly list of best-selling discs.
4. an artist's first performance.

WORD BANK

to deter ▫ to persuade not to do something
to grip ▫ to hold very tightly
to launch ▫ to start
oblivion ▫ obscurity, nothingness
to split ▫ to separate
youngster ▫ young person

books, calendars and posters, 10,000 Hear'Say dolls were produced and a range of clothing was planned.

In the summer of 2001, however, rumours started appearing in the newspapers of divisions within the group, and their second album, *Everybody*, only reached number 24. In January 2002, Kym left the group (having earned over £1 million in less than a year). Widely-publicised auditions were held to choose a replacement for her, but in October 2002 the group finally ▫split, complaining that 'fans' were booing them at their concerts and shouting abuse at them in the streets.

So what became of Hear'Say? Kym married a soap star and is still singing, and Myleene has ▫launched a new career in classical music, but the other members of the group have faded into ▫oblivion. There have even been rumours that they are working in ordinary low-paid jobs again.

But despite the obvious fact that the record and TV companies made the most money from the Hear'Say experience, this didn't ▫deter thousands more young people queuing up for places on the second series of *Popstars*, or its imitators *Pop Idol* and *Fame Academy*. It would appear that for many ▫youngsters, a taste of fame is more important than artistic recognition or financial security.

The UK music industry

10% of all world music sales are generated by the UK, whose huge pop music industry brings in £4.5 billion each year and accounts for 4% of all UK exports. These are the five richest pop stars currently living in Britain.

Paul McCartney £670 million

Madonna £225 million

Mick Jagger £175 million

Elton John £170 million

Sting £165 million

5. a collection of songs released for sale.
6. when an artist has to perform so that he/she can be judged.
7. people who follow and support an artist.
8. to make an angry noise showing that you don't like an artist's performance.

Reading

5 Answer the questions about Hear'Say. How much/How many:

1. people auditioned for the first series of *Popstars*?
2. people were there in Hear'Say?
3. albums did Hear'Say release?
4. copies did their first single sell?
5. singles did they make that reached the top ten?
6. Hear'Say dolls went on sale?
7. money did Kym earn from Hear'Say?
8. months did Hear'Say exist as a group?

Speaking

6 Do you have bands like Hear'Say and programmes like *Popstars* in your country? What do you think of them? Do you think that the members of manufactured pop groups are being exploited?

Writing

7 Write a profile of your favourite singer or band. Try to find out statistics about how many records they sell and, if possible, how much they earn.

Language & Culture

Business letters

Sports Window UK
29 High Street
Higher Hepburn
Herts.
HH1 2HO

19.10.2005

The Manager
Sports Window US
2751 Beach Boulevard
San Antonio
California
USA
115002

Stock and sales levels

Dear Sir/Madam,
We have been looking at stock and sales levels for the previous year. Have you completed your checks yet? If so, can you compare your output with ours?
Our levels were as follows:
▶ Tracksuits: 1,570 sold but this was only 65% of the total stock.
Total sales: £47,000
Most popular colour: blue
▶ Trainers: 4,750 pairs sold. This was 95% of the total stock. No returns.
Total sales: £190,000
▶ Football tops: 3,251 sold. This was the equivalent of 71.5% of the total stock.
Total sales: £97,530
▶ Sports bags: 91 sold. This was the equivalent of 51.5% of the total stock.
Total sales: £1,820
We took a total of 3,421 phone orders, only 65 were cancelled.
Are your figures similar? Do you think cut backs should be made in next year's stock levels?
I look forward to receiving your reply in the near future. Perhaps we can meet some time in the autumn?
Yours faithfully,
Jon Runner
Store Manager

Sports Window US
2751 Beach Boulevard
San Antonio
California
USA
115002

10.27.05

Sports Window UK
29 High Street
Higher Hepburn
Herts.
HH1 2HO

Stock and sales levels

Dear Sir,
I am writing in reply to your letter dated October 19th. Here is the information you require:
▶ Tracksuits: 3,120 sold, which represent 82.5% of the total stock. No returns.
Total sales: $78,000
Most popular color: black
▶ Trainers:10,500 pairs sold. This was 100% of the total stock.
Total sales: $262,500
▶ Basketball tops: 1,797 sold. This was the equivalent of 35% of the total stock.
Returns: 63
Total sales: $44,925
▶ Sports bags: 325 sold. This was the equivalent of 65% of the total stock. No returns.
Total sales: $3,900
We took a total of 7,500 orders online, 121 were canceled. Did you check your online orders yet? I think it may be better to review stock levels overall. We can arrange to meet with you later in the fall and go through the stock sheets.
I trust this information is helpful for you in the meantime.

Sincerely,
J D Foster
Store Manager

GRAMMAR

1 Look at the letters quickly. Which one was written by a manager in the UK and which one was written by a manager in the US?

2 Match the following words with numbers in the letters.
1. seventy one point five per cent
2. one hundred and ninety thousand pounds
3. two hundred and sixty-two thousand five hundred dollars
4. ninety seven thousand five hundred and thirty pounds
5. forty four thousand nine hundred and twenty-five dollars
6. eighty two point five per cent
7. one thousand eight hundred and twenty pounds
8. three thousand nine hundred dollars

SKILLS

3 Read each letter again and identify the following:
1. the sender's address.
2. the recipient's address.
3. the date.
4. the subject line.
5. the opening salutation.
6. the closing salutation.

What differences can you find between these aspects of the letters?

4 Read the letters and find:
1. two examples of spelling differences in US and British English.
2. one difference in a vocabulary item in US and British English.
3. one difference in the use of a tense in US and British English.

5 Imagine that you are the manager of a Sports Window shop in your country. Write a letter to either the UK or the US manager telling him your sales figures.

1. Tracksuits: five thousand six hundred and seventy-two sold. Sixty-two point five per cent of total stock.
2. Most popular colour: black.
3. Trainers: six thousand one hundred and fifty-two pairs sold. Ninety-five per cent of total stock.
4. Football tops: seven thousand nine hundred and ninety-nine sold. Ninety-nine point five per cent of total stock.
5. Sports bags: one thousand and thirty-three sold. Fifty-seven per cent of total stock.

Try to arrange a meeting in November to discuss the figures. Remember to use the letter-writing conventions that you identified in exercise 3.

Module 7 Sport and leisure

IN THIS MODULE YOU WILL READ AND HEAR ABOUT:

- the Commonwealth Games
- extreme sports in Australia
- shopping malls in the USA and UK
- reality TV in the UK
- popular types of holidays for British and American people
- Australia's national sports
- the activities available at a UK gym

School holidays: England	
Late July - August	**6 weeks**
October half-term	**1 week**
Christmas	**2 weeks**
February half-term	**1 week**
Easter	**2 weeks**
May half-term	**1 week**
Total	**13 weeks**

School holidays: USA	
Mid June - mid August	**8 weeks**
Christmas	**$1\frac{1}{2}$ weeks**
Easter	**1 week**
Total	**$10\frac{1}{2}$ weeks**

1 How are the people in the photographs spending their leisure time?

2 Look at the typical school holiday dates for England and the USA. How do they compare with your own school holidays? In which country do schoolchildren have the most holidays?

Topic ▫ The Commonwealth Games
Countries ▫ Britain and its ex-colonies
Vocabulary ▫ Names of countries/Sports
Links ▫ 1f, 3b, 3f, 5f, 7f

The Friendly Games

What are the Commonwealth Games?

The Commonwealth is a voluntary organisation of 54 independent countries who all share a common history as part of Britain's imperial past. The countries are as diverse as Canada, New Zealand, Pakistan, Barbados, Sri Lanka and Zambia, and Queen Elizabeth is head of the organisation. Today the Commonwealth works to advance democracy, human rights and social and economic development, and organises special programmes to help promote trade, science, health, young people and many other specific issues in its member countries.

The Olympic-style Commonwealth Games are held every four years in a different member country. Known as the Empire Games until 1950, the first event was held in Hamilton, Canada in 1930. There were only eleven participating countries, and the sports included athletics, boxing, bowls, rowing, swimming and wrestling.

England has only ▫hosted the Games twice: in London in 1934 and in Manchester in 2002. They have only been held twice outside of Canada, Britain or ▫Australasia – in Jamaica in 1966 and in Malaysia in 1998. The number of countries participating in the Games has slowly grown to over 70, and thousands of athletes now participate. Without competition from the USA and the major European countries, Australia, Canada and the British countries (which compete separately) usually win the most medals.

As happens for the Olympics, ▫host countries usually build special new facilities for the Games. Manchester spent 20 years preparing for the 2002 Games and built a new 48,000-seat stadium which cost over £100 million. Luckily, the Games attracted around 1 million visitors to the city and were a financial success.

The Commonwealth Games have their own version of the Olympic torch ceremony. On Commonwealth Day (May 11th) in a Games year, the Queen hands a ▫baton containing a message to an athlete. This is then passed in relay style to other athletes. They run through different Commonwealth countries until they reach the host nation. The baton is opened and the Queen's message is read out at the opening ceremony of the Games.

Before you read

1 Can you name the sports or the people in the pictures? At what international event can you regularly see these sports? Do you know of any other big international athletics events?

Reading

2 EP Read the text *The Friendly Games*. Are these sentences true or false?

1. The British monarch is head of the Commonwealth.
2. The Commonwealth Games take place every year.
3. The first Games were in 1950.
4. The Games are always held in Canada, Britain, Australia or New Zealand.
5. England, Scotland, Wales and Northern Ireland compete as four separate countries in the Games.
6. 48,000 people came to the Games in Manchester.
7. Commonwealth Day is in May.
8. Lots of different runners carry the Queen's message to the Games' host country.

WORD BANK

Australasia – Australia, New Zealand and their neighbouring islands in the Pacific
baton – a cylindrical stick
host – someone who accommodates other people
to host – to accommodate
lap – a circuit of a sports track or field
to run away with – to easily win
sprinter – an athlete who runs short distances very quickly
stir – controversy

Commonwealth heroes

Cathy Freeman Australia (1994 Games in Victoria)

In 1994 Cathy Freeman became the first aboriginal sprinter to win a gold medal in the Commonwealth Games and the first athlete in Commonwealth history to win golds in both the 200m and 400m events. She caused a stir after the races, too, by carrying the aboriginal flag as well as the Australian flag in a lap of victory. She was voted Australian of the Year in 1998, and in 2000 she was chosen to light the Olympic flame in Sydney.

Alan Wells Scotland (1978 Games in Edmonton, 1982 Games in Brisbane)

Alan Wells has won three Commonwealth medals, but that's not what he's most famous for. In a strange incident in the Brisbane 200m final he was jointly awarded the gold medal with Englishman Mike McFarlane when computers registered their times as identical - 20.43 seconds. Wells also won gold at the 100m in the Moscow Olympics, making him one of the most successful Scottish athletes ever.

Lennox Lewis Canada (1986 Games in Edinburgh)

Back in 1986, an unknown heavyweight boxer fighting under the Canadian flag ran away with the gold medal at the Edinburgh Games. Two years later he also took gold at the Seoul Olympics. Now a professional and fighting for Britain, where he was born, Lewis was the first boxer to win both world heavyweight titles since Mike Tyson.

Vocabulary

3 Make a list of all the Commonwealth member countries that are mentioned in *The Friendly Games* text.

4 Find the names of these sports in the text.

 a
 b
 c
 d
 e
 f
 g

Reading

5 Read about the three Commonwealth heroes. Match the columns to make true sentences.

1. Cathy Freeman is	a British	boxer	who won two gold medals	at the 1982 Games	in Victoria.
2. Alan Wells is	a Scottish	runner	who won a gold medal for Canada	at the 1986 Games	in Edinburgh.
3. Lennox Lewis is	an Australian	runner	who won a joint gold medal	at the 1994 Games	in Brisbane.

Writing

6 Write a paragraph about one of your sporting heroes. Mention their achievements at international events.

Extreme sports

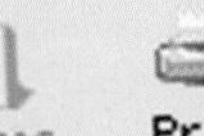

Back Forward Reload Home Search My Net Images Print Security Shop Stop

Go To: http:// www.x-ox.com

X-OZ.COM

Welcome to Australia's top extreme sports site!

▫Check out this year's top four x-sports. Click on the links to learn more.

1. Kite surfing

What do they do? Surf on a surfboard attached to a power kite that can take them into the air. Kitesurfers have to learn to control both the surfboard and the kite at the same time, and perform tricks and turns while in the air.

Where do they do it? The Whitsunday Islands, 74 tropical islands between the mainland and the Great Barrier Reef, are ideal for beginner kitesurfers thanks to the warm, flat water that surrounds them. The islands have become such a popular destination that Whitehaven Beach there is now known as Kitehaven Beach!

Danger rating: 3/5

2. Freestyle motocross

What do they do? Perform ▫stunts on special light, powerful, off-road bikes. Using ramps, riders can jump over obstacles up to 35m. While in the air they perform special moves such as the "whip" (turning the bike sideways in the air), the "superman" (kicking their legs out behind them and flying parallel to the bike) and the "cliff hanger" (fixing their feet under the ▫handlebars and releasing their hands).

Where do they do it? There will be a whole day of motocross at the Planet X Summer Games in Sydney this November – the ▫thrill-seekers' Olympics!

Danger rating: 4/5

3. Street luge

What do they do? Lie on their backs on large skateboards only 4cms from ground, travelling on the road at speeds of nearly 130kph. The boards are specially built to fit each rider, who must wear a leather suit and a full motorbike helmet. Riders use their feet as ▫brakes. Roads are closed for competitions, but not for practice sessions, so a car always follows each luger in case of accidents.

Where do they do it? Melbourne has lots of clubs that practise most Saturdays. See our message board for details.

Danger rating: 4/5

4. Base jumping

What do they do? Jump off tall structures (BASE = buildings, antennae, span (bridges), earth) and land with a parachute. To begin base jumping you have to already be a ▫competent skydiver, with experience of 150 parachute jumps. Base jumping has a controversial reputation. Jumpers have a 95% chance of ending up in hospital at some point in their career. The sport is even illegal in some countries, including the USA.

Where do they do it? Anywhere (often illegally)! Frenchman's Cap in Tasmania (a 340m high cliff) is a popular spot.

Danger rating: 5/5

WORD BANK

brake ▪ device for reducing speed
to check out ▪ to look at, investigate
competent ▪ able to do something well
handlebar ▪ the part of a bike that you hold with your hands
stunt ▪ dangerous trick
thrill ▪ excitement

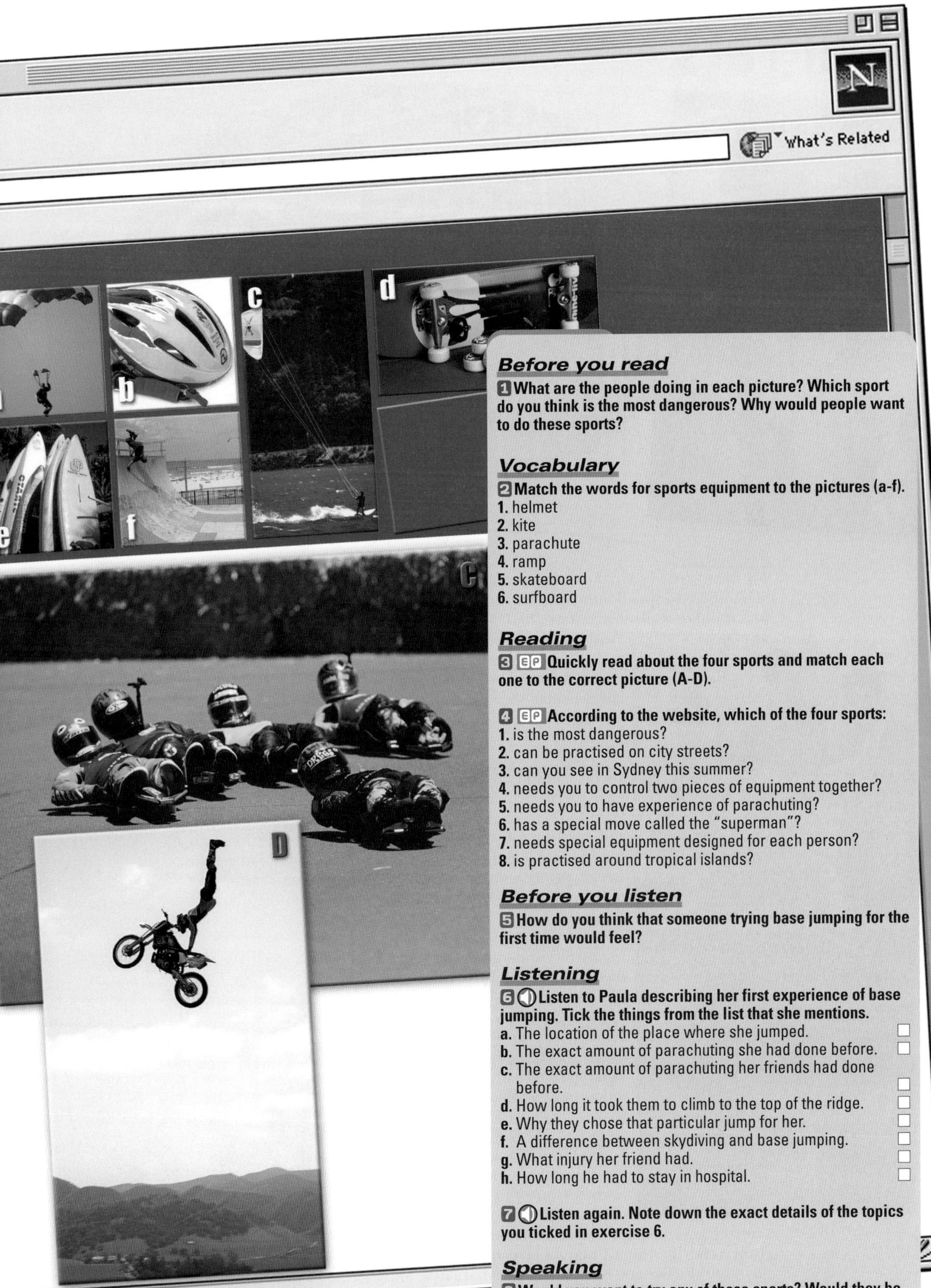

Before you read

1 What are the people doing in each picture? Which sport do you think is the most dangerous? Why would people want to do these sports?

Vocabulary

2 Match the words for sports equipment to the pictures (a-f).

1. helmet
2. kite
3. parachute
4. ramp
5. skateboard
6. surfboard

Reading

3 EP Quickly read about the four sports and match each one to the correct picture (A-D).

4 EP According to the website, which of the four sports:

1. is the most dangerous?
2. can be practised on city streets?
3. can you see in Sydney this summer?
4. needs you to control two pieces of equipment together?
5. needs you to have experience of parachuting?
6. has a special move called the "superman"?
7. needs special equipment designed for each person?
8. is practised around tropical islands?

Before you listen

5 How do you think that someone trying base jumping for the first time would feel?

Listening

6 Listen to Paula describing her first experience of base jumping. Tick the things from the list that she mentions.

a. The location of the place where she jumped. ☐
b. The exact amount of parachuting she had done before. ☐
c. The exact amount of parachuting her friends had done before. ☐
d. How long it took them to climb to the top of the ridge. ☐
e. Why they chose that particular jump for her. ☐
f. A difference between skydiving and base jumping. ☐
g. What injury her friend had. ☐
h. How long he had to stay in hospital. ☐

7 Listen again. Note down the exact details of the topics you ticked in exercise 6.

Speaking

8 Would you want to try any of these sports? Would they be interesting to watch as a spectator? Do you think they really are sports, or are the people who do them just crazy?

Topic ▫ Leisure time spent in shopping malls
Countries ▫ USA and UK
Vocabulary ▫ Leisure facilities
Links ▫ 1d, 1e, 5c

Mall rats

mall rat /mɔːl ræt/ American teenager who spends all of his or her time at the shopping mall with friends.

NANCY

My friends and I go to the mall every day after school. It's just somewhere to spend time with your friends. We usually just ▫hang out or walk up and down looking in the clothes shops. We don't often buy anything. We go to the mall at the weekends, too, and go to the movie theater there or hang out in the ice cream parlor. We always make sure we look good when we go to the mall in case there are any ▫cute boys there!

THE KOWALSKIS

We take the kids to the mall every weekend because they often have special activities there, like children's shows and games. We also go to the bowling alley there too, and the kids love eating at the food court – there's so much choice: Mexican, Italian, Thai – and plenty of fast food, of course! We get the weekly ▫groceries at the mall too, and sometimes Vanessa goes to the spa there. It's great having everything under one roof.

TYLER

My friends and I go to the mall about twice a week. We play the games in the arcade, and we like to check out the latest DVDs and computer games in the shops. You can even listen to the music or try out the new games in some shops. And we like to buy the latest sports clothes, too. Sometimes, if it's raining at the weekend, we go to the indoor skate park at the mall, too.

CONNIE

I go to the mall every Saturday. I don't go for any particular reason, but I like to look in the designer shops and the cosmetics shops, and I usually end up buying something. Sometimes when I get it home I realise that I didn't really want the thing I bought – or that it doesn't go with anything else I've got! But I like to see what's new, and there's a really good atmosphere there.

WORD BANK

crèche ▪ place where you can leave small children to be looked after by other people for a short time
cute ▪ good-looking
groceries ▪ food and other everyday items of shopping
to hang out ▪ to spend time together, not doing anything in particular

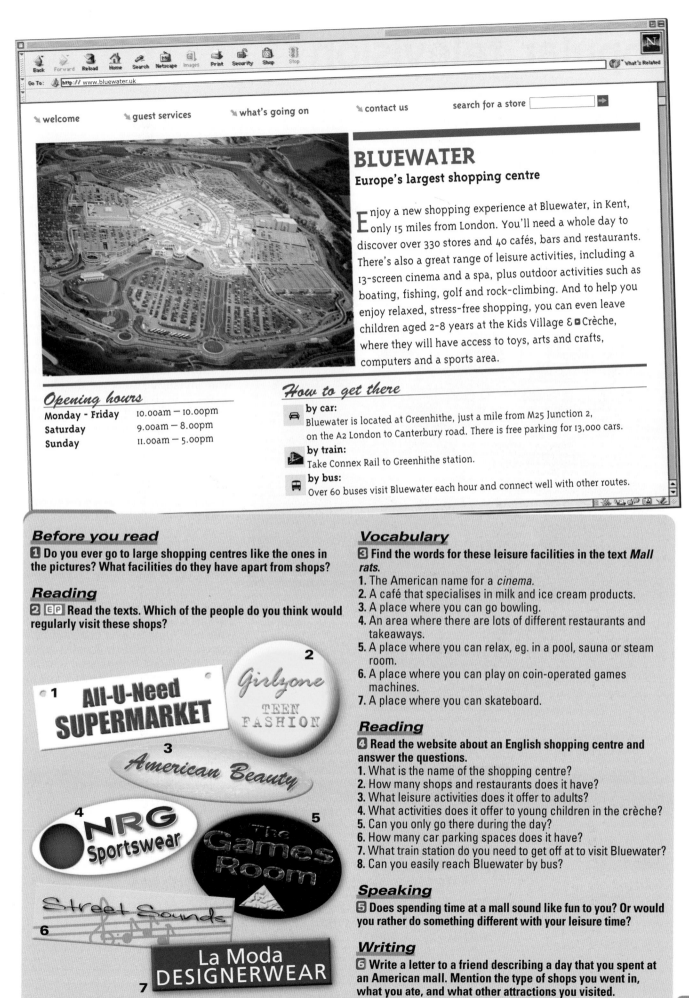

Back Forward Reload Home Search Netscape Images Print Security Shop Stop

Go To: http:// www.bluewater.uk

welcome | guest services | what's going on | contact us | search for a store

BLUEWATER

Europe's largest shopping centre

Enjoy a new shopping experience at Bluewater, in Kent, only 15 miles from London. You'll need a whole day to discover over 330 stores and 40 cafés, bars and restaurants. There's also a great range of leisure activities, including a 13-screen cinema and a spa, plus outdoor activities such as boating, fishing, golf and rock-climbing. And to help you enjoy relaxed, stress-free shopping, you can even leave children aged 2-8 years at the Kids Village & ▪ Crèche, where they will have access to toys, arts and crafts, computers and a sports area.

Opening hours

Monday - Friday	10.00am – 10.00pm
Saturday	9.00am – 8.00pm
Sunday	11.00am – 5.00pm

How to get there

by car:
Bluewater is located at Greenhithe, just a mile from M25 Junction 2, on the A2 London to Canterbury road. There is free parking for 13,000 cars.

by train:
Take Connex Rail to Greenhithe station.

by bus:
Over 60 buses visit Bluewater each hour and connect well with other routes.

Before you read

1 Do you ever go to large shopping centres like the ones in the pictures? What facilities do they have apart from shops?

Reading

2 EP Read the texts. Which of the people do you think would regularly visit these shops?

Vocabulary

3 Find the words for these leisure facilities in the text *Mall rats.*

1. The American name for a *cinema.*
2. A café that specialises in milk and ice cream products.
3. A place where you can go bowling.
4. An area where there are lots of different restaurants and takeaways.
5. A place where you can relax, eg. in a pool, sauna or steam room.
6. A place where you can play on coin-operated games machines.
7. A place where you can skateboard.

Reading

4 Read the website about an English shopping centre and answer the questions.

1. What is the name of the shopping centre?
2. How many shops and restaurants does it have?
3. What leisure activities does it offer to adults?
4. What activities does it offer to young children in the crèche?
5. Can you only go there during the day?
6. How many car parking spaces does it have?
7. What train station do you need to get off at to visit Bluewater?
8. Can you easily reach Bluewater by bus?

Speaking

5 Does spending time at a mall sound like fun to you? Or would you rather do something different with your leisure time?

Writing

6 Write a letter to a friend describing a day that you spent at an American mall. Mention the type of shops you went in, what you ate, and what other attractions you visited.

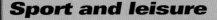

Popular television

TV gets real

In 1974 the BBC ▫broadcast a new TV programme called *The Family*. In 12 episodes, everyday scenes from the lives of the working-class Wilkins family in Reading were shown to the nation. Some television executives feared that it couldn't possibly be a success – who would be interested in watching something so boring? But *The Family* was instantly a huge hit. Known then as 'fly-on-the-wall' documentaries, and now as 'docusoaps' or 'reality TV', such programmes now dominate the TV schedules and regularly attract millions of viewers.

In the 1990s, house and garden ▫makeover programmes such as *Changing Rooms* were particularly popular, while docusoaps such as *Driving School* made overnight stars out of likeable ordinary people such as Maureen Rees, possibly the worst driver in the world.

In the new millennium, however, reality TV programmes have tended to become more personal and humiliating. *Fat Club*, for example, followed the ups and downs of eight ▫overweight people desperate to lose weight at a remote health club, and *Wife Swap* took the simple but explosive idea of two women ▫swapping places in each other's families for two weeks. For the first week they had to live according to the other woman's rules, but for the second week they could dictate how the house was run. In 2003, reality humiliation reached a new low with *How Clean is your House?*, a surprise hit involving two women who investigate some of the dirtiest homes in the country, then return later to see if the inhabitants are still following their cleaning advice.

With reality TV also came interactive TV, starting with the mother of them all, *Big Brother*. Following the model of that programme, in which viewers decide each week by vote who stays and who goes, many other elimination shows quickly appeared. The most popular ones were *Pop Stars*, *Fame Academy* and *I'm a Celebrity – Get me Out of Here*, where a group of celebrities attempt to survive for two weeks in the jungle together, performing various tasks along the way. Celebrities, especially those seeking to ▫boost their careers, seem particularly ▫keen to appear on reality shows, as successful celebrity versions of *Big Brother*, *Driving School*, *Fat Club* and *Fame Academy* have proved.

Tonight's TV programmes

BBC1 8pm
....
The Taylors from Windsor give their neighbours' home a Victorian ▫feel with the help of regular designers Linda and Anna. Will they be impressed with the results?

Channel 4 8.30pm
....
Prepare to be disgusted, as Kim and Aggie visit a family with seven children who claim that they never have any time for tidying.

ITV 8pm
....
Who will have to swim among crocodiles in order to win tonight's food for the group? Will it be model Catalina or footballer John? - you decide!

ITV 9pm
....
There's trouble this week as fitness trainer Harvey gets ▫tough with the group, especially Simon, who has gained some weight. Some of the group plan a rebellion.

BBC1 8.30pm
....
Dave's feeling nervous and stressed as his wife prepares for her seventh test. Will she finally pass this time?

Channel 4 9pm
....
This week Tracey, who has one child and works full-time, changes places with Kate, a stay-at-home mum with five children.

Before you read

1 What are your favourite TV programmes? Do you have *Big Brother* in your country? What do you think of it?

Reading

2 EP Read the text *TV gets real* and complete the TV guide with the names of programmes from the text.

3 Answer the questions.

1. What was the name of the BBC's first 'docusoap'?
2. Was it successful or not?
3. Which docusoap did Maureen Rees appear in?
4. Name four British TV programmes where viewers vote on who has to leave the programme each week.
5. Name five British reality TV programmes which famous people have appeared in.
6. Name three British TV channels.

WORD BANK

to boost ▫ to make more successful
to broadcast ▫ to transmit
feel ▫ atmosphere
keen ▫ entusiastic
makeover ▫ to completely transform and improve the appearance of something or someone
overweight ▫ too heavy or fat
to swap ▫ to exchange
to take off the air ▫ to stop broadcasting
tough ▫ strict, severe
TV ratings ▫ audience statistics

Soap power

Despite the success of the new reality TV shows, it is still soap operas that regularly attract the biggest audiences each week. The term 'soap opera' (always shortened these days to just 'soap') was created in the USA to describe early daytime radio and TV drama serials – then aimed at housewives – whose storylines were sentimental or sensational, and which were usually sponsored by the manufacturers of washing powder.

Soaps in Britain have come and gone over the years as British society has changed. *Brookside*, centred on a housing estate in Liverpool, began in the 1980s and mirrored the social issues of the time – Thatcherism and unemployment. It was very popular in that decade, but in the new millennium it gradually declined in popularity and its storylines became more outrageous. It was finally ▫taken off the air in 2003. Other soaps have proved more enduring. The battle for the top of the weekly ▫TV ratings is always between Britain's two favourites – *EastEnders* and *Coronation Street*. Both of these soaps are set in urban working-class areas; *EastEnders* in the fictional Albert Square in the East End of London, and *Coronation Street* in the equally fictional town of Weatherfield – a suburb of Manchester. Both programmes feature strong characters and well-written scripts which often deal convincingly with personal dilemmas and topical issues. The programmes – each shown four times a week – usually have audience figures of 12–13 million, and are supposedly watched even by the Queen. *EastEnders* has been running since 1985, but *Coronation Street* is the soap champion. Shown continuously since 1960, it is the longest-running TV series in the world.

The original cast of *EastEnders*.

Brookside in the 1980s.

A cast reunion on the set of *Coronation Street*.

Before you listen

4 In groups, try to think of an idea for a new reality TV show.

Listening

5 EP Listen to three TV executives discussing a possible new reality TV show. What is the best title for the show?

a. *Football academy*
b. *Sports academy*
c. *Celebrity football academy*
d. *Celebrity sports academy*

6 Listen again and answer the questions.

1. How long would the young people stay in the training school?
2. Why don't they want to have a programme on just football?
3. What would the programme concentrate on, apart from the sports?
4. What would the winner get?

Reading

7 EP Read the text *Soap power*. Which of the soap operas mentioned in the text:

1. were first broadcast in the 1980s?
2. can no longer be seen on TV?
3. are based in the north of England?
4. is based in London?
5. has been shown for over 40 years?

Speaking

8 What type of reality TV programmes do you think will appear in the future?
Will they become more extreme?
Will soaps continue to be popular?
Will people stop making more serious programmes?

Holidays

1

2

3

A

Dear Gemma,

I'm having a great time here in Magaluf, even though my parents are here too! Everything's been planned for us – the flights, the hotel, excursions, barbecues, beach parties – it's fantastic! And the weather is brilliant. I wanted to practise my Spanish, but everyone here speaks English anyway. In fact, there are more British people here than Spanish!

How's life back in Glasgow?!

love, James

B

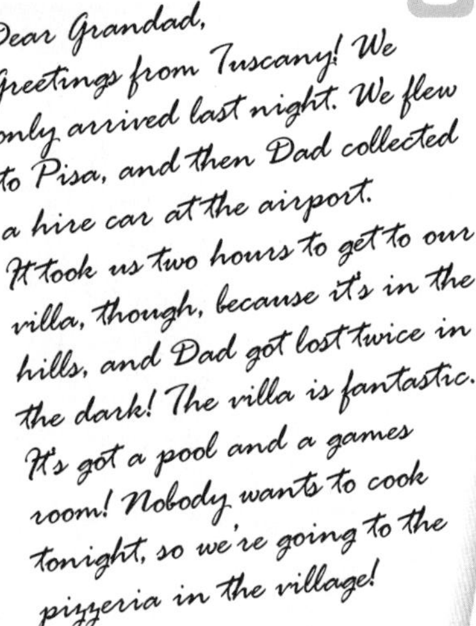

Dear Grandad,

Greetings from Tuscany! We only arrived last night. We flew to Pisa, and then Dad collected a hire car at the airport. It took us two hours to get to our villa, though, because it's in the hills, and Dad got lost twice in the dark! The villa is fantastic. It's got a pool and a games room! Nobody wants to cook tonight, so we're going to the pizzeria in the village!

love, Lisa

C

Dear Mom and Dad,

Sorry we didn't write before, but we're really busy here at Camp Redwood! There's so much to do every day. Yesterday we tried white-water rafting and on Monday night we went on a night hike. It was quite scary, and we didn't get back to camp until 3 am! The dormitories aren't very comfortable, and the food is terrible, but we don't mind! See you in August!

love,
Ritchie and Paul

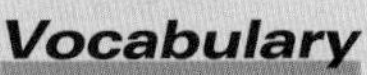

Vocabulary

1 Match the photos 1-6 to the different types of holiday.

a. Backpacking
b. Caravan park
c. Summer activity camp
d. Package holiday
e. Self-catering villa
f. Sight-seeing tour

Before you read

2 EP Which of the types of holiday in exercise 1 would you recommend to these people?

1. Mr and Mrs Mills want to go abroad with their son, but they prefer to have everything organised for them. They want to go somewhere hot.
2. Mr and Mrs Ellis want a quiet holiday abroad with their daughter. They don't want to stay in a hotel, and they don't mind driving abroad.

WORD BANK

dormitory ▫ room where lots of people sleep together
foothills ▫ smaller mountains grouped around a larger one
scary ▫ frightening
slide ▫ transparent photograph that you can project onto a wall
spacious ▫ having a lot of space

4

D

Dear Harry,
We finally made it to Nepal! I can't believe that it's June already – the weeks have flown by. What a fantastic experience! Pakistan, India, Tibet, and finally the ▫foothills of Mount Everest! Life will never be the same again! I'll tell you all about it when we get home – we'll have hundreds of ▫slides.
I hope this postcard reaches you before we do!
love,
Barbara

5

E

Dear Mum,
Here we are at Golden Sands again. The weather isn't very good, but we're having a good time. The caravan is great – really ▫spacious. There's plenty of room for all four of us inside. And the kids are loving it here. It's great for young children – lots of organised activities, and entertainment in the evening. Sometimes Jeff and I even get some time to ourselves!
See you soon
Love,
Sarah

6

F

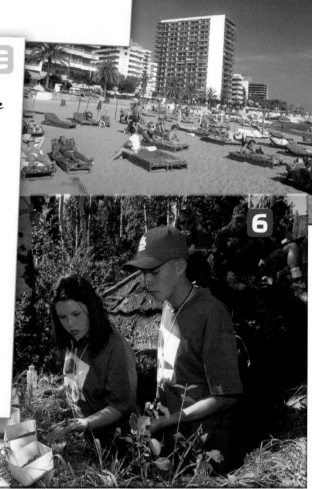

Dear Elizabeth,
This is the fifth day of our tour, and the sixth country we've visited! This really is a dream come true. You must come to Europe some day – it's so different from home. Just imagine – the Tower of London, the Eiffel Tower, the Coliseum, the Acropolis – all in ten days!
Don't forget to water my plants!
love,
Mom

3. Mrs Graham, of New York, wants her two sons to have a summer holiday in the country, but she and her husband have to work all summer.
4. Mr and Mrs Abbot, of Birmingham, want a cheap holiday with their two small children. They can't afford to go abroad or to stay in a hotel.
5. Mrs Wyatt, of Denver, is interested in the culture and history of Europe, but she doesn't want to travel alone.
6. Barbara Marriot, of Chicago, wants to travel to remote parts of the world with a friend. She doesn't mind very basic accommodation and food.

Reading

3 Read the postcards and check your answers to exercise 2. Who is each postcard from?

4 EP Are these sentences true or false?

1. James is speaking a lot of Spanish on his holiday.
2. Lisa doesn't like the villa she is staying in.
3. Ritchie and Paul are bored at Camp Redwood.
4. They like the food at Camp Redwood.
5. Barbara has already visited India.
6. She has a lot of pictures of her trip.
7. There is a lot for children to do at the Golden Sands caravan park.
8. The sight-seeing tour of Europe lasts ten days.

Listening

5 Listen to a family discussing what type of holiday to have. What is their final decision?

Writing

6 Write a postcard to an English-speaking friend from your ideal holiday destination. Describe what type of holiday it is, and what you are doing.

Speaking

7 Are these types of holiday popular with people from your country? Which type of holiday would you prefer?

Topic ▪ Sport in Australia
Countries ▪ Australia
Vocabulary ▪ Sports and equipment
Links ▪ 2d, 7a, 7b

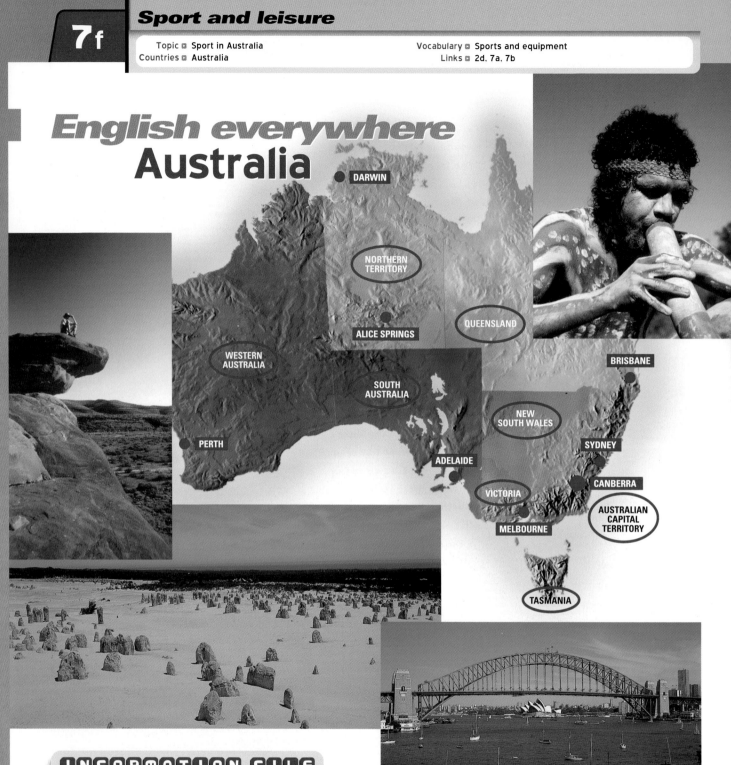

Australia

Australia

Total area ▪ 7.7 million sq. km
Total population ▪ 20 million
Ethnic mix ▪ 92% White
7% Asian
1% Aborigine
Capital ▪ Canberra
Popul. of capital ▪ 330,000
Government ▪ A federation of six states and two territories. Australia was a British colony until 1901. It is still a monarchy (Britain's monarch is also Australia's) but it is now an independent state.
Climate ▪ Coasts: fertile, mountainous
North: tropical
Centre: desert (known as 'the bush' or 'the outback')

Before you read

1 Do you know anything about Australia? Can you name any famous Australians? Think about sport, film, music, etc.

Reading

2 Look at the map and read the Information File on Australia, then answer the questions.

1. How many people live in Australia? Does this figure surprise you?
2. Why are all the major Australian cities on the coast?
3. Who are the people in the photographs?
4. What is the city in the photograph? Is it the capital of Australia?
5. Do you think Canberra is a large city?
6. Who is Australia's current monarch?

WORD BANK

ashes ▫ the powder that remains when something is burned
to bounce ▫ to throw something to the ground so that it comes up again
to bowl ▫ to throw a ball carefully in a specific direction
challenging ▫ difficult
goalposts ▫ vertical poles that represent the goal in a sport
rough ▫ quite violent
stumps ▫ groups of three vertical sticks that cricket players must run between
yacht ▫ a large racing boat with a sail

SPORT

Australia has plenty to offer the sports fan all year round. For example, Australians play at least four types of football! But before you book your sporting holiday, don't forget that Australia is in the southern hemisphere – December and January are high summer, and July is mid-winter!

Australian rules football

Always known as 'Aussie rules', this game is unique in the world. It's played by teams of 18 players on an oval field with an oval ball, like a rugby ball. Unlike normal football or rugby, however, the ball can be passed in a variety of ways: kicked, hit with the hand, ▫bounced and carried! It's a fast, skilful and often ▫rough game. To score a goal, the ball must be kicked through ▫goalposts at the side or the centre of the field. Melbourne is the centre of Aussie rules, and matches regularly attract crowds of over 50,000.

SPORT

Cricket

International cricket matches are played every summer in Australia, and Melbourne has the biggest cricket ground in the world. Cricket is played by teams of 11 players. The bowler from one team ▫bowls the ball to a player from the other team, who tries to hit the ball and run between the two sets of ▫stumps before the other team can return the ball. The Australian team is one of the best in the world and has a long-running competition with England known as The ▫Ashes, because Australia's victory over England in London in 1882 was considered to be the death of English cricket.

Sailing

Australia is a favourite destination for fans of all kinds of sailing. The Sydney to Hobart Yacht Race takes place each year over the Christmas and New Year period, and is one of the world's most exciting and ▫challenging races. On Boxing Day, 26th December, the ▫yachts leave Sydney Harbour, accompanied by boats of all shapes and sizes in a carnival atmosphere. They hope to arrive in Hobart, Tasmania around New Year's Day to a Mardi Gras party.

Vocabulary

3 Can you identify any of the sports in the photos? Can you find the following things in the pictures?

yachts *an oval ball* *a bat* *stumps*

Reading

4 Now read the texts and try again to identify the things in exercise 3.

5 Answer the questions.

1. Which city is a centre for both Aussie rules and cricket?
2. Can you touch the ball with your hands in Aussie rules?
3. What is The Ashes? Why is it called that?
4. When does the Sydney to Hobart Yacht Race begin?
5. Where is Hobart?

Vocabulary

6 The east coast of Australia is famous for its watersports. Match the equipment to the sports.

Sports	Equipment	
scuba diving	flippers	sailboard
surfing	mask	surfboard
waterskiing	motor boat	waterskis
windsurfing	oxygen tank	

Listening

7 Listen to Caroline talking about her favourite watersport. Which of the sports in exercise 6 is she describing?

Writing

8 In groups, make a list of your country's national sports, famous sports grounds and well-known competitions. Prepare an entry in a guide book for your country similar to the one on this page.

Grammar ◘ Phrasal verbs
Skills ◘ Speaking: making suggestions and inviting

Language & Culture

Fitz Gym
Bored at the weekends?
Then why not come along and find out what we can offer you?

◆ Do you want to take up a new sport? Have you considered badminton, table tennis or short tennis?

◆ Do you want to start your own team? Then get in touch with our local team director for football, basketball or volleyball.

◆ Fancy some underwater action? Why not look into our full range of water classes? We offer water aerobics, swimming lessons for all levels and water polo sessions.

◆ All classes take place between 9.00 am and 10.00 pm every day so there's always time to fit them in between work, studies or a busy homelife.

◆ The first month is absolutely free if you sign up before the end of the month. After that it costs £35.00 per month.

◆ Need to know more? Then look up our website, pick up a leaflet from any of your local shops or come along and see us!

GRAMMAR

1 Read the text quickly and find all the sports and activities that Fitz Gym offers.

2 Match the phrasal verbs underlined in the text to these definitions.

a. to happen
b. to start doing an activity, usually for pleasure
c. to arrive
d. to sign an agreement to do something
e. to take away
f. to discover
g. to investigate something
h. to do something at a time that does not affect other arrangements
i. to find a piece of information in a book or on the Internet
l. to make contact with someone

3 Complete the sentences with the phrasal verbs you identified in exercise 2. You may need to change the tense.

1. I thought I might try and *get in touch with* my old friends from university. I haven't seen them for years.
2. My sister has just decided to ...... painting as a hobby.
3. The Olympic Games ...... in a different country every four years.
4. Have you ...... those new words in the dictionary yet?
5. Has she ...... if she can get a day's holiday yet?
6. Did you ...... a cinema programme when you were in town yesterday?
7. The police said they were ...... the crime.
8. I don't know how you ...... all the things you have to do every day!
9. Have you ...... for the tennis lessons yet?
10. Is your brother going to ...... to the party tonight?

SKILLS

4 Read the dialogue and complete it with the phrases below.

I like the sound of that *why don't you* *what about*
~~what shall we do~~ *I'd rather not* *we could go*
how about *I'm not keen on*

A: OK. (1) *What shall we do* this weekend?
B: Well, (2) ...... to the cinema and see that new Bond film.
C: No, thanks. I've already seen that. (3) ...... having a barbecue?
A: (4) .... We don't know what the weather's going to be like. It might rain. (5) ...... joining that new gym in the High Street?
B: I'm not sure. (6) ...... keeping fit and I haven't got much money just now. How much does it cost each month?
C: I saw an advert for it and I think it said the first month is free and it's £35 a month after that.
B: That's too much money for me. (7) ...... go and we can meet afterwards?
A: OK. We'll go and sign up and then we'll meet you for a drink at say 8.00pm.
C: OK. (8) ...... !
B: Great! I'll see you later then.

5 In small groups, invite your friends to do something this weekend or suggest doing something else. Use the topics below to help you. Remember to use phrases from the dialogue in exercise 4.

go swimming *play football* *watch TV* *hire a video*
go the gym *organise a party* *go to the cinema*
have a barbecue *go to a concert* *go to a nightclub*

Module 8 The arts

IN THIS MODULE YOU WILL READ AND HEAR ABOUT:

- modern artists at a school in Scotland
- the book *The Lord of the Rings* and other epic stories
- stage musicals in London's West End
- child actors in Hollywood
- breakdancing and hip-hop culture
- film music
- a film review

1 **Match these arts to the photographs: music, dance, theatre, art, film, literature.**

2 **Are you interested in any of the arts in the photos? Have you got a talent for any of them?**

3 **Which of the six arts mentioned are these words connected with? Use a dictionary if you don't know. Some words are connected with more than one art.**

box office canvas cast choreography composer conductor exhibition plot script set

Topic ▫ Modern art
Countries ▫ Scotland
Vocabulary ▫ Art
Links ▫ 5a, 5e, 11f

A child could do that

YOUNG MASTERS

At a recent art exhibition at the West Highland Museum in Scotland, a picture called *The Future is Gone* by Jodie Fraser, depicting three ghostly planes over the New York skyline, attracted a lot of attention. *911*, another work by Jodie on the same subject, won an individual Barbie Prize for modern art in 2002. *911* consists of a grey ▫canvas covered with 3,000 burnt matches, one for each person who died in the terrorist attacks on the World Trade Center. The main £20,000 Barbie Prize was won by the collected work of Jodie and her schoolfriends at Caol Primary School near Fort William – because Jodie is only 10 years old.

Children in Room 13.

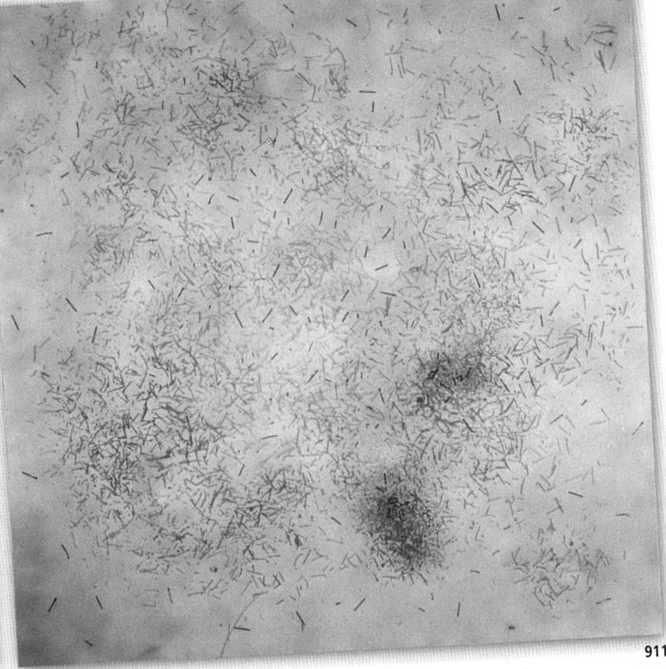

911.

The Turner Prize

The Turner Prize, the adult version of the Barbie Prize, is awarded every year to an artist in Britain aged under 50, for outstanding work in the last 12 months. These are the winners of recent years.

year	artist	typical work
2002	**Keith Tyson**	*The Thinker* (computer equipment placed inside a ▫pillar makes a ▫humming sound)
2001	**Martin Creed**	*The Lights Going On and Off* (lights turn themselves on and off in an empty room)
2000	**Wolfgang Tillmans**	57 everyday events photographed from unusual angles and positioned ▫randomly across a wall
1999	**Steve McQueen**	*Drumroll* (a film made by rolling a videocamera in an ▫oil drum through the streets of New York)

The Thinker by Keith Tyson.

WORD BANK

canvas ■ the fabric that you use oil paints on
committee ■ a group of people who control an organisation
employee ■ someone who works for another person
to flood out ■ to come out in great quantities
grant ■ money given free
to hum ■ to make a buzzing noise, like a bee
oil drum ■ an empty cylinder that contained oil
to patronise ■ to treat someone too simply, as if they were a child
pillar ■ a tall column, usually used to support the roof of a building
randomly ■ not in a fixed order

One of Rob Fairley's rules is "Never teach them art!"

The Magic Yellow Elephant.

The art that has ■flooded out of Caol Primary School's art club, Room 13, has amazed the modern art world. Room 13 is open to any child at playtime, lunchtime or after school. On Fridays, if the children have completed all their schoolwork, they can spend all day there, and some children stay there from 9am to 6pm. The only adults involved are artist Rob Fairley and his assistant Claire Gibb, but they aren't the children's teachers. They are their ■employees.

Room 13 is an independent business, separate from the school, and has a ■committee (all under the age of 11) who manage their own finances, apply for ■grants, order art materials and give lectures. They have even lectured at the Tate Modern gallery in London. But some banks and arts organisations are not prepared to deal with a committee who are not yet teenagers, so Room 13 often has financial problems, and their orders for art materials are sometimes ignored.

Ivan Massow, head of the judges of the Barbie Prize (a junior version of the annual Turner Prize for Modern Art), says "It was obvious that the children had been asked to think about things and express themselves through art. And the quality of the work was exceptional. If I had bought *911* and put it in my London flat, no-one would have thought that it was the work of a 10-year-old".

The children are not looking forward to studying art at secondary school, where they will have to use cheaper materials and follow a strict exam syllabus. They know that they have a unique freedom in Room 13. One of Rob Fairley's rules is "Never teach them art!", and their headteacher doesn't interfere with their work. As their managing director, Danielle Souness, said at a recent conference: "Room 13 proves that if you give us the chance we can organise our education and we are tired of being ■patronised with your idea of what we can understand".

You can visit Room 13 at www.room13scotland.com

Before you read

1 Look at the works of art in the photos. What do you think of them? What do you think they 'mean'? Do you prefer more traditional styles of art?

Reading

2 Read the text quickly. What is unusual about:

1. Jodie Fraser's success as an artist?
2. the committee of Room 13?
3. the children's relationship with Rob Fairley and their headteacher?

3 EP Match these headings with the paragraphs of the text.

a. Day-to-day activity in Room 13
b. The children's opinion of art teaching
c. The committee's work
d. One pupil's work
e. An art expert's opinion of the children's work

4 EP Are these statements true or false?

1. The Barbie Prize is a special art prize for young people.
2. *911* is a work that represents dead people.
3. Rob Fairley decides what happens in Room 13.
4. There are some teachers on the committee of Room 13.
5. Some adults don't treat the committee of Room 13 seriously.
6. The children think that they will get a better education at secondary school.

5 EP Read the list of recent Turner Prize winners. Whose work:

1. involves film-making?
2. involves photography?
3. involves electronics?

Speaking

6 What do you think of the descriptions of the Turner Prize winners' work?

7 Discuss the following questions.

1. Why have the children of Room 13 produced such interesting art?
2. Can you teach subjects like art and music, or are they talents that people are born with?
3. Should children be allowed to 'organise their education' in any way?

The Lord of the Rings

The turn of the millennium produced a number of polls of "The nation's favourite...".
The winner of three national British polls, Amazon.com's "Book of the Millennium", Channel 4's "Book of the Century" and BBC's "Big Read", was Tolkien's *The Lord of the Rings*, and Tolkien himself was voted "Author of the Century" in several other surveys.
The film versions of Tolkien's trilogy have widened his readership even further.
But why does the book have this phenomenal reputation?

A story for all time

First published in 1954, J.R.R.Tolkien's *The Lord of the Rings* tells the story of how the most powerful object in the universe, the One Ring, falls into the hands of Frodo Baggins, a young human-like creature. Frodo must then begin a long and dangerous journey to take the Ring to the only place where it can be destroyed forever. The book has been translated into 25 languages and has sold nearly a hundred million copies. People regularly name it as their favourite book – but what can explain its enduring popularity? Of course *The Lord of the Rings* offers readers a complete fantasy world with its own geography and language, but its story is also based on timeless themes and characters that re-occur through all literature.

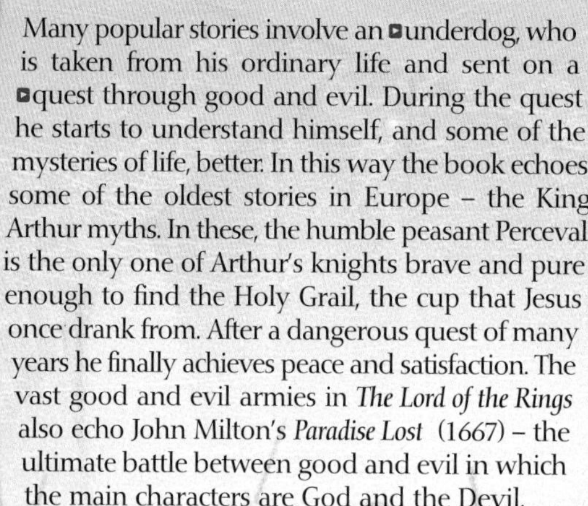

Many popular stories involve an ◘underdog, who is taken from his ordinary life and sent on a ◘quest through good and evil. During the quest he starts to understand himself, and some of the mysteries of life, better. In this way the book echoes some of the oldest stories in Europe – the King Arthur myths. In these, the humble peasant Perceval is the only one of Arthur's knights brave and pure enough to find the Holy Grail, the cup that Jesus once drank from. After a dangerous quest of many years he finally achieves peace and satisfaction. The vast good and evil armies in *The Lord of the Rings* also echo John Milton's *Paradise Lost* (1667) – the ultimate battle between good and evil in which the main characters are God and the Devil.

Many critics now look back on *The Lord of the Rings* as an ◘allegory of the two World Wars, when brave small countries defended themselves against fascist dictators and their armies. Some even see the One Ring as symbolising man's control of the nuclear bomb. The book has also helped to shape other, more modern myths. Both the *Star Wars* films and the *Harry Potter* books have similarities to *The Lord of the Rings*, with their plots based around the attractiveness of the 'dark side', and their small heroes battling evil opponents much more powerful than themselves.

WORD BANK

allegory ▫ symbolic story
to cast ▫ to throw
dint ▫ impression
grasp ▫ reach
grimly ▫ darkly
quest ▫ mission
sledge-hammer ▫ heavy hammer used for breaking stones
to spring ▫ to jump
to strike ▫ to hit
underdog ▫ someone in a position of inferiority
will ▫ (noun) resolution, (verb) to decide
wits ▫ intelligence

Power too great and terrible

In Chapter 2 of The Fellowship of the Ring, *Gandalf the wizard gives the Ring to Frodo and explains its significance.*

Frodo weighed the Ring in his hand, hesitating, and forcing himself to remember all that Gandalf had told him; and then with an effort of ▫will he made a movement, as if to ▫cast it away – but he found that he had put it back in his pocket.

Gandalf laughed ▫grimly. 'You see? Already you, too, Frodo, cannot easily let it go, nor ▫will to damage it. And I could not make you – except by force, which would break your mind. But as for breaking the Ring, force is useless. Even if you took it and ▫struck it with a heavy ▫sledge-hammer, it would make no ▫dint in it. It cannot be unmade by your hands, or by mine.

[...]

'There is only one way: to find the Cracks of Doom in the depths of Orodruin, the Fire-mountain, and to cast the Ring in there, if you really wish to destroy it, to put it beyond the ▫grasp of the Enemy for ever.'

'I do really wish to destroy it!' cried Frodo. 'Or, well, to have it destroyed. I am not made for perilous quests. I wish I had never seen the Ring! Why did it come to me? Why was I chosen?'

'Such questions cannot be answered,' said Gandalf. 'You may be sure that it was not for any merit that others do not possess: not for power or wisdom, at any rate. But you have been chosen, and you must therefore use such strength and heart and ▫wits as you have.'

'But I have so little of any of these things! You are wise and powerful. Will you not take the Ring?'

'No!' cried Gandalf, ▫springing to his feet. 'With that power I should have power too great and terrible. And over me the Ring would gain a power still greater and more deadly.' His eyes flashed and his eyes were lit as by a fire within. 'Do not tempt me!'

Before you read

1 Have you read *The Lord of the Rings*, or seen any of the films? Do you know what the story is about?

Reading

2 Read the introductory paragraph on page 108. Which three specific polls did *The Lord of the Rings* win at the turn of the millennium?

3 EP Quickly read the text *A story for all time*. Choose the best way to complete the summary of the text.

The Lord of the Rings is so popular because:

a. it takes its readers into a fantastic world completely different from their world.
b. it is part of a literary tradition and can be interpreted in a variety of ways.
c. its readers can recognise aspects of modern history in its story.

4 EP According to the text *A story for all time*, which of these themes can be found in *The Lord of the Rings*?

a. The father-son relationship.
b. An ordinary person goes on a quest.
c. The battle between good and evil.
d. The search for the right person to love.
e. How dangerous it can be to have power.
f. What happens after you die.

5 Answer these questions about *A story for all time*.

1. When was *The Lord of the Rings* first published?
2. Who is its author?
3. How many languages has it been translated into?
4. What is the name of its hero?
5. What must he do with the One Ring?
6. Which of King Arthur's knights finds the Holy Grail?
7. Who are the main characters in *Paradise Lost*?
8. Which science fiction films have similarities with *The Lord of the Rings*?

6 Read the extract from *The Lord of the Rings* and answer the questions.

1. What does Frodo try, but fail, to do with the Ring in the first paragraph?
2. Could Gandalf destroy the Ring himself if he wanted to?
3. How does Frodo feel about his quest?
4. Why doesn't Gandalf want the Ring?

Speaking

7 Can you think of any more fantasy books or films that have similar themes and characters to *The Lord of the Rings*?

West End musicals

Hot tickets

The 'West End' is London's theatreland – home to over forty theatres. London's plays, shows and operas attract around 11 million visitors per year and, with tickets costing around £30 each, they bring a lot of income into the capital. The biggest West End attractions are always musicals. *Cats* ran for 21 years, and *Les Miserables* is currently celebrating its 18th year in the West End. Here are some of the hottest tickets in town today.

My Fair Lady is based on G. B. Shaw's 1916 play *Pygmalion* and tells the story of Eliza Doolittle, the ◘Cockney flowerseller chosen from the streets by a professor of ◘linguistics and transformed into a lady. This current production opened in 2001 starring Martine McCutcheon from the TV soap *EastEnders*. It features well-known songs such as "I'm getting married in the morning" and "On the street where you live".

Bombay Dreams is based in the Indian film industry and features an all-Asian cast. The story centres around Akaash, a poor boy played by Raza Jaffrey, who becomes a film star and falls in love with the daughter of one of Bombay's greatest film directors. The show features modern Indian pop music, such as "Shakalaka Baby", and ◘dazzling costumes and choreography. It opened in 2002 and quickly became one of the most popular shows in London.

We Will Rock You opened in 2002. This musical, with a script by comedian Ben Elton, takes place in the future, when rock music is illegal. The story is based on famous songs by Queen such as "Bohemian Rhapsody" and "I Want to Break Free", the set resembles a rock concert and there are plenty of special effects. And Tony Vincent, who plays the hero Galileo Figaro, sounds very like Queen's lead singer, Freddie Mercury.

Before you read

1 Have you ever been to the professional theatre? Do you know what sort of productions you can see at the moment in your capital city /your city?

Vocabulary

2 Match these words connected with the theatre to their definitions.

1. musical
2. script
3. box office
4. to open
5. to run
6. special effects
7. choreography
8. matinee
9. set
10. cast

a. the planning of the dance moves in a show
b. when a show begins in a theatre
c. the spoken dialogue in a show
d. when a show lasts for a time in a theatre
e. an afternoon performance of a show
f. all the performers in a show
g. the background and scenery for a show
h. a show with singing and dancing
i. technical illusions
j. a theatre's ticket-selling service

WORD BANK

cockney ▪ a working-class person from the East End of London
dazzling ▪ very bright and colourful
linguistics ▪ the study of languages

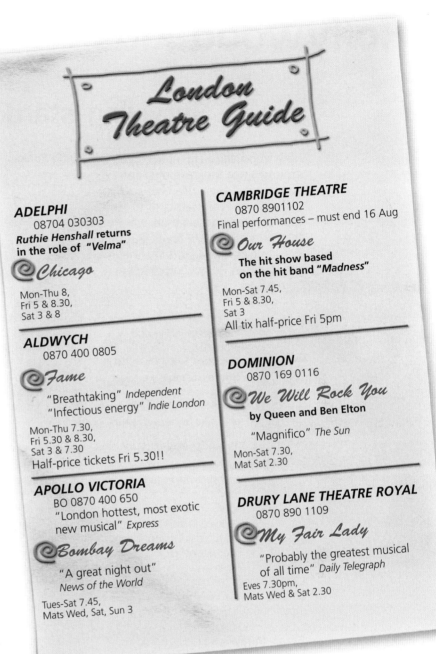

ADELPHI
08704 030303
***Ruthie Henshall* returns in the role of "Velma"**

Mon-Thu 8,
Fri 5 & 8.30,
Sat 3 & 8

ALDWYCH
0870 400 0805

"Breathtaking" *Independent*
"Infectious energy" *Indie London*

Mon-Thu 7.30,
Fri 5.30 & 8.30,
Sat 3 & 7.30
Half-price tickets Fri 5.30!!

APOLLO VICTORIA
BO 0870 400 650
"London hottest, most exotic new musical" *Express*

Bombay Dreams

"A great night out"
News of the World

Tues-Sat 7.45,
Mats Wed, Sat, Sun 3

CAMBRIDGE THEATRE
0870 8901102
Final performances – must end 16 Aug

The hit show based on the hit band "Madness"

Mon-Sat 7.45,
Fri 5 & 8.30,
Sat 3
All tix half-price Fri 5pm

DOMINION
0870 169 0116

We Will Rock You
by Queen and Ben Elton

"Magnifico" *The Sun*

Mon-Sat 7.30,
Mat Sat 2.30

DRURY LANE THEATRE ROYAL
0870 890 1109

My Fair Lady

"Probably the greatest musical of all time" *Daily Telegraph*

Eves 7.30pm,
Mats Wed & Sat 2.30

Reading

3 Read the *Hot tickets* text and find the names of the musicals in the photos.

4 EP Complete this table with information about the three musicals.

Show	My Fair Lady	We Will Rock You	Bombay Dreams
Opening year	....	....	....
Main character	....	....	....
Actor who plays him/her	....	....	....
Songs from the show	....	....	....

5 Find the following information in the theatre guide.

1. The names of the theatres where you can see the three musicals from exercise 4.
2. How many performances of *Chicago* there are on a Friday.
3. When you can get cheap tickets to see *Fame*.
4. Abbreviations for 'box office', 'matinées' and 'tickets'.
5. When you can see *Bombay Dreams* at the weekend.
6. When *Our House* will leave the Cambridge Theatre.
7. What the Daily Telegraph newspaper thought about *My Fair Lady*.
8. On which days there are matinées of *My Fair Lady*.

Before you listen

6 What are the different ways that you can get tickets for theatre shows? What do you think is a reasonable price for a theatre ticket?

Listening

7 EP Listen to a recorded phone message from the *We Will Rock You* box office. Note down the different prices for the different days and times.

Speaking

8 Which of these shows would you like to see? Why? How much would you be prepared to pay?

Hollywood kids

Surviving stardom

Hollywood child stars have been around since the days of silent cinema, but they often have difficult, or even tragic, lives, and their fans can desert them when they enter their late teens. But here are some ex-child stars that have survived the Hollywood machine.

During the Depression era of the 1930s, Hollywood produced many child stars. The most famous of all was **Shirley Temple** – a talented singer and tap dancer who made her first film at the age of 4. She became the first child to win an Oscar, but the film studios lost interest in her when she hit her 20s, and she was already a ▫divorcee at 21. As an adult, however, she became involved in politics and had a successful career as an international diplomat. She represented the USA at the United Nations, and also served as an ambassador to Ghana and Czechoslovakia.

Elizabeth Taylor starred as a child in several sentimental films of the 1940s, including the *Lassie* series about a faithful, clever dog. She was ▫stunningly beautiful, and her film roles continued into her adult life. By the 1960s she was one of the biggest stars in Hollywood, and she became notorious for her many marriages – eight in total (twice to the same man, actor Richard Burton). In the 1970s Elizabeth suffered from alcoholism and weight problems, but in the 1980s she discovered a new role as ▫campaigner and ▫fund-raiser for AIDS charities.

Jodie Foster amazed critics and was nominated for an Oscar for her role, aged 12, in the disturbing 1976 film *Taxi Driver*. Following her appearance in this film, Jodie was ▫stalked by a mad fan, John Hinckley. In 1981 Hinckley shot President Reagan in an attempt to re-enact the film. In her adult life Jodie has had an accomplished career as an actress and a director, winning two Oscars – for *The Accused* in 1988 and *The Silence of the Lambs* in 1991. Today she is known as one of the most secretive and publicity-shy actresses in Hollywood.

Drew Barrymore comes from a large acting family. Her grandfather John was a classical British actor in the 1930s, and her father is also an actor. When she was 7, Drew starred in the ▫blockbuster movie *ET*, directed by her ▫godfather Steven Spielberg. But following the success of *ET*, Drew had serious problems with drugs. By the age of 16 she had already been in ▫rehab, attempted suicide and separated from her parents. But she has now put her problems behind her, and since the age of 21 she has made a number of successful films, including the popular *Scream* and *Charlie's Angels*.

In the 1990s, the *Home Alone* films made 10-year-old **Macaulay Culkin** the most highly-paid child star ever. With his father as his manager, Macaulay earned an estimated $30 million. In 1994, his parents separated and there was a bitter ▫custody battle over their six children. As a result, Macaulay obtained a legal separation from his father and gained control over his own finances. In 1997 he got married at the age of 17, but divorced two years later. Although he hasn't made a film since 1994, Macaulay has had successful roles in the theatre.

WORD BANK

blockbuster ▪ extremely successful film
campaigner ▪ someone who tries to get support for a cause
custody ▪ legal possession of something or a child
divorcee ▪ a divorced woman
fund-raiser ▪ someone who raises money for a cause
godfather ▪ a man who is selected by the parents at a child's christening to help look after the child
rehab ▪ (= rehabilitation) treatment and cure of an addiction
to stalk ▪ to follow and give constant unwanted attention to someone
stunningly ▪ extremely

A star is born

NAME: HALEY JOEL OSMENT
DATE OF BIRTH: ....
FIRST FILM: MIXED NUTS
YEAR: ....
MOST FAMOUS FILM: THE SIXTH SENSE
YEAR: ....
CO-STAR IN THAT FILM: BRUCE WILLIS

OTHER FILMS, YEARS AND CO-STARS:
FORREST GUMP (19...........) WITH TOM HANKS
BOGUS (19...........) WITH WHOOPI GOLDBERG AND GERARD DEPARDIEU
.... (200...........) WITH JUDE LAW
ANY OSCAR NOMINATIONS? YES (FOR ....)/NO

Before you read

1 Do you recognise any of the films in the photos? Do you recognise the child actors? Do you know what they are doing these days?

Reading

2 Quickly read the text *Surviving stardom*. What different problems have the child stars had in their lives?

3 EP Read the text again. According to the text, which child star(s):
1. haven't made any films since their childhood?
2. have had successful careers as adult film stars?
3. have had a successful career or role outside of films or acting?
4. separated from their families?
5. had a famous grandfather?
6. had drug problems while still a child?
7. had problems with a fan?
8. earned the most money as a child?
9. was married a lot of times?
10. has also directed films?

Before you listen

4 Can you think of any other films that have children as their stars? How good are the child actors?

Listening

5 EP Listen to the information about Haley Joel Osment, a current child star, and complete the notes about him above.

Writing

6 Imagine that, at your age, you are already a famous film star. Complete a table like the one above with notes about your own experience.

Speaking

7 With a partner, take turns to interview each other about your life as a child star. Complete all the information in the table about your partner, then ask each other how you feel about being a star, and if you have had any problems.

Topic ▪ Breakdancing
Countries ▪ USA
Vocabulary ▪ Movement
Links ▪ 1e, 2f

Dancing in the streets

Hip-hop terms

breaking/breakdancing: dancing to hip-hop music, often close to the ground, or even on your hands or your head
b-boy/b-girl: breakdancer
crew: breakdance team
battle: breakdance competition
MC: a rapper, someone who speaks rhythmically over a beat
DJ: someone who plays records for people to rap or dance to
scratching: when a DJ moves a record with his hand to interrupt or repeat the music

Breaking and battling

Breakdancing emerged in New York in the 1970s. The style of movement, which combines dance, gymnastics and boxing, was performed by kids, often in teams, in competitions at street corners. Breakdancing was part of the larger hip-hop culture that also incorporated rappers, DJs and graffiti artists. The Rock Steady Crew from the Bronx were one of the first hip-hop groups and became world famous. The group still organise a Rock Steady Crew Anniversary every year in New York to celebrate hip-hop culture, and its main focus is always a street dance competition.
The Anniversary attracts competitors of all different ethnic types from all over the world, and over 20,000 observers.

Before you read

1 What type of dancing is shown in the photos? Do you know what city it originated in?

Reading

2 EP Read the text *Breaking and battling* and the table of hip-hop terms. Are the following statements true or false?
1. Breakdancing began in the 1980s.
2. Breakdancing is an athletic style of dance.
3. Breakdancing is competitive.
4. The Rock Steady Crew only formed recently.

What's on

Rap & Hip-Hop

Don't miss the annual Rock Steady Anniversary, which is happening this weekend in New York.

THURSDAY 24TH JULY:
11am Celebrity benefit basketball game
9pm MC challenge

FRIDAY 25TH JULY:
1pm-5pm: Film festival
3pm: B-boy/b-girl battle (invited crews only)
+ 'Punk rock rap' fashion show
a fusion of street and skate culture, with a stage designed by set designer and graffiti artist Ernie Vales.
Models will be real b-boys/girls and street skaters.

SATURDAY 26TH JULY:
1pm: Free outdoor concert

SUNDAY 27TH JULY:
3pm: B-boy/b-girl battle final

1

2

3

4

5

6

Breakdance moves

donkey: jumping onto your hands from a standing position, and then flipping back onto your feet again
flares: supporting yourself on your hands and swinging your legs round
handglide: spinning on one hand
headspin: spinning on your head
popping: making sliding movements, like a robot
windmill: spinning on your back, without using your hands

5. You can watch street dance at the Rock Steady Crew Anniversary.
6. Only Americans compete at the Anniversary.
7. A 'b-boy' is a male dancer.
8. A 'battle' is a rapping competition.

3 Read the program of events for the Rock Steady Anniversary. On which day(s) can you see:

1. a breakdance competition?
2. a clothes show?
3. a concert?
4. a rapping competition?
5. a sports match?
6. films about hip-hop?

Vocabulary

4 Read the definitions of breakdance moves and find words that mean:

1. moving smoothly along the floor without taking your feet off the floor, like on ice.
2. turning very quickly.
3. moving from side to side, or in a circular motion.
4. making a quick movement where you reverse your position.

5 EP Match the pictures of the breakdance moves to their descriptions.

Speaking

6 Can you dance? What styles of dance can you do? Which famous people do you think are good dancers?

Soundtrack
Cinema music

Top scores

From the earliest days of the movies, films have traditionally used music to ▫heighten the drama of the action on screen. The first cinemas came equipped with a piano or an organ, and the silent films of the 1920s had live musical accompaniment. The pianist or organist had to watch the screen closely all the time to make sure that the music he or she was playing matched the action of the film.

With the arrival of sound, it became possible to put music as well as dialogue onto a film's ▫soundtrack. It is difficult to think of a single film made since then without some sort of background music. Film musicals were spectacularly popular from the 1930s to the 1960s, with extravagant screen productions of popular stage musicals such as *Oklahoma* (1955) and *My Fair Lady* (1964) involving hundreds of singers and dancers. Although it became less popular at the end of the 20th century, the film musical has recently been revived through box-office successes such as *Moulin Rouge* (2001) with Nicole Kidman, and *Chicago* (2003) with Renée Zellweger.

Film music has also become popular away from the cinema. Many soundtracks become best-selling records, and film ▫scores are now studied seriously and played by classical

Speaking

1 Can you name any of the films in the photos? If you have seen them, can you remember what their music was like?

Reading

2 Answer these questions about the text.

1. What sort of instruments used to accompany old silent films?
2. What did the musician have to do while he or she played?
3. When did film musicals start to lose popularity?
4. Which two modern films have helped to make the musical popular again?
5. Which types of film tend to have commercially successful scores?

WORD BANK
acclaimed ◘ liked and praised
to heighten ◘ to make more intense
score ◘ music specially written for a film
soundtrack ◘ the recorded version of a film's sound (specifically its music)

The best film soundtracks of all time

(chosen by the listeners of Britain's Classic FM radio station)

1 The Lord of the Rings *(Howard Shore 2001)*
2 Star Wars *(John Williams 1977)*
3 Schindler's List *(John Williams 1993)*
4 The Empire Strikes Back *(John Williams 1980)*
5 Gladiator *(Hans Zimmer 2000)*
6 ET *(John Williams 1982)*
7 Out of Africa *(John Barry 1985)*
8 Lawrence of Arabia *(Maurice Jarre 1962)*
9 Dances with Wolves *(John Barry 1990)*
10 Titanic *(James Horner 1997)*

orchestras and radio stations. The most ◘acclaimed and popular film music in recent years has often been the scores of epic or science-fiction films such as *Star Wars* (1977), *ET* (1982), *Gladiator* (2000) and *The Lord of the Rings* (2001), many of which have been composed by American composer John Williams.

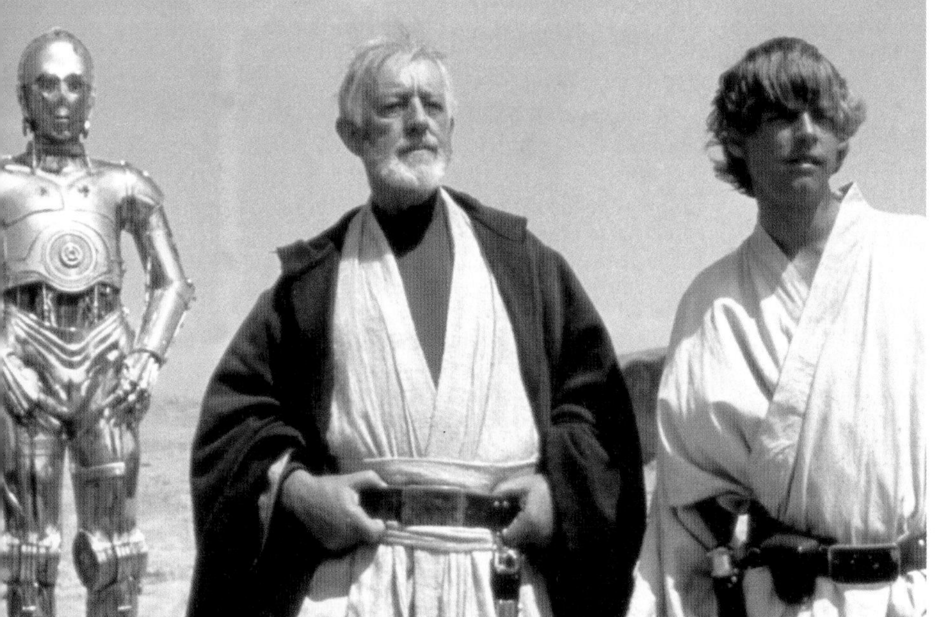

◆ John Williams

John Williams was born in New York, but studied music at the University of California at Los Angeles. He trained as a classical pianist, and also worked as a jazz musician before entering the film industry. Williams has composed the music for nearly 80 films, and has won five Oscars for his scores. He has written scores for several of the most famous films of recent years, including *Jaws, ET, Close Encounters of the Third Kind* and *Jurassic Park*, plus the Indiana Jones and the Harry Potter series. He is also an orchestral conductor and he has written several classical orchestral pieces.

3 Read the text about John Williams and find out:
1. where he was born.
2. where he studied.
3. an instrument that he can play.
4. how many film scores he has written.
5. how many Oscars he has won.
6. another musical talent he has, apart from writing and playing music.

4 Look at the Classic FM list of top ten film scores. How many of the films have you seen? How many have scores written by John Williams?

Writing

5 Write a paragraph about a film that you particularly liked because of its music or its songs. Mention who wrote the music, and how it added to the general effect of the film.

Language & Culture

I capture the castle

[1] This film is an adaptation of Dodie Smith's 1948 novel. It is directed by the first-time feature director Tim Fywell and there are some lively performances from the main characters. The screenplay by Heidi Thomas has some very funny lines.

[2] The plot is simple and the director has worked hard to remain faithful to Dodie Smith's novel. The plot moves quickly and a romantic sub-plot is very neatly introduced when the landlord of a castle dies and it is inherited by an American family. The American family have two extremely handsome sons and Mortmain, the main character, has two beautiful daughters.

[3] The main characters are Mortmain, a promising novelist who lives with his family in a rented ruined castle. In fact, he never does any writing. This role is played by Bill Nighy. Nighy acts more convincingly here than in his previous film and television roles. His strangely eccentric wife, and the stepmother of his daughters, Topaz, is played by Tara Fitzgerald. She has some of the funniest scenes in the film and she plays her part well. The two daughters are Cassandra and Rose. Romola Garai and Rose Byrne play the two sisters very differently. The handsome American boys are played by Henry Thomas and Marc Blucas. When both girls fall for the same boy, it is easy to see how things will turn out.

[4] The castle setting is unconvincing but the filming of Cassandra is beautifully done and allows us to get to know her character very well. The costumes are very convincing and precisely evoke the England of the 1930s.

[5] I can't imagine how the period could have been more realistically depicted. If you like the1930s and good acting then this is a film worth watching.

GRAMMAR

1 Read the film review quickly and find out the names of the main characters in the film.

2 Complete the table with adverbs from the text.

Adjective	Adverb
1. hard	*hard*
2. quick	………..
3. neat	………..
4. extreme	………..
5. convincing	………..
6. strange	………..
7. good	………..
8. different	………..
9. beautiful	………..
10. precise	………..
11. realistic	………..

3 Read the review again and find the two examples of comparative adverbs.

4 Complete the sentences with the correct adverbs. Use the adjective in brackets to form the adverb.

1. She speaks English ….. . She never makes mistakes. (good)
2. Did you see the match last night? Juventus lost because they played so ….. . (bad)
3. My brother always behaves ….. . He's really annoying! (sensible)
4. The children played ….. on the beach for hours. (happy)
5. I'm not very good at thinking ….. . (logical)
6. ….., we couldn't go to the park because it was raining. (unfortunate)
7. The thief was acting very ….. and the police caught him ….. . (suspicious/easy)
8. Maria always answers questions very ….. . (intelligent)
9. Doesn't he write ….? (nice)

SKILLS

5 Read the review of *I capture the castle* again and circle examples of special vocabulary relating to films.

6 Match these topics to the paragraphs (1-5) of *I capture the castle*.

a. Conclusion – general opinion of the film
b. The setting, camerawork and costumes
c. Introduction
d. The plot
e. The main characters and the actors who played them

7 Now write a review of a film you have seen. It can be one you loved or one you hated. Use the film review above and the words you identified in exercise 5 to help you.

Module 9 Communication and technology

IN THIS MODULE YOU WILL READ AND HEAR ABOUT:

- British newspapers
- sending text messages
- innovations for Internet use
- using the Internet for schoolwork
- how new technology is affecting the English language
- the computer industry in the Republic of Ireland
- new technology for the home and car

Communications in the new millennium

	USA	UK	Ireland
Homes with an Internet connection	59%	47%	40%
People with a mobile phone	45%	80%	79%

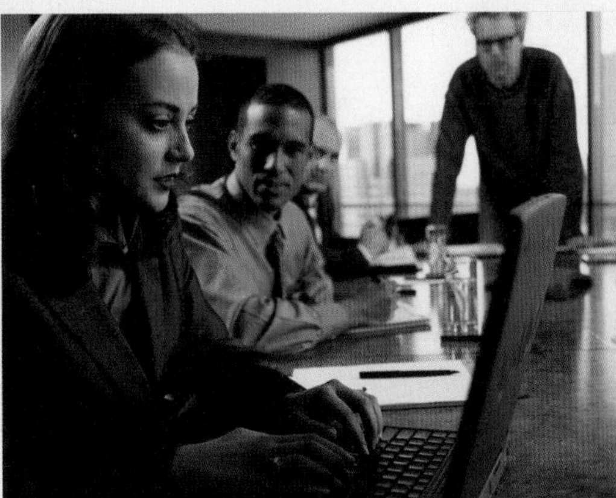

1 Can you find the following things in the photographs?

keyboard laptop electronic notebook mobile phone monitor mouse screen

2 Do most people have access to this technology in your country?

3 Look at the table. Do you think that the equivalent statistics would be higher or lower in your country?

Topic UK tabloid and broadsheet newspapers
Countries UK
Vocabulary Heat and hot weather
Links 2d, 3e

The UK press

Britain's National Daily Newspapers

The broadsheets (or "qualities") (2.9 million sales per day)
The Telegraph
The Times
The Financial Times
The Guardian
The Independent

The middle-market tabloids (3.4 million sales per day)
The Daily Mail
The Daily Express

The popular tabloids (7 million sales per day)
The Sun
The Daily Mirror
The Daily Star

THE DAILY STAR

SUNDAY ROAST BRITAIN

TEMPERATURE 38 °C 101 °F

Millions chill out at 100 °F

SIZZLING Sunday had Brits steaming yesterday on the hottest day EVER.

The temperature officially reached 37.9 °C (100.2 °F) at Heathrow Airport, topping the 37.1 °C recorded in 1990 – but elsewhere thermometers rose to 101 or even higher.
Bookies got a £1 million roasting as punters cleaned up on the temperature soaring past the 100 °F mark for the first time.
Travellers and workers at Heathrow were grabbing stocks of ice creams, lager and soft drinks as they wilted in the heat.
"All our chocolates are melting," moaned sales assistant Martin Stankiwicz. "But ice cream sales have gone through the roof."
One traveller, Aaron Rouse, 25, said: "There's half a dozen ambulances outside because people keep dehydrating."
Elsewhere, shoppers huddled around supermarket chiller cabinets to cool off.
Roads in Great Leighs, Essex, melted, leaving the surface "like syrup".
Ambulance crews in Hampshire treated 27 pensioners who collapsed from the heat in church.
Faced with paying out £250,000 on the record being broken and the temperature passing 100 °F, a spokesman for bookies William Hill moaned: "It's the worst weather result we have ever seen."

The UK's tabloid newspapers are particularly fond of stories about Britain's royal family. The late Princess Diana was an extremely popular subject.

Before you read

1 What different newspapers do you have in your country? Are they national papers or local ones? What are the differences between them?

2 Look at the headlines of the two newspaper articles. One is from *The Daily Star* (a tabloid paper) and the other is from *The Independent* (a broadsheet paper). What story are they both reporting?

Vocabulary

3 These words are all connected with heat. Match them to their definitions.

1. centigrade
2. fahrenheit
3. to dehydrate
4. to melt
5. to roast
6. to sizzle
7. to soar
8. to wilt

a. when something solid turns to liquid because of the heat
b. to suddenly go up
c. when a plant bends over because it is too hot and dry
d. a scale for measuring temperature where freezing point is 0 and boiling point is 100
e. to make a hissing noise (like sausages in a pan)
f. to lose water
g. to cook food using dry heat
h. a scale for measuring temperature where freezing point is 32 and boiling point is 212

WORD BANK

bookies (= bookmakers) people who professionally take bets and pay money if the bet is successful
to chill to cool (also has a slang meaning = to relax)
to clean up (*slang*) to make a good profit
to get a roasting (*slang*) to be badly beaten
to go through the roof (*slang*) to go up suddenly
to grab to take quickly, with force
to huddle to group closely together
lager light beer
to moan (*slang*) to complain
to pay out a sum of money that is paid
punter (*slang*) someone who makes a bet with a bookmaker
steadily gradually
sweltering extremely hot

THE INDEPENDENT

100 °F: Britain's hottest day

BRITAIN ENTERED a new hot-weather era yesterday when the temperature record was broken by a substantial margin, the thermometer exceeding the 100 °F mark for the first time. In the mid-afternoon of a sweltering day in southern England, the temperature at Heathrow airport was recorded at 37.9 °C (100.2 °F), higher than the previous record of 37.1 °C (98.8 °F) set at Cheltenham in August 1990. It was the hottest temperature since records began in 1659.

Nigel Reed, head of the operations centre at the UK Met Office in Bracknell, Berkshire, said that although no individual weather event could be directly attributed to global warming, "this was consistent with what we would expect to happen with climate change".

Although there can be no direct proof that yesterday's record temperature was the result of climate change, many observers see it as part of a steadily warming pattern affecting the world, not least because of the margin by which the previous UK record was broken – nearly a whole degree centigrade and nearly a degree-and-a-half fahrenheit. Bookmakers will have to pay out an estimated £ 500,000 to hundreds of people who put money on the heat hitting 99 °F and 100 °F. William Hill faces having to pay out up to £ 250,000. "It will be as big a payout as one of the White Christmas ones," said Graham Sharpe, William Hill's spokesman.

Reading

4 EP Read the news articles. Which article reports the following things: *The Daily Star, The Independent*, or both?

a. The actual temperature that was reached on the previous day.
b. The previous temperature record in the UK.
c. The possible link to global warming.
d. The effect of the hot temperatures on bookmakers.
e. How certain people suffered from the heat.
f. Damage to roads.
g. A quote from a bookmaker.

5 Which of the articles do you find easier to understand? Why do you think this is?

6 Read the articles again carefully with the glossary. Which article includes the most:

a. slang words?
b. longer, Latin-based words?
c. puns (word-based jokes)?
d. direct quotes from people?
e. long sentences?

Before you listen

7 Look at the table of statistics about British newspapers on page 120. Which type of newspaper sells the most copies each day? Why do you think this is?

Listening

8 Listen to three British people talking about which newspapers they buy. For each person find out:

a. what paper(s) they buy;
b. how often they buy them;
c. why they buy them.

Speaking

9 Which types of stories do you think tabloid newspapers concentrate on? Choose from the following:

› the economy
› the private lives of famous people
› crime
› politics
› TV and pop music
› sport
› the arts

Are there similar newspapers or magazines in your country?

Texting

WAN2 TXT?

Before the new millennium, the English word *text* was just a noun, but these days *texting* is one of Britain's favourite activities. It's short for *text-messaging*, the everyday phrase for what mobile phone companies officially call *SMS*, or 'short messaging service'. The UK is the world's texting champion, with 60 million messages being sent each day, most of them by the 77 percent of teenagers who own a mobile phone. Because texting is hard work on the thumbs, it has also developed its own language of abbreviations, often incomprehensible to adults. And texters aren't limited to just words – nowadays they can add graphics, or even photos, to their messages too.

WAN2 MEET
L8R? TXT ME
BAC
SAM
TELE-GRAFIX
New generation pictures and animation for your mobile!!
141732 It's not easy being a princess
141733 I am nuts about you
141734 I LOVE U MUM
141735 Almost an Angel
141736 No Msg Just a KISS!
141737 Guess Who's On the Way?
141738 LOVE U LOTS
141739 Best Mum in the World
141740 Little Devil
141741 I Miss You Babe
SMS ORDER: Text PICT+Number to 89020 (eg: PICT 141732)

Before you read

1 Look at the text message and the title of the first text. Can you 'translate' them into normal English? (Check your answers on page 128.)

2 Look at the mobile phone graphics above. What type of person would send each graphic, and who to?

Reading

3 Read the text *WAN2 TXT*? Find out:

1. what *SMS* means.
2. which country in the world sends the most texts.
3. how many texts are sent in the UK each day.
4. how many British teenagers own a mobile phone.
5. why texters use a lot of abbreviations in their messages.

WORD BANK

to back ▫ to support
chiropractic ▫ medical treatment based on manipulation of the spine
shrug ▫ movement of the shoulders up and down
strain ▫ injury caused by too much use
surge ▫ dramatic increase

Back Forward Reload Home Search Netscape Images Print Security Shop Stop

Go To: http:// www.phone.org.uk

Texting boom 'could lead to injuries'

The popularity of text messaging on mobile phones is continuing to rise, but experts are warning that sending too many could lead to hand injuries.

In February, a record 1.4 billion messages were sent in the UK – 100 million more than in January. The ▫surge is attributed to a boom in messages sent on Valentine's Day. The Mobile Data association, which compiles the figures, says the 57.5 million messages sent by amorous texters on 14th February was more than double the number sent on the same day last year.

However, the increase could lead to finger and wrist injuries from repetitively pushing the tiny buttons on mobile phones, say medical experts.

A safe text guide with exercises for avoiding injury, including shoulder ▫shrugs and neck-muscle stretches, has now been launched by Virgin Mobiles. The guide is ▫backed by the British ▫Chiropractic Association and the Repetitive ▫Strain Injury Association. A spokesman from the BCA said "Text messaging regularly, over a long period of time, could cause repetitive strain and lead to injuries in later life".

26th February 2002

4 EP Read the web page. Are the following sentences true or false?

1. 100 million messages were sent in February 2002.
2. 57.5 million messages were sent on Valentine's Day 2002.
3. A lot more messages were sent on Valentine's Day 2001.
4. Repetitive finger movements can cause injuries.
5. Virgin Mobiles have suggested some exercises to prevent texting injuries.

Before you listen

5 Why do you think that the majority of texters are teenagers? Why do they enjoy texting so much? Discuss with your classmates.

Listening

6 Listen to four teenagers talking about their texting habits. Who sends the most texts?

1. Adam **2.** Hayley **3.** Elizabeth **4.** William

7 EP Listen again. Match the teenagers in exercise 6 to the reasons why they like texting.

a. It is usually easier to write a message than to say it.
b. It is cheaper than making phone calls.
c. You can contact more than one person at the same time.
d. You can send messages in private.

Speaking

8 In groups, discuss the advantages and disadvantages of these forms of communication:

› letters.
› phone calls.
› faxes.
› emails.
› texts.

Topic: New Internet technology
Countries: USA
Vocabulary: Telecommunications, computers
Links: 5d, 9b, 9d, 9e

Internet innovations

WAP, broadband, wi-fi, 3G – phone technology and the Internet change so rapidly that we barely have time to get used to one new concept before it is immediately replaced by another and becomes outdated!

WHAT'S NEW?

THIS WEEK WE LOOK AT THE LATEST TECHNOLOGICAL ADVANCES FOR THE INTERNET. BE PREPARED! BY 2010, YOU'LL WONDER HOW WE EVER MANAGED WITHOUT THEM.

BROADBAND

What is it? A combination of the latest cable and radio technology means that huge amounts of electronic data can now be transmitted from computer to computer at incredibly high speeds. It's like changing from a narrow pipe delivering your water to a much broader pipe.

Benefits for the user: much faster, more reliable Internet connection; it's turned on all the time (you pay a fixed sum every month, so you don't have to keep dialling up); you can do two Internet operations at the same time (eg. collect emails and download a picture from the Internet).

WIRELESS

What is it? Computing without phone lines, similar to cordless phone technology.

Benefits for the user: the freedom to use a laptop or notebook without connecting it to a phone line (as long as you don't go too far away from the wireless hub – the main unit of the network that is connected to a phone line).

3G

What is it? 'Third generation' mobile technology (still in development) that will be able to transmit data quickly to your phone.

Benefits for the user: access to the complete, real Internet (not the mobile-only WAP network) quickly and in colour over your mobile; the ability to download music and video to your mobile.

WORD BANK

broad ▫ wide
chalk ▫ writing material, traditionally used by teachers on blackboards
geek ▫ (slang) person obsessed with computers and technology
hobo ▫ a homeless vagrant
hub ▫ the centre of a wheel or network
to leak out ▫ to escape by accident
node ▫ a point of connection on a network
to scrawl ▫ to draw quickly and carelessly
to take off ▫ to be a big success
top hat ▫ old-fashioned tall black hat
WAP (Wireless Application Protocol) ▫ a network of information and services that can be accessed via a mobile phone

War-Chalking

By CLIVE THOMPSON

Back in the Depression, ▫hobos would draw ▫chalk marks on the walls of houses to show where a generous stranger lived. A ▫top hat meant "kind gentleman lives here"; a cross meant "religious talk will get you a meal."

This summer, the British designer Matt Jones created a new set of hobo symbols for the Internet age. Jones is a fan of "Wi-Fi" (short for "wireless fidelity"), the new technology that lets you take your broadband connection and broadcast it around your home or office. Wi-Fi signals can travel more than 1,000 feet, which means that your private connection often ▫leaks out into the street. If you're feeling generous, you can leave it "open" for anyone passing by to use. … Presto: free high-speed access!

The only problem is that Wi-Fi radio signals are invisible. You might be near a ▫node right now. But how can you tell?

Easy. You look for one of Jones's symbols ▫scrawled on the wall. If you see two back-to-back half-circles, it means some ▫geek has discovered an open node nearby. ...

Within weeks of Jones's invention, war-chalking ... ▫took off. The Schlotzsky's Deli chain began war-chalking its restaurants, and the state of Utah announced it would mark up its conference rooms. Wireless companies, in contrast, reacted with alarm: Nokia called war-chalking "theft, plain and simple", and some cable companies have sent warning letters to users who openly share their Internet connections.

Yet the growth of Wi-Fi seems unstoppable. ... Consider it a lesson from the hobos: in a world full of generous strangers, sometimes there really is such a thing as a free lunch.

Before you read

1 Do you use the Internet? How often do you use it? Do you know how much your family spends on Internet use?

Vocabulary

2 Match these technological words to their definitions.

1. to dial up
2. to download
3. wireless
4. laptop
5. notebook
6. network

a. without cables or wires
b. a small mobile computer, about the size of a large book
c. a very small mobile computer that will fit in your hand
d. to make a connection to a phone line
e. a group of computers that are connected
f. to copy something from the Internet on to your computer

Reading

3 Read the *What's New?* text and answer the questions.

1. Is broadband quicker than an ordinary Internet connection?
2. How do you pay for a broadband connection?
3. What are the advantages of wireless technology?
4. What are the limits of wireless technology?
5. Has 3G technology been completely developed yet?
6. What will you be able to do with 3G technology on your mobile?

4 Answer the questions about *War-Chalking* text.

1. Why did hobos leave chalk marks for other hobos on houses during the Depression?
2. How far can Wi-Fi signals travel?
3. What does this mean for anyone near your building with a laptop?
4. What symbol do people leave on walls when they discover a free Wi-Fi connection?
5. Why did restaurants and hotels war-chalk their buildings?
6. How did telecommunications companies react to the war-chalking phenomenon?

Speaking

5 How do you think computer and Internet technology will develop over the next 50 years? Discuss with your classmates.

Writing

6 Imagine that it is 2050. Write a short article like the *What's New?* text. List some of the computer innovations that you imagine for that year and describe their benefits.

7 Find out from your classmates how interested they are in computers and how often they use them. Follow your teacher's instructions, then report the results to the class.

Internet cheats

Cheating.com

These days lots of students use the Internet for help with their homework and assignments, and there is no doubt that the Web has become a valuable academic tool. But now that ▫cutting and pasting is so easy, there can often be a fine dividing line between using the Net for research and plagiarising material directly from it. There are even some unscrupulous sites (often called ▫'paper mills') that offer students ready-made downloadable essays on a number of popular topics – usually for a payment. But most teachers are now aware of Internet plagiarism, and there is even a variety of software that schools can use to detect it. But teachers can often spot plagiarists simply by following their own suspicions. For example:

- a high-school student ▫turns in an essay using language and ideas more suitable for a university student.
- a weak student suddenly turns in an ▫outstanding essay.
- the same work occurs in a number of different students' assignments.
- the essay doesn't quite fit the question or title that the teacher has ▫set the class.
- American students produce essays written in British English, or vice versa.

The price of plagiarism can be high, especially in the USA, where it is not uncommon for students to be expelled, particularly at college level.

Before you read

1 Do you ever use the Internet to help you with your schoolwork? How is studying with the Web different to studying with books?

Vocabulary

2 Find words in the text *Cheating.com* to complete the table.

Activity	Verb	Person who does it
plagiarism *(= copying something directly without admitting it)*	to pl.............	pl.............

Reading

3 EP Read the text *Cheating.com* and choose the correct answers to the questions.

1. What are 'paper mills'?
   a. Software programs that detect plagiarism.
   b. Websites that offer ready-made essays.
2. Do you always have to pay to download an essay?
   a. Yes.
   b. No, not always.
3. When would a teacher start to suspect plagiarism?
   a. If the level of a student's work seemed too high.
   b. If the level of a student's work seemed too low.
4. When would a British teacher become suspicious?
   a. If one of their students turned in an essay with lots of spelling mistakes.
   b. If one of their students turned in an essay with lots of American spellings.
5. What can happen to students who are found guilty of plagiarism?
   a. They can be thrown out of their school.
   b. They can be taken to the police.

WORD BANK

- to browse – to look through something on the Internet in a random way
- to cut and paste – to make a copy of information on a computer and insert it in a new position
- outstanding – excellent
- paper mill – a factory that produces paper from wood. This is a play on the word 'paper', which can also mean an essay.
- to set – to assign
- to turn in – to give, submit

There are many websites, designed to appeal to students and teachers, that are devoted, in one way or another, to Internet plagiarism.

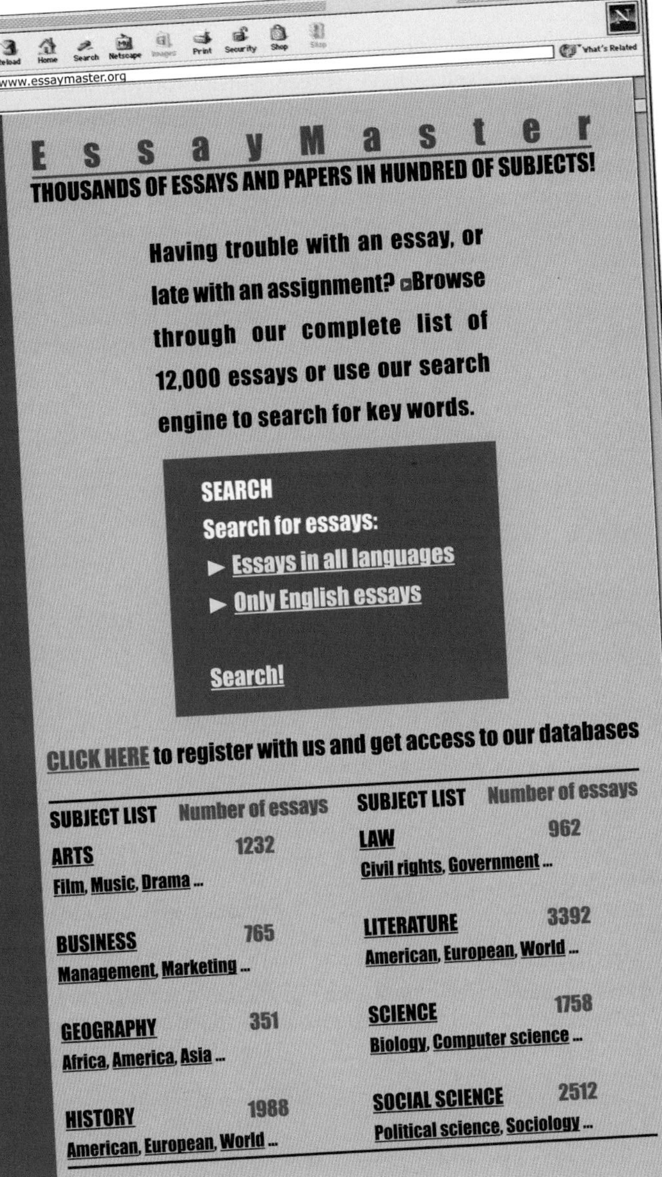

http:// www.essaymaster.org
EssayMaster
THOUSANDS OF ESSAYS AND PAPERS IN HUNDRED OF SUBJECTS!
Having trouble with an essay, or late with an assignment? Browse through our complete list of 12,000 essays or use our search engine to search for key words.
SEARCH
Search for essays:
Essays in all languages
Only English essays
Search!
CLICK HERE to register with us and get access to our databases
SUBJECT LIST Number of essays
ARTS 1232
Film, Music, Drama ...
BUSINESS 765
Management, Marketing ...
GEOGRAPHY 351
Africa, America, Asia ...
HISTORY 1988
American, European, World ...
SUBJECT LIST Number of essays
LAW 962
Civil rights, Government ...
LITERATURE 3392
American, European, World ...
SCIENCE 1758
Biology, Computer science ...
SOCIAL SCIENCE 2512
Political science, Sociology ...

4 Look quickly at the two websites. Which site is offering:

a. downloadable essays?
b. help to fight plagiarism?

5 Answer the questions about the websites.

1. How many essays does the EssayMaster site offer?
2. Which subject does it offer the most essays for?
3. How do Turnitin.com check an essay for plagiarism?
4. What do they give to the teacher after their check?
5. What did James Hunter discover about the essay that they analysed for him?

Speaking

6 Are there any school subjects that you would be tempted to cheat in? Discuss the different reasons why plagiarising an essay would be wrong. Talk about:

› why it is wrong to tell lies.
› unfairness to your teacher.
› unfairness to other students.
› learning how to think and work independently.
› how you can learn by making mistakes.

turnitin.com

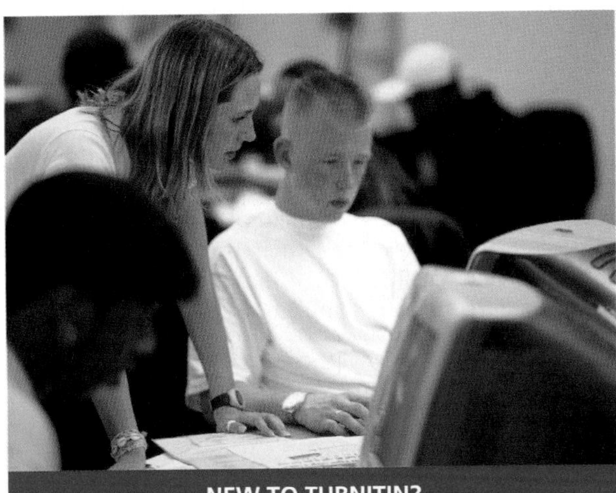

NEW TO TURNITIN?

WHAT IS TURNITIN.COM?

Turnitin.com is an online resource for educators and students concerned with developing quality writing and research skills. We do this by:

- providing a reliable, efficient and powerful deterrent to Internet-based plagiarism.
- detecting digital plagiarism when and where it occurs.
- helping educators and students fight plagiarism with guidelines for good research.

HOW DOES OUR WEBSITE STOP PLAGIARISM?

We prevent and detect plagiarism by comparing submitted papers to billions of Internet pages and our own databases. For each paper submitted we produce a special 'originality report', which we send to the relevant educator.

"The first paper I turned in was full of material from three Internet sources. I knew that the work was not from the student, but the report made it quite painless for me to confront him. There was no argument, and we could then deal with the issues regarding plagiarism."
James Hunter, North High School

Language change

Welcome to Weblish!

..... New technology always brings changes and new additions to the language, but the telecommunications revolution of the last few years has caused some of the most rapid and widespread changes yet seen.

..... New words, such as *webcast*, are entering the language all the time to put a name to concepts that haven't existed before, and existing words are being used in a new way. For example, the words *access* and *text*, previously used only as nouns, are now commonly used as verbs in phrases such as *to access the Internet* and *to text someone*. Other words, such as *chat*, which used to mean 'casual verbal communication' but now means 'live email communication', have taken on entire new meanings.

..... In addition, many of these English words – the most obvious being *computer* itself – have spread outside of the English-speaking world and become part of a global language of technology. Thanks to the influence of the American computer industry, users of British English have abandoned some British spellings in favour of their American equivalents, such as *program* instead of *programme* and *disk* instead of *disc*.

..... Finally, the style and tone of the language itself is changing. Although they are written forms of communication, the immediacy of emails and text messages means that their language is usually much more informal than a letter would be, even in a business context. And, to the concern of many people, spelling and punctuation are becoming much more unconventional.

New words

blog *(web + log)* a personal on-line diary or journal that anyone can access.

cyberspace the imaginary 'space' through which Internet messages travel.

dotcom an Internet business.

spam unwanted emails sent to you by commercial companies.

webcam *(web + camera)* a videocamera that can transmit images live over the Internet.

webcast *(web + broadcast)* a live 'television programme' on the Internet, broadcast by a webcam.

Text message shortcuts

The senders of text messages have invented a unique language of abbreviations. Here are some of the most common:

CU	See you
GR8	great
L8R	later
MSG	message
NE	any-
R	are
THX	thanks
TXT ME BAC	Text me back
U	you
UR	your/you're
WAN2...?	Do you want to...?
Y	Why?
2DAY	today
2MORO	tomorrow

Vocabulary

1 How many English words can you list that are connected to computers and the Internet? Do the words have an equivalent in your own language?

2 Read the *New Words* text. Insert the words into the correct sentences below.

1. Did you know you can watch a live .... of *Big Brother* 24 hours a day?
2. 'Did you get any interesting emails this morning?' 'No, just a lot of ....'
3. My sister works for Web Systems in London – it's one of the new ....s.
4. They're putting up a .... in the City Hall so they can broadcast the concert on the Internet.
5. Have you read this girl's .... today? Some of her views are really extreme.
6. 'I never received that email you sent me.' 'Didn't you? It must have got lost in ....'

Reading

3 EP Read the text *Welcome to Weblish!* and match these titles to the four paragraphs.

a. The spread of American English
b. A period of huge change for English
c. Changing style and tone
d. Changing words and meanings

WORD BANK
concern ▫ worry
unconventional ▫ non-standard, unusual
widespread ▫ common across a large area

Relaxing attitudes

The ease and speed of new forms of communication have brought a much more relaxed attitude to formality and correctness in written English.

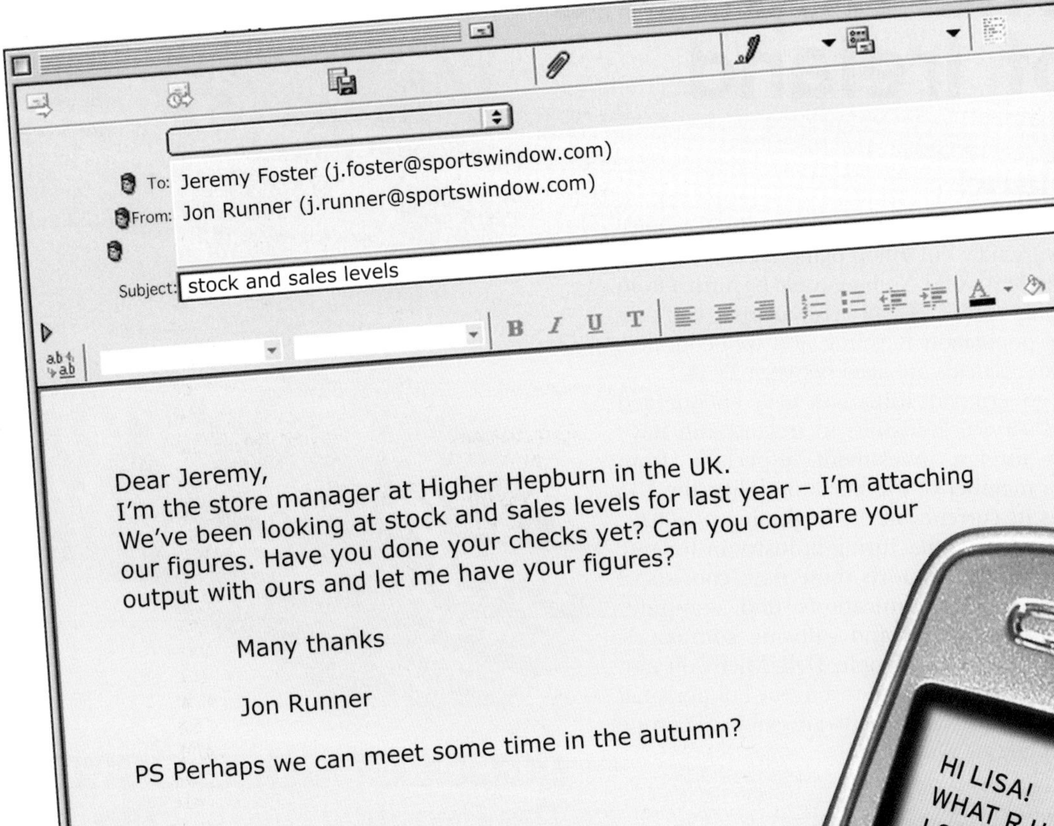

To: Jeremy Foster (j.foster@sportswindow.com)
From: Jon Runner (j.runner@sportswindow.com)
Subject: stock and sales levels
Dear Jeremy,
I'm the store manager at Higher Hepburn in the UK.
We've been looking at stock and sales levels for last year – I'm attaching our figures. Have you done your checks yet? Can you compare your output with ours and let me have your figures?
Many thanks
Jon Runner
PS Perhaps we can meet some time in the autumn?

HI LISA!
WHAT R U DOING
L8R 2DAY? WAN2
DO NETHING WITH
US? OR MAYBE
2MORO? SEND ME
A MSG.
CU
EMMA

4 EP Complete the table about changes to the English language.

Language change

Before computers	**In the computer age**
access was only a noun	*access* is now also a ....
text was only a noun	*text* is now also a ....
.... meant a .... form of communication	.... can mean a written form of communication
British people used the spelling *programme*	British people use the spelling ....
British people used the spelling	British people use the spelling *disk*
most written communication was formal	a lot of written communication is ....
.... and .... were very correct	.... and .... are not so correct

5 Look at the email above. Compare it to the first business letter on page 90. What differences in style can you find?

Writing

6 Look at the second business letter on page 90 and rewrite it as an email. Use the email on this page to help you. (Don't include all the sales figures from the letter.)

7 Look at the text message abbreviations. on page 128, then read the text message on this page. Rewrite it in full using standard English.

Topic ▫ The computer industry in Ireland
Countries ▫ Republic of Ireland
Vocabulary ▫ The computer industry
Links ▫ 2a, 2f, 3b, 4e

English everywhere
The Republic of Ireland

Wired Ireland

The stereotypical view of Ireland is of a rural, agricultural country where the people are friendly, but ▫short of money and not very ▫in touch with the modern world. Nothing could be further from the truth. Today, only about 8% of Irish people work in agriculture, and the population is young and well-educated. Nearly a third of Irish residents are aged between 25-44.

In the last decade, government initiatives have encouraged manufacturing and service industries in Ireland and have brought in much foreign investment, especially from Europe. Ireland is a member of the EU and, unlike the UK, adopted the euro as its currency at the beginning of 2002.

Electronics is the largest manufacturing industry in Ireland, and a third of the country's exports these days consists of products from the telecommunications and computer industries. About 300 computer and software companies, including world leaders such as Apple, Dell, Microsoft and Intel, have operations in Ireland. Almost a third of personal computers and 60% of packaged software sold in Europe comes from Ireland.

INFORMATION FILE

The Republic of Ireland

Total area ▫ 70,000 sq. km
Total population ▫ 4 million
Ethnic mix ▫ 98% White
2% Other
Capital ▫ Dublin
Popul. of capital ▫ 1 million
Government ▫ A democracy with a president
Climate ▫ Mild, cool, cloudy

Different aspects of Ireland: Dublin city centre, the famous green countryside and historical ruins.

WORD BANK

call centre ▫ office where the principal activity is answering customers' telephone calls
headquarters ▫ principal office
in touch with ▫ in contact with
short of ▫ not having enough

A bite of the Apple in Ireland

In 1980, the American computer manufacturer Apple opened a factory in Cork, Ireland's second city, in order to produce and distribute Apple Mac computers for Europe. In 1999, the huge demand for Apple's new product, the iMac computer, led them to add a ▫call centre to their operations in Cork in order to process customers' orders and queries, and in 2002 the Apple Centre in Cork became Apple's ▫headquarters for Europe. Although there is less manufacturing done in Cork today, the Centre currently employs 1,200 people working in the areas of sales, financial management, planning, software development and testing, and customer service.

The call centre has now expanded to cover the whole of Europe. This means that anyone in a European country phoning Apple with a query or technical problem with their Apple computer will speak directly to one of the multi-lingual operators in Cork. Call centres in general are a huge growth industry in Ireland, and have become one of the country's top employers.

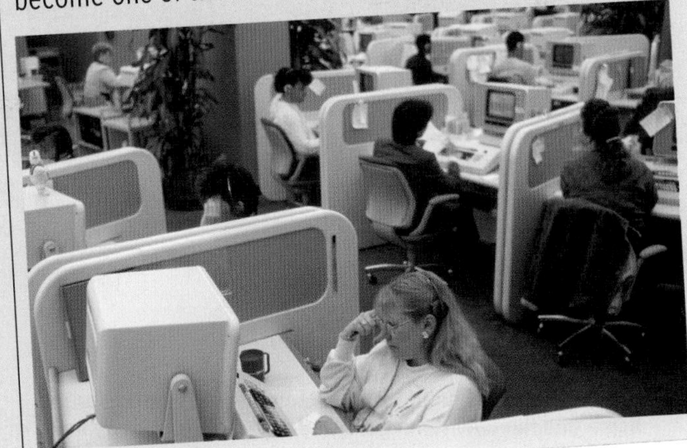

◄ A view of Cork, where Apple have their European headquarters.

Before you read

1 Can you name any places in Ireland, or any famous Irish people?

Reading

2 Look at the map and read the Information File on Ireland. Answer the questions.

1. Where, in the country, is Ireland's capital?
2. What percentage of Irish people live in Dublin?
3. Is Ireland part of the UK?
4. Do you think that Ireland experiences much hot weather?

3 Read the text *Wired Ireland* and answer the questions.

1. What proportion of the Irish population are aged between 25-44?
2. What currency does Ireland have?
3. What proportion of Ireland's exports are connected to computers and telecommunications?
4. What proportion of Europe's software originates in Ireland?

4 EP Read the text *A bite of the Apple in Ireland* and put these events in the correct order.

a. Apple opened a call centre in Cork.
b. Apple first opened a branch of their business in Cork.
c. Cork became Apple's European headquarters.
d. Apple produced the iMac computer.

5 EP Are these sentences about the text true or false?

1. Cork is the most important city in Ireland.
2. Apple's original business in Ireland was manufacturing.
3. The iMac computer was a very popular product.
4. Manufacturing is still Apple's main business in Cork.
5. Over a thousand people work at the Apple Centre in Cork.
6. The call centre only takes phone calls from the UK and Ireland.
7. There are employees at the call centre who speak foreign languages.
8. Call centres employ a lot of people in Ireland these days.

Speaking

6 Discuss what can go wrong when you are using a computer, and why you might have to phone a call centre for technical support.

Grammar ▫ Future tense review (*will, be going to*, present continuous)
Skills ▫ Speaking: phone conversations

Language & Culture

The networked home

Talking fridges and intelligent central heating systems could become standard in houses all over the UK within a few years. The UK government announced that it is spending a budget of £40 million on new technologies over the next few years. The fridges and central heating systems will be able to speak to a service centre when they need a new part or when there is a problem. Some of the new types of fridges will also be programmed to inform the owner when they are running out of certain food items. These fridges will speak to the owner when the owner opens the door and will tell them what they need to buy.

Televisions on wristwatches, the Internet on microwave ovens and DVD players on fridges will all be potential future products. Scientists might also develop energy-saving systems to reduce bills and the cost to the environment. Research is already taking place to find out what those costs will be.

The home isn't the only focus for new developments: researchers are going to develop cars that talk to service stations and personal digital shopping assistants. They are going to program the shopping assistants not only to do the shopping but also to deliver it to people's homes.

So going shopping and buying spare parts for your fridge may become a thing of the past.

Powering the Network

In the future, high-speed Internet access (1) *will be/is being* essential in order to power the networked home. However, there (2) *will be/are going to be* problems because certain parts of the country (3) *are never having/will never have* this sort of technology.
The government says it (4) *will give/is giving* £30 million to provide broadband to all parts of the UK, especially rural areas, over the next three years. However, critics say this (5) *isn't being/isn't going to be* enough.
'People (6) *will have/are going to have* problems,' said one critic, 'when they buy an item for their networked home but can't use it because there is no broadband in the area where they live.'
The total budget (7) *is splitting/is going to be split* equally between the government and industry.

GRAMMAR

1 What new technologies are scientists developing for the home and the car? Read the text *The networked home* quickly and find the answer.

2 Complete the table with the examples of future tenses from the text. Then explain why each tense is used.

Will	Be going to	Present continuous
will be able to	....	....
....	....	
....		
....		
....		
....		

3 Now read the text again quickly and find three modal verbs which are used to express possibility or uncertainty about the future.

4 Read the text *Powering the Network* and circle the best future form (1-7).

SKILLS

5 Complete the phone conversation with the words and phrases below.

I didn't catch what you said · *I just wanted to ask you* · *I said* · *I think I'll* · *I'd better go* · *I'll call you tomorrow night* · *It's me* · *No problem* · *Oh, hi* · *Pardon* · *See you* · ~~*Is that you?*~~

Laura: Alison, (1) *is that you*? (2).........., Laura.
Alison: (3) ....! How are you?
Laura: Fine thanks. Look, I'm on a train. (4) .... if you're going to the gym tonight.
Alison: Well, I'm not sure. Lee phoned me and asked me to go for a drink with him.
Laura: (5) ....? We were in a tunnel then. (6) ....
Alison: (7) .... Lee has asked me to go for a drink tonight.
Laura: Oh. So are you going out with him or going to the gym?
Alison: (8) .... go for a drink with him if that's okay.
Laura: Yeah. (9) .... I'll go to the gym on my own.
Alison: OK. (10) .... Maybe we could go together then.
Laura: Fine. Look, Alison, (11) .... I'm losing the signal.
Alison: OK. (12) ....
Laura: Bye!

6 In pairs, act out the phone conversation in exercise 5.

7 Now choose one of the situations below and act out a phone conversation with your partner.

› You are phoning a friend to arrange to go to the cinema.
› You are phoning the doctor's to make an appointment.
› You are phoning your mother to tell her you will be home late.
› You are phoning your brother/sister who is studying in a different town.

Module 10 Society

IN THIS MODULE YOU WILL READ AND HEAR ABOUT:

- positive discrimination for disadvantaged students in the UK
- immigration to the USA
- globalisation
- working mothers in the English-speaking world
- the care of old people in the UK
- how pop music reflects changes in society
- a business providing services to old people in the UK

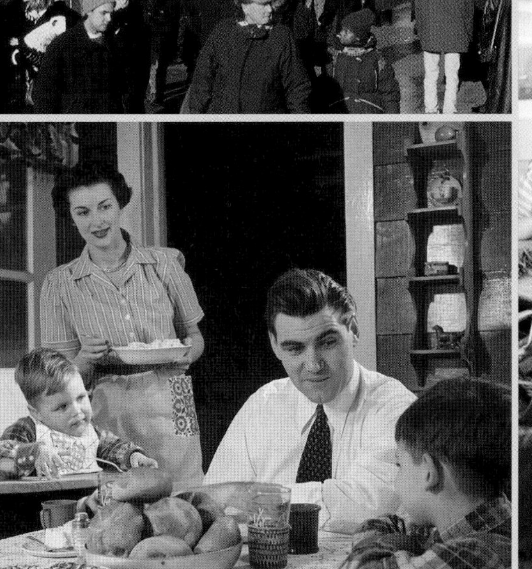

1 Compare the pairs of photographs. Do you think they show the UK or the USA? What date would you give to the older photos?

2 What changes to society do the photographs illustrate?

3 Can you guess at any of the following statistics?

1. The number of immigrants who apply each year for British citizenship.
2. The average number of children per family in the USA.
3. The percentage of British families where both the mother and the father work.
4. What percentage of the UK population are aged over 60.

By the end of the module you'll know whether or not your guesses were correct.

Positive discrimination

HCS news

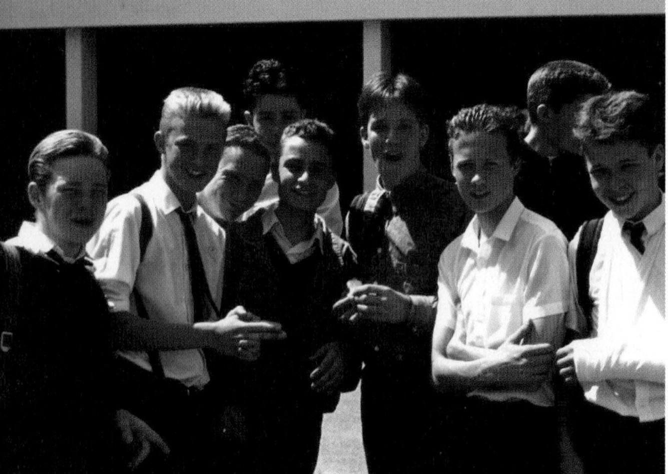

A VIEW FROM YEAR 10

I'm Daniel Yates and I go to Hanbury Comprehensive School in Birmingham. Comprehensive schools are paid for by the state. There are 1,500 pupils here and the classes are quite big – about 25 pupils in a class. This year's A-level results were quite good – 40% of the students got A or B grades. About 50 pupils from Hanbury manage to get in to university each year, but not many go to places like Oxford or Edinburgh. I think there was a pupil two years ago who got into Cambridge, but that's unusual.

THE CHALFONT COLLEGE GAZETTE

First impressions of Chalfont

My name's Harriet Fisher and I'm a pupil at Chalfont College for Girls. The school is 150 years old, and it's an independent school for girls. That means that our parents pay for our education, not the state. The fees here are about £6,000 per term if you are a ▪boarder, or about £4,000 per term if you are a ▪day pupil. I'm lucky to be here because it's a fantastic school. We have small class sizes (about 1 teacher for every 9 pupils), the exam results are usually excellent, and every year lots of pupils get into top universities like Oxford and St Andrew's.

State and private education in the UK

UK pupils at state schools	93%
UK pupils at independent (private) schools	7%
Students at Oxford and Cambridge Universities from state schools	49%
Students at Oxford and Cambridge Universities from private schools	51%

Before you read

1 Do you have state schools and private schools in your country? What type of parents tend to send their children to private schools? What type of school often has the best teachers and the best exam results?

2 What do you think that 'positive discrimination' means? How could it be used in the context of schools or universities?

Reading

3 Read the table of statistics and the profiles of the two pupils. Find out:

1. how much it costs to send a girl to Chalfont College for Girls each term, if they don't live at the College.
2. if a comprehensive school is a private or a state school.
3. the proportion of teachers to students at Chalfont College for Girls.
4. the names of four top UK universities.
5. what percentage of UK pupils go to a private school.
6. what percentage of students at Oxford and Cambridge Universities come from private schools.

WORD BANK

alleged ▫ spoken about as if it was true
boarder ▫ a pupil who lives at his or her school
to boycott ▫ to officially refuse to take part in something
day pupil ▫ a pupil who lives with his or her family and only comes to school during lesson hours
guidelines ▫ recommendations
impeccable ▫ perfect
income ▫ how much money you earn
intake ▫ the proportion that it admits
quota ▫ percentage that has been officially agreed

School heads ▫boycott Bristol University

Bristol University is being boycotted by top independent schools because of its ▫alleged policy of positive discrimination. Surveys reveal that record numbers of the best independent students have been rejected by Bristol this year, despite having ▫impeccable grades, and the Headmasters' and Headmistresses' Conference and the Girls' Schools Association are now advising their A-level students not to apply to the university. Angry teachers say that Bristol is deliberately choosing state school students with lower grades instead in order to meet government "▫quotas".

In its defence, the university said that it was under pressure from the government to increase its ▫intake of state school pupils. At present, the government issues ▫guidelines to universities regarding the proportion of state school pupils that they should admit, but universities could soon be under even more pressure to admit poorer students. The government plans to replace the current system with specific targets based on students' parents' ▫income and whether their parents went to university.

4 Read the text above. Which of these sentences best summarises it?

a. Bristol University has been accused of taking too many of its students from private schools and not enough from state schools.
b. Bristol University has been accused of rejecting pupils from private schools because it wants to be more open to pupils from state schools.
c. Bristol University has been accused of rejecting pupils from private schools because they don't work very hard at university.

5 Answer the questions about the text. Why:

1. are some private schools advising their students against applying to Bristol University?
2. do some head teachers think that Bristol is rejecting their pupils' applications?
3. does Bristol feel that it has to admit a certain number of state school pupils?
4. might students soon have to tell their preferred universities how much their parents earn?

Vocabulary

6 Match the words to their definitions.

1. admissions
2. applicants
3. credits
4. elite

a. points, marks
b. the system where a university chooses its students
c. only open to a few, top people
d. people who want to get into a university

Listening

7 EP Listen to the report about Edinburgh University and choose the correct alternatives in the sentences.

1. Edinburgh University *wants/doesn't want* people to think of it as an elite university.
2. The University is changing its *admissions/exams* system.
3. Applicants will be asked about their parents' *jobs/money*.
4. Applicants will get extra credits if *no-one/someone* in their family has already been to university.
5. Applicants will get extra credits if they have had a *tragedy/academic success* in the family.

Speaking

8 What do you think about the idea of using positive discrimination to help students from poorer schools get into university? Can you think of any cases of positive discrimination in your country? Think about:

› schools.
› jobs.
› politics.
› representation in the media: TV, magazines, adverts, etc.

Immigration

Becoming American

Immigrants to the USA have to obtain a 'green card' if they want to live permanently in the country. After obtaining a green card, immigrants can apply to become full US citizens – a process called 'naturalization'. Naturalization can take anything from 6 months to 2 years, at the end of which there is a ceremony where the new citizen takes the Oath of Allegiance to the US. The naturalization process involves an exam set by the Immigration and Naturalization service. This consists of an interview, an English dictation test, and a written exam with questions about the constitution and history of the USA. The UK is currently introducing a citizenship exam for immigrants based on the US model.

The United States Immigration Service Citizenship: an overview

A citizen of the United States is a native-born, foreign born or naturalized person who owes allegiance to the United States and who is entitled to its protection.

As a citizen, you get unique rights and privileges which include the right to vote, having a US passport, the US government's protection when abroad and the right to petition for green cards for your children and close relatives. As a US citizen, you cannot be deported or lose your citizenship even if you commit a crime or choose to live elsewhere in the world.

Naturalization is the way immigrants become citizens of the United States. The general requirements for administrative naturalization include:

- a period of continuous residence and physical presence in the United States
- an ability to read, write and speak English
- good moral character
- attachment to the principles of the US Constitution
- favorable disposition toward the United States

All naturalization applicants must demonstrate good moral character, attachment and favorable disposition. The other naturalization requirements may be modified or waived for certain applicants, such as spouses of US citizens.

WORD BANK

allegiance ▫ loyalty
cabinet ▫ group of ministers who decide government policy
compulsory ▫ obligatory
to deport ▫ to remove someone from a country as a punishment
to be entitled to ▫ to have the right to possess
etiquette ▫ polite behaviour
favorable disposition ▫ positive opinion
NHS ▫ National Health Service
oath ▫ solemn promise
to petition for ▫ to ask for
spouse ▫ husband or wife
to waive ▫ to deliberately ignore

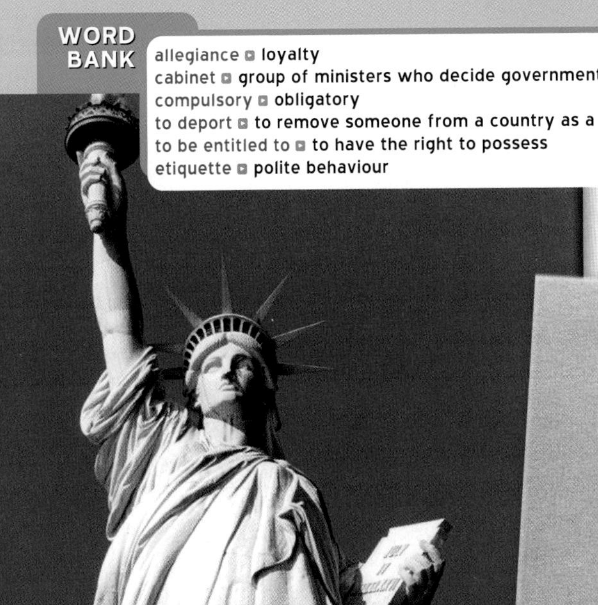

Some sample questions from the US CITIZENSHIP EXAM

1 How many stars are on the US flag?
2 What colour are the stripes on the US flag?
3 How many states are there in the Union?
4 What is the 4th of July?
5 From what country did the American colonies declare Independence?
6 Who was the first President of the United States?
7 Who is the President of the United States today?
8 Who is the Vice President of the United States?
9 For how long do we elect the President?
10 What is the Constitution?

The Guardian

Citizenship test to be practical

Nicholas Watt

A Home Office committee, set up last year to devise a ▫compulsory citizenship programme for the 110,000 immigrants who apply each year to become naturalised Britons, yesterday recommended that the citizenship test should focus on practical issues, such as housing and the ▫NHS, rather than on British history.

On the controversial areas of British history and compulsory language lessons, the committee responded to fears that the citizenship test could become a form of 'culture colonialism'. Learning history should be optional and new citizens will be encouraged, rather than compelled, to learn English. They will instead be taught how to cope with life in Britain, how to find a job and be paid the minimum wage, and how to use the NHS and social services.

The committee recommended that new citizens were also taught about how Britain is a "changing multicultural society". This will include ▫"etiquettes of everyday life, what makes for good neighbours, the changing status of women and the assumption of equality between the sexes". There will also be a political lesson on British national institutions, including the monarch, the prime minister, parliament and the ▫cabinet.

Before you read

1 What do immigrants to your country have to do if they want to become full, permanent citizens? Do you know what they have to do in the US or in Britain?

Reading

2 EP Read the texts *Becoming American* and *Citizenship: an overview*. Are the following statements true or false?

1. You have to have a green card before you can apply to become a US citizen.
2. Naturalised citizens have to promise to be loyal to the USA.
3. The citizenship exam is an oral exam.
4. Naturalised citizens can automatically get green cards for their families.
5. Your citizenship can be taken away from you if you are sent to prison.
6. The foreign wife of a US citizen could be given citizenship even if she couldn't speak English.

3 Read the sample questions from the US citizenship exam. How many of them can you answer?

4 Read the British newspaper article on this page. What is the basic difference between the US citizenship exam and the proposed British citizenship exam?

5 Answer the questions about the text.

1. How many immigrants apply each year for British citizenship?
2. What did the committee recommend about British history lessons for immigrants?
3. What did they recommend about English language lessons?
4. What will immigrants learn about employment in Britain?
5. Will immigrants learn about the Queen?

Speaking

6 Do you think that making immigrants take citizenship exams is a good idea? How far should immigrants integrate into the culture of their host countries? How far should they keep their own customs?

Globalisation

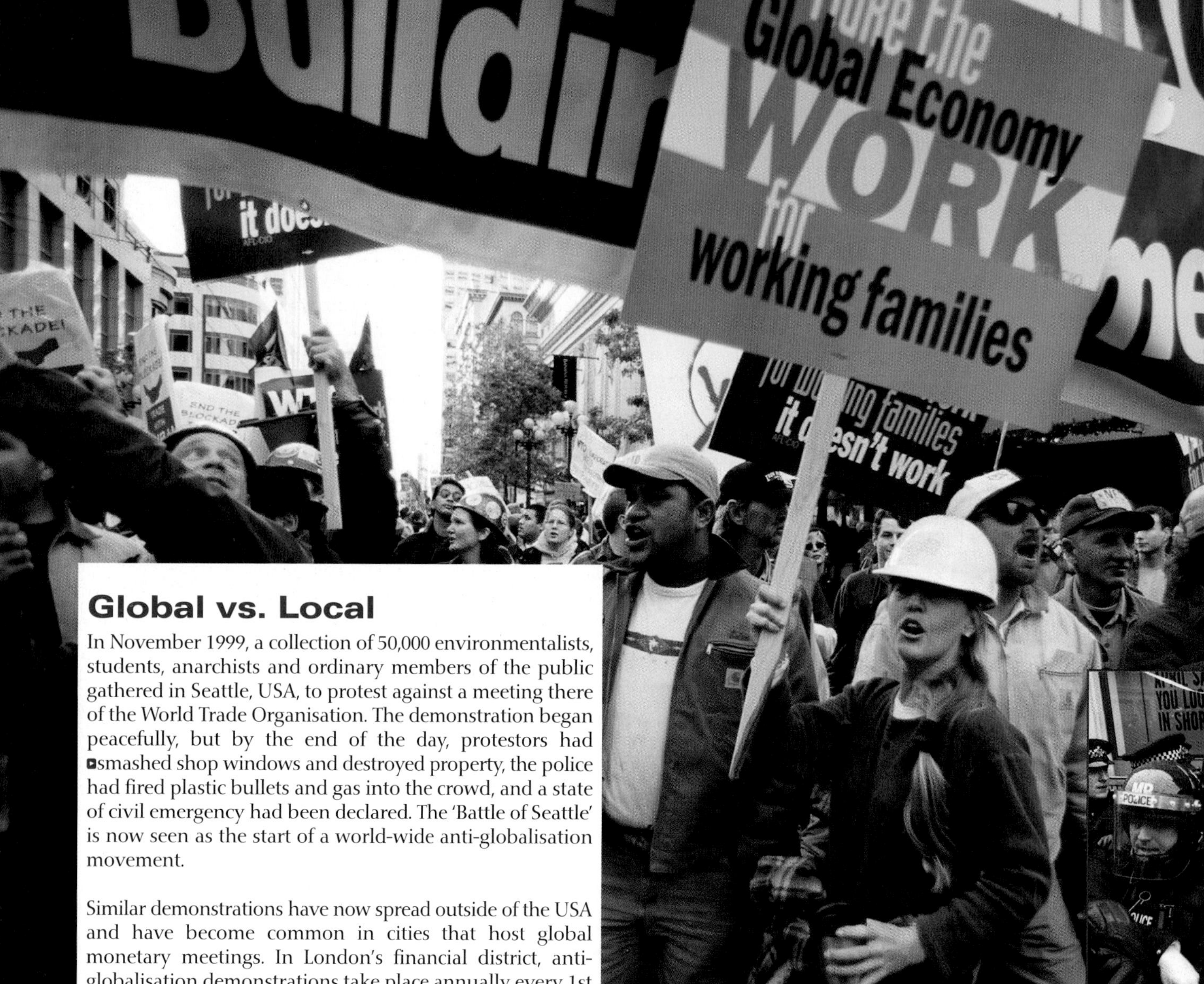

Global vs. Local

In November 1999, a collection of 50,000 environmentalists, students, anarchists and ordinary members of the public gathered in Seattle, USA, to protest against a meeting there of the World Trade Organisation. The demonstration began peacefully, but by the end of the day, protestors had ▫smashed shop windows and destroyed property, the police had fired plastic bullets and gas into the crowd, and a state of civil emergency had been declared. The 'Battle of Seattle' is now seen as the start of a world-wide anti-globalisation movement.

Similar demonstrations have now spread outside of the USA and have become common in cities that host global monetary meetings. In London's financial district, anti-globalisation demonstrations take place annually every 1st of May. The largest protest so far took place in Genoa, Italy, in 2001, where 300,000 demonstrators ▫clashed with police in a violent conflict: one person died and hundreds were injured.

Anti-globalisation protestors are protesting about the dominance in the world economy of large (usually American) multi-national companies. They consider that these companies spread their own western culture at the expense of other cultures, and that they exploit developing countries and the environment in general.

Targets for violence and vandalism are often American companies such as McDonald's, GAP and Starbucks. In 1999, José Bové, a French farmer who had been in the Seattle protest, became a national hero when he demolished a new McDonald's as a protest about the standardisation of food, the impact of McDonald's on local businesses and the high level of US taxes on imported European food.

Before you read

1 Look at the photos. What do you think the people are protesting about? Where are they? Do they look peaceful or violent?

2 Can you match these American company names to their products?

1. Calvin Klein	**a.** fast food
2. GAP	**b.** jeans
3. Levi's	**c.** sports clothes
4. Mattel	**d.** cola
5. McDonald's	**e.** designer clothes and perfume
6. Nike	**f.** coffee
7. Pepsi	**g.** casual clothes
8. Starbucks	**h.** dolls

Can you buy these companies' products in your country? Do you like them?

WORD BANK

ABC ▫ American television channel
brand ▫ name and image of a product
breed ▫ type
to clash ▫ to confront with violence
to enhance ▫ to make better
Girl Guide ▫ female equivalent of a boy scout
highlight ▫ key, important feature
juniper berries ▫ the fruit from which gin is made
porch ▫ shelter over the front door of a house
screwdriver ▫ tool used for putting screws in wood
sidewalk ▫ pavement
to smash ▫ to break into pieces

No Logo

The American writer Naomi Klein's best-selling book *No Logo* (1999) explores how, since the 1980s, multinational corporations have created global brands and used marketing to spread their influence throughout the world. Here are two extracts from the first chapter of the book.

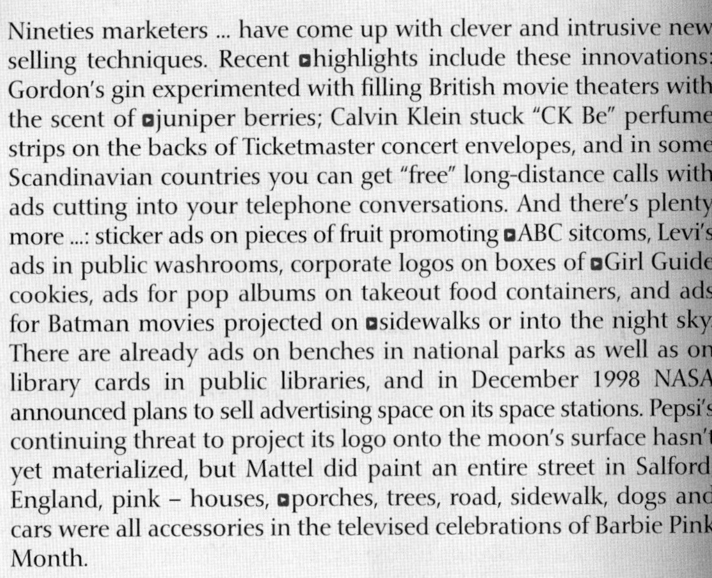

Nineties marketers ... have come up with clever and intrusive new selling techniques. Recent highlights include these innovations: Gordon's gin experimented with filling British movie theaters with the scent of juniper berries; Calvin Klein stuck "CK Be" perfume strips on the backs of Ticketmaster concert envelopes, and in some Scandinavian countries you can get "free" long-distance calls with ads cutting into your telephone conversations. And there's plenty more ...: sticker ads on pieces of fruit promoting ABC sitcoms, Levi's ads in public washrooms, corporate logos on boxes of Girl Guide cookies, ads for pop albums on takeout food containers, and ads for Batman movies projected on sidewalks or into the night sky. There are already ads on benches in national parks as well as on library cards in public libraries, and in December 1998 NASA announced plans to sell advertising space on its space stations. Pepsi's continuing threat to project its logo onto the moon's surface hasn't yet materialized, but Mattel did paint an entire street in Salford, England, pink – houses, porches, trees, road, sidewalk, dogs and cars were all accessories in the televised celebrations of Barbie Pink Month.

...

With this wave of brand mania has come a new breed of businessman. One who will proudly inform you that Brand X is not a product, but a way of life, an attitude, a set of values, a look, an idea. And it sounds really great – much better than that Brand X is a screwdriver, or a hamburger chain, or a pair of jeans, or even a very successful line of running shoes. Nike, Phil Knight announced in the late eighties, is "a sports company"' its mission is not to sell shoes but to "enhance people's lives through sports and fitness" and to keep "the magic of sports alive."

Reading

3 EP Read the text *Global vs. Local*. Match these titles to the four paragraphs.

a. The spread of the anti-globalisation movement
b. Protests against specific companies
c. The first anti-globalisation demonstration
d. What the protests are about

4 Answer these questions about the text.

1. Why was Seattle chosen for the first anti-globalisation demonstration?
2. Was the demonstration completely peaceful?
3. When do anti-globalisation demonstrations regularly take place in London?
4. When was there a large demonstration in Genoa?
5. How many people died in that demonstration?
6. What sort of companies are anti-globalisation protestors protesting about?
7. Which three specific companies does the text mention?
8. What did José Bové do to protest about globalisation in France?

5 EP Read the *No Logo* text. Which company has used or thought of these advertising techniques?

1. Putting stickers on envelopes containing concert tickets.
2. Putting advertisements in public toilets.
3. Projecting an advertisement onto the moon.
4. Spraying smells in cinemas.
5. Painting a street pink.
6. Putting stickers on fruit.

Speaking

6 How, according to the second paragraph from *No Logo*, do companies try to market their products these days? Is it important to you what brands you buy (for example, for your clothes)? Are teenagers influenced too much by marketing and branding?

Working mothers

Birthrate figures	USA	UK	Australia
Average age of mothers giving birth	27	30	29
Average age for having a first baby	25	28	27
Average number of children per family	1.9	1.64	1.75

Who's holding the baby?

These days, better education and career opportunities for women in the English-speaking world mean that many women are leaving it until the age of 30, or even 40, to start a family. By this age, many women already have successful careers which they are often reluctant to give up. These days there are a number of men, especially those in couples where the woman earns the most money, who are happy to stay at home in the traditional role of the "housewife", but for a large proportion of couples this is not an option. Financial pressures, particularly in the UK, where house prices have reached ▫astronomical heights, mean that many couples cannot ▫afford to give up one of their ▫salaries when a baby arrives. In 39% of British couples with children, both parents work, and some women return to work when their babies are only three or four months old. So who is holding the baby for these couples?

Jenny Cope

childminder, Lincoln, England

"I look after five different children in total, but they come on different days of the week, so I only ever have three each day. My house isn't big enough for any more! Today I'm ▫minding Kieran, who's three, Toby, who's two, and George, who's fourteen months. Their parents all work full-time, and they bring them at different times of the day. For example, Kieran arrives here at half past seven and his mum collects him at six o'clock in the evening. I play with them, give them their meals, do some educational stuff with them and let them watch videos. We go out a lot, too – for walks or picnics."

Before you read

1 Look at the table of birthrate figures. How do you think these statistics might have been different 30 years ago? Why do you think that these statistics have changed in recent years?

2 Who looked after you before you started school? Did your mother work when you were little?

Reading

3 Read the first paragraph of *Who's holding the baby?* and answer the questions.

1. Why are some women in the English-speaking world having babies later in life?
2. What sometimes happens in couples where the woman earns more than the man?
3. What causes particular financial pressure on families in the UK these days?
4. In what percentage of British families do both the mother and the father work?

Vocabulary

4 Quickly read the profiles of the three women and match the words to their definitions.

1. childminder
2. day care center
3. nanny
4. nursery

a. a special type of 'school' where parents can leave very young children all day (American English)
b. a special type of 'school' where parents can leave very young children all day (British English)
c. someone who looks after one family's children in the family's home
d. someone who looks after various people's children in their own home

WORD BANK

to afford ▫ to have enough money for
astronomical ▫ extremely high
to get someone up ▫ to get someone out of bed and dress them
to have time off ▫ to have free time
to mind ▫ to look after
to pick someone up ▫ to collect
salary ▫ the money that your employer pays you
tea ▫ a light meal in the late afternoon or early evening

Tricia Durham

day care assistant, Pittsburgh, USA

"I work here at Daisies Day Care Center, doing the early shift. That means that I work from eight in the morning until four in the afternoon, although the center is open until six in the evening. We take children from birth to five years. Their parents leave them here at the center and ▫pick them up after work. We have five different rooms – one is for the babies to play in, two are for the older children to play in, one is for the babies to sleep in and one is where we serve their meals. Of course there's also a big playground outside. We do a lot of educational activities with the older children – music, painting, nature studies. They don't just play with toys all day."

Annette Stills

nanny, Adelaide, Australia

"I live with the Carter family and look after their two daughters: Amy, who's three, and Ella, who's eighteen months. Not all nannies live with their employers, but I've got my own room and bathroom in the Carters' house. Mr and Mrs Carter leave the house really early to go to work, so I ▫get the children up and give them their breakfast. After that I take Amy to nursery and then I go to the shops with Ella. I pick Amy up again at half past twelve, and then we usually take sandwiches to the park. We go home after lunch so Ella can have a sleep and I can do some cleaning, then I take Amy to ballet and music classes on Tuesdays and Thursdays. I give the children their ▫tea at about 5 o'clock and I give them a bath before their parents come home. Their parents put them to bed while I start the dinner. I ▫have Saturday afternoon and all Sunday off."

Reading

5 EP Which of the three women:

1. regularly starts work at half past seven?
2. looks after very small babies?
3. takes a child to various classes?
4. looks after three children each day?
5. gives the children a bath in the evening?
6. helps with the housework too?

Before you listen

6 How do you think that working mothers who leave their children with other people feel about the situation? Discuss with your classmates.

Listening

7 Alison and Beth both leave their children at Daisies Day Care Center. Listen to what they say and answer the questions.

1. How many children does each woman have?
2. How long do their children spend at Daisies each week?
3. How do the women feel about their children being there?

Speaking

8 Look again at the birthrate statistics on page 140. Do you think that the statistics are similar or different for your country?

9 Do you agree or disagree with these statements?

1. Women these days have babies too late in their lives.
2. Women who have young children shouldn't continue to work.
3. It's OK for men who have young children to continue to work.
4. Men who look after their children while their wives work are ridiculous.
5. It's wrong to pay someone else to look after your young children while you work.

Caring for the elderly

The UK, like many European countries, has an ageing population. At the start of the new millennium, 18% of the British population were aged over 60. As a result, the UK has a booming care home industry, with approximately a quarter of a million old people currently resident in 13,000 different institutions where they receive varying degrees of nursing care.

The Beeches Nursing Home

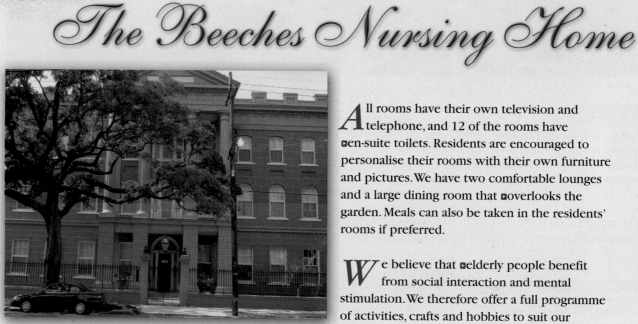

All rooms have their own television and telephone, and 12 of the rooms have ▫en-suite toilets. Residents are encouraged to personalise their rooms with their own furniture and pictures. We have two comfortable lounges and a large dining room that ▫overlooks the garden. Meals can also be taken in the residents' rooms if preferred.

We believe that ▫elderly people benefit from social interaction and mental stimulation. We therefore offer a full programme of activities, crafts and hobbies to suit our residents. There are also regular trips to local shops and places of interest and a local ▫vicar comes to the home to give a church ▫service once a week.

The Beeches is a beautiful Victorian house converted into a 25-bed nursing home. Nursing care is provided by a professional team, but we aim to provide a relaxed, intimate atmosphere. There are no restrictions on visiting hours – relatives and friends are always welcome.

WORD BANK

- elderly ▫ old
- en-suite ▫ private and connected
- out of sight ▫ hidden
- to overlook ▫ to have a view over
- service ▫ religious ceremony
- staff ▫ group of employees of the same company
- vicar ▫ a priest in the Church of England

A home from home?

Who's looking after your grandparents? Do they still live at home, or are they in an old people's home? Or maybe they even live with you and your parents. This week we look at different teenagers' experiences, and the relationships between the generations.

Zoe Hayes, Eastbourne

My gran is 82 and she lives at Broadmead Nursing Home. She's been there for about four years now. She decided that she couldn't cope any longer living in a big house on her own. Mum used to go and visit her about three times a week at home, but it was obvious that she needed more care, and mum had noticed that she was starting to get confused mentally.

She couldn't come and live with us, because we didn't have a bedroom for her. Gran was very sad to leave her home – she'd lived there all her life – and she had to sell the house to pay for her care in Broadmead. We visit her there every Sunday. I don't mind going there. The ▫staff are very nice and there's quite a good atmosphere. I'm sure it isn't the same as living in your own house, though.

Daisy Won, Liverpool

My gran is 75 and she lives with us in our house. She came to stay with us when my grandad died, in 2001. I had to move out of my bedroom and share a room with my sister instead, but it's normal in our culture to look after old people within the family. After all, Gran looked after my dad when he was a child, so it's right that he should look after her now. I don't agree with putting old people into care homes. I think that's just a way to put them ▫out of sight so you can forget about them. I visited a local nursing home with my school recently, and I didn't like it at all. The old people there looked bored, and some of them never have any visitors. I couldn't ever live in a place like that.

Before you read

1 What happens to old people in your country when they can't look after themselves in their own houses, or they become mentally confused?

Reading

2 EP Read the introductory paragraph and the brochure for The Beeches, an old people's home in the UK. Are the following sentences true or false?

1. The Beeches is a modern building.
2. It's got twelve bedrooms.
3. Residents' families can visit when they want.
4. All the rooms have a private toilet.
5. Residents can bring their own furniture and pictures when they arrive.
6. Residents must eat in the dining room.
7. Residents have the opportunity to go outside of the home.
8. Residents are taken to a church every week.

Speaking

3 What general impression does the brochure give of life in a nursing home? Do you think that it gives a realistic picture? What advantages and disadvantages could there be in living in a care home?

Reading

4 EP Read about Zoe's and Daisy's experiences. Which of them:

1. has the oldest grandmother?
2. has a grandmother who lives with her?
3. doesn't mind visiting a care home?
4. had a bad impression of a care home she visited?
5. shares a room with her sister?
6. thinks that putting old people into care homes is wrong?

Speaking

5 Discuss these questions.

1. Do you think that the number of old people in British care homes is high?
2. Why do you think that putting elderly family members into a care home is quite common in the UK?
3. Do special institutions for old people exist in your country? Are they used by many people? What sort of reputation do they have?
4. Do you think it is wrong to put old people into care homes? Why (not)?

Writing/Speaking

6 Imagine that one of your relatives needs to go into a care home. Write a list of questions that you would like to ask the manager. Then use the questions that you have prepared to role play an interview with a partner, who takes the part of the care home manager. When you have completed the interview, swap roles with your partner.

Soundtrack
Changing societies

The lyrics of pop songs always reflect the attitudes and the preoccupations of their day, and many of them take a critical view of a society that they consider to be gradually ■deteriorating. These two songs comment on worrying social problems of their own times and of our own – pollution, urban development and an over-dependence on technology.

⏭Big Yellow Taxi

Joni Mitchell, 1969

In this song, Joni Mitchell, a folk-influenced American singer, protests about various forms of damage to the environment. Some people consider the song to be about Hawaii, where an enormous pink hotel dominates the ■waterfront in Honolulu.

1

They paved paradise
And put up a parking lot
With a pink hotel, a boutique
And a swinging hot spot

Don't it always seem to go
That you don't know what you've got till it's gone
They paved paradise
And put up a parking lot

2

They took all the trees
Put them in a tree museum
And they charged the people
A dollar and a half just to see them

Don't it always seem to go
That you don't know what you've got till it's gone
They paved paradise
And put up a parking lot

3

Hey farmer, farmer
Put away that ■DDT now
Give me spots on my apples
But leave me the birds and the bees
Please!

Don't it always seem to go
That you don't know what you've got till it's gone
They paved paradise
And put up a parking lot

4

Late last night
I heard the screen door slam
And a big yellow taxi
Took away my old man

Don't it always seem to go
That you don't know what you've got till it's gone
They paved paradise
And put up a parking lot
They paved paradise
And put up a parking lot

WORD BANK

DDT ▪ a controversial pesticide, now illegal
to deteriorate ▪ to get worse
Judgement Day ▪ in the Christian religion, the day on which God will appear and decide the fate of all humans
limp ▪ without strength or movement
to make it ▪ to arrive
mighty ▪ powerful
to pick ▪ to choose
through ▪ finished
twinkling ▪ shining
waterfront ▪ where the land meets the sea

⏭In the year 2525

Zager and Evans, 1969

This song, with its pessimistic view of the future of mankind, was the only hit for the American folk duo Denny Zager and Richard Evans.

In the year 2525
If man is still alive
If woman can survive
They may find...

In the year 3535
Ain't gonna need to tell the truth, tell no lies
Everything you think, do, or say
Is in the pill you took today

In the year 4545
Ain't gonna need your teeth, won't need your eyes
You won't find a thing to do
Nobody's gonna look at you

In the year 5555
Your arms are hanging ▪limp at your sides
Your legs got nothing to do
Some machine is doing that for you

In the year 6565
Ain't gonna need no husband, won't need no wife
You'll ▪pick your son, pick your daughter too
From the bottom of a long black tube

In the year 7510
If God's a-comin' he ought to ▪make it by then
Maybe he'll look around himself and say
Guess it's time for the ▪Judgement Day

In the year 8510
God's gonna shake his ▪mighty head
He'll either say 'I'm pleased where man has been'
Or tear it down and start again

In the year 9595
I'm kinda wondering if man's gonna be alive
He's taken everything this old earth can give
And he ain't put back nothing...

Now it's been 10,000 years
Man has cried a billion tears
For what he never knew
Now man's reign is ▪through
But through the eternal night
The ▪twinkling of starlight
So very far away
Maybe it's only yesterday...

Speaking

1 What pollution problems do we experience in our world today? Can you think of any areas near where you live that have been spoilt by new buildings?

Vocabulary

2 Look at the Joni Mitchell song. Match these words to their definitions.

1. pave
2. parking lot
3. swinging
4. hot spot

a. nightclub
b. lively and fashionable
c. cover in concrete
d. car park

Listening

3 Listen to the Joni Mitchell song. Which two lines of the song summarise its main message?

4 EP Match these topics to the verses (1-4) of *Big Yellow Taxi*.

a. Chemicals in the environment
b. The singer's boyfriend leaving her
c. Building in places of natural beauty
d. Creating artificial landscapes

Before you listen

5 How long do you think the human race will survive? What do you think might finally destroy it?

Listening

6 EP Listen to the song *In the year 2525*. Match the singers' predictions to these years.

1. 3535
2. 4545-5555
3. 6565
4. 7510-8510
5. 9595

a. Man will have destroyed the earth.
b. God will decide whether or not to destroy the human race.
c. Babies will be manufactured artificially.
d. Humans will be controlled by drugs.
e. Human bodies will be useless.

Speaking

7 Do you agree with the singers' pessimistic view of society's future? Do you think that any of the predictions in this song are already coming true?

8 Do you think that the social problems highlighted in these two songs are worse or better today than in 1969, when both songs were recorded? Are there other problems in today's society that you feel are just as important?

Writing

9 Write some song lyrics about a problem in your own society. Before you start, make lists of English words that rhyme (eg. *buy/high*), then try to use them in your lyrics.

Language & Culture

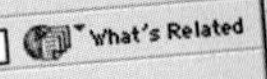

The Saga story

When Sidney and Margery De Haan bought a 12-bedroom hotel in Folkestone after the Second World War, they did not realise that they were going to change the lives of many pensioners in the UK.

The holiday industry in the UK was revolutionised in 1951 by a man called Sidney De Haan. De Haan invented Saga, a package holiday company for older and retired people. His vision was to recognise the value of older people as a customer group and to make their needs and interests the focus of his business. If De Haan had not recognised this market, life for the over-50s would have been very different.

The De Haans' hotel business was not good in the autumn and winter, and the hotel was threatened with closure. However, Margery De Haan noticed that most of the people who used park benches in the town during the year were elderly. She realised that these people were using the park benches because they had nowhere else to go and nothing else to do. If there was nowhere else to go, there was a market for creating that place for old people.

De Haan decided to target elderly people offering them cheap accommodation in his hotel. He thought, 'If I offer these people cheap holidays and organise everything, they will want to travel.' He was right. His initial idea expanded and he started to offer coach trips with a stay in his hotel. This appealed to pensioners because it was very cheap and it meant they could travel in a way they had never had the opportunity to do before.

Over the years, Saga holidays offered older people the chance to travel abroad for weeks at a time, or the chance to visit France for a day for those who didn't have passports. Nowadays pensioners can choose to travel to the US for a weekend, cruise the Mediterranean or go wine-tasting in the South African vineyards. If pensioners want to travel to particular places, they will find all the information they need in the Saga travel magazine or on the Saga website.

De Haan decided that if the holidays worked, other business ideas for the over 50s would work too. In 1984, he relaunched the Saga magazine. It dealt with topics of general interest to pensioners as well as holiday information, and soon achieved a circulation of 1.2 million. De Haan then developed Saga newsletters, Saga websites, Saga financial advice services and insurance, and a Saga radio station.

All of this means that the over-50s and the retired can have active lives and active holidays wherever and whenever they want.

GRAMMAR

1 Read the text *The Saga story* quickly and list six areas of business which Sidney De Haan developed.

2 Read the text and underline the five conditional sentences. Then rewrite them on the correct line below.

Zero: ....
First: ....
....
Second: ....
Third: ....

3 Complete the dialogue with the verbs in brackets in the correct tense.

A: Did your parents enjoy their Mediterranean cruise?
B: Yes, thanks. They loved it. If you (1) ..... (not give) them that Saga brochure, they (2) ..... (never think) of going on a cruise!
A: That's great! Which ports did the boat stop in?
B: Well, the first port was Marseilles. They saw quite a few of the sights, but if they (3) ..... (have) more time they (4) ..... (go) to a football match!
A: I don't believe it! Where did they go after that?
B: After that they stopped off in Barcelona. They saw the Sagrada Familia Church and Mount Tibidabo. They didn't see any nightclubs! I'm sure if I (5) ..... (can) afford to go to Barcelona I (6) ..... (visit) all the night clubs.
A: OK - we know you like dancing! And where did they go after Barcelona?
B: Well, the final port was Naples. They loved it!
A: It all sounds great! So if you (7) ..... (take) me on holiday next year what (8) ..... (we/see)?
B: Nightclubs, football grounds and a few famous buildings!

SKILLS

4 Complete the dialogue with the opinion phrases below.

In my opinion *we'll have to agree to disagree* ~~*I think*~~
What about you *I don't think* *I think it depends on*
Sorry, I don't agree with you

A: I heard the government are proposing to allow retired people to work part-time after they retire. (1) *I think* that's a very good idea. (2) ......?
B: (3) .... I think old people should retire when they have to and allow younger people to take their jobs.
A: But what about all the experience older people have? (4) ......, if retired people came back into the workforce, everyone would benefit from it.
B: But (5) ...... that it's fair on young people. Retired people have had their opportunity to work and they should stay retired.
A: (6) ...... the person and the skills and experience they can offer. Age doesn't matter.
B: OK, well I guess (7) ...... on this one then!

5 In pairs, act out the dialogue in exercise 4.

6 Choose a topic from the list below and discuss it with a partner. Remember to use the opinion phrases from exercise 4.

a. Old people are not looked after well in this country.
b. The government should increase pensions for old people.
c. Everyone should help old people by visiting them more and taking them out at least once a week.
d. Old people should be allowed to return to part-time employment, if they want, after they retire.

Module 11 Links to literature

IN THIS MODULE YOU WILL READ AND LISTEN TO:

- a patriotic speech from *Henry V* by William Shakespeare
- two poems by William Wordsworth
- an extract from *Emma* by Jane Austen
- an extract from *The Last of the Mohicans* by James Fenimore Cooper
- an extract from *Uncle Tom's Cabin* by Harriet Beecher Stowe
- an extract from *Nicholas Nickleby* by Charles Dickens
- an extract from *Pygmalion* by G. B. Shaw
- a poem about the First World War by Wilfred Owen
- an extract from *A Room of One's Own* by Virginia Woolf
- an extract from *The Grapes of Wrath* by John Steinbeck
- a poem by Dylan Thomas
- an extract from *White Teeth* by Zadie Smith

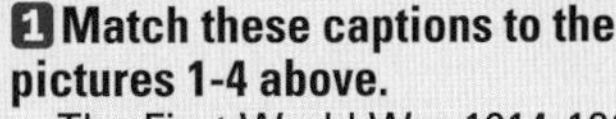

1 Match these captions to the pictures 1-4 above.

a. The First World War 1914-1918
b. The Victorian era 1837-1902
c. The Elizabethan era 1558-1603
d. The French Revolution 1789

2 Can you match these English writers to the dates in exercise 1?

A Charles Dickens
B Wilfred Owen
C William Shakespeare
D William Wordsworth

William Shakespeare (1564-1616)

Harry, England and Saint George

HENRY: Once more unto the breach[1], dear friends,
once more;
Or close the wall up with our English dead.
In peace there's nothing so becomes a man[2]
As modest stillness and humility:
But when the blast[3] of war blows in our ears,
Then imitate the action of the tiger;
Stiffen the sinews[4], summon up[5] the blood,
Disguise fair nature with hard-favour'd rage[6];
Then lend the eye a terrible aspect;
...
... On, on, you noblest English.
Whose blood is set from fathers of war-proof[7]!
Fathers that, like so many Alexanders[8],
Have in these parts from morn till even[9] fought
And sheathed[10] their swords for lack of argument:
Dishonour not your mothers; now attest
That those whom you call'd fathers did beget you[11].
Be copy[12] now to men of grosser blood,
And teach them how to war. And you, good yeomen[13],
Whose limbs were made in England, show us here
The mettle of your pasture[14]; let us swear
That you are worth your breeding; which I doubt not;
For there is none of you so mean and base,
That hath[15] not noble lustre in your eyes.
I see you stand like greyhounds in the slips[16],
Straining upon the start. The game's afoot[17]:
Follow your spirit, and upon this charge
Cry 'God for Harry, England, and Saint George!'

From *Henry V*, Act III, Scene I

GLOSSARY

1 battle
2 nothing suits a man better
3 noise of the trumpet
4 make your muscles tense
5 call to
6 put on an appearance of determined anger
7 whose ancestors proved their worth in war
8 an ancient Greek warrior and hero
9 from morning until evening
10 put back in their covers
11 prove that the men you call fathers really are your fathers
12 be a model
13 independent working men
14 the quality of your homeland
15 has
16 like racing dogs waiting to race
17 the game has just started

Shakespeare's works

Shakespeare worked as a professional actor and playwright with a group in London known as the Lord Chamberlain's Men. His 37 plays are based on a number of sources including ancient Greek and Latin writings and historical chronicles. They include tragedies (*Hamlet*, 1601), comedies (*A Midsummer Night's Dream*, 1595-96), histories (*Henry V*, 1596-97) and fantasies (*The Tempest*, 1611).

The text

In this speech, one of the most famous pieces of patriotic English literature, King Henry V addresses the English soldiers before they face the French at the Battle of Agincourt (1415) during the Hundred Years War (1337-1453).

Links 2a, 3a, 3c, 4e, 5c, 6d, 6e, 11i

Reading

1 According to Henry, what animal should a man resemble when he goes into battle? What physical changes should happen to him?

2 What part of the speech tells you that England and France have been at war for a long time?

3 What second animal are the men compared to at the end of the speech? How might they resemble this animal?

Your analysis

4 How many references does Henry make to the soldiers' fathers? Why do you think he does this?

5 From what social class would most of Henry's soldiers come? Why, then, does Henry twice refer to them as *noble*?

6 What makes Henry a good speech-maker? What effect have his words had on the soldiers by the end of the speech? How do you know? What do you imagine happens immediately after this speech is finished?

Contemporary links

7 Can you think of any leaders in today's world who make good speeches and have a good effect on crowds?

8 How important is it these days for politicians to say the right thing and to have the right image in today's media? Is this more important than their actual policies?

William Wordsworth
(1770-1850)

Composed upon Westminster Bridge, Sept. 3, 1802

Earth has not anything to show more fair[1]:
Dull would he be of soul[2] who could pass by
A sight so touching in its majesty:
This City now doth like a garment[3] wear
The beauty of the morning; silent, bare,
Ships, towers, domes, theatres, and temples lie
Open unto the fields, and to the sky;
All bright and glittering[4] in the smokeless air.
Never did sun more beautifully steep[5]
In his first splendour valley, rock, or hill;
Ne'er saw I, never felt, a calm so deep!
The river glideth at his own sweet will[6]:
Dear God! the very houses seem asleep;
And all that mighty heart is lying still!

GLOSSARY

1 beautiful
2 he would be unfeeling and unresponsive
3 an item of clothing
4 shining
5 soak, as if with a liquid
6 flows in the way that it wants to
7 multitude
8 yellow flower (narcissus)
9 waving
10 change shape while shining, like a star
11 a large galaxy
12 throwing their heads in an energetic dance
13 were better than
14 joy
15 happy
16 cheerful
17 stared
18 often
19 appear suddenly in the mind or memory
20 joy

I Wandered Lonely as a Cloud

I wandered lonely as a cloud
That floats on high o'er vales and hills,
When all at once I saw a crowd,
A host[7], of golden daffodils[8];
Beside the lake, beneath the trees,
Fluttering[9] and dancing in the breeze.

Continuous as the stars that shine
And twinkle[10] on the milky way[11],
They stretched in never-ending line
Along the margin of a bay:
Ten thousand saw I at a glance,
Tossing their heads in sprightly dance[12].

The waves beside them danced; but they
Out-did[13] the sparkling waves in glee[14]:
A poet could not but be gay[15],
In such a jocund[16] company:
I gazed[17] – and gazed – but little thought
What wealth the show to me had brought:

For oft[18], when on my couch I lie
In vacant or in pensive mood,
They flash upon that inward eye[19]
Which is the bliss[20] of solitude;
And then my heart with pleasure fills,
And dances with the daffodils.

Wordsworth's works

With Samuel Taylor Coleridge, Wordsworth wrote the collection of poems *Lyrical Ballads* (1798), which is usually seen as marking the beginning of the Romantic era in English literature. Wordsworth's themes include the beauty and sublimity of nature, divine inspiration, and the conflict between man's feelings and his reason.

The text

In the first poem, Wordsworth surveys the panoramic view of London from Westminster Bridge. In the second, he remembers a beautiful sight that he saw near his home in northern England's Lake District.

Links 2e

Reading

1 In the first poem, what time of day is it, and what is the weather like? Is there much activity in the city? Find the words and phrases in the poem that tell you this.

2 What effect does the view of the city have on the poet?

3 In the second poem, what various things are the daffodils compared to?

4 How did the poet feel when he first saw the daffodils? How does the beauty of the daffodils still have an effect on him now?

Your analysis

5 What is the poet saying in lines 1 and 9-10 of the first poem? Why is this unusual? How is the second poem a more traditional subject for a poet?

6 Which of these sentences do you think reflects Wordsworth's feelings?
a. Beauty can only be found in natural things.
b. Beauty can be found everywhere if you look for it.
c. The city is more stimulating than the country.

Contemporary links

7 Many Romantic poems idealise life in the country and paint a bad picture of city life. What arguments can you think of to oppose this view? Discuss the good points of the city and the bad points of the country.

Jane Austen
(1775-1817)

Emma passes judgement

"But did you never see him? He is in Highbury every now and then, and he is sure to ride through every week on his way to Kingston. He has passed you very often."

"That may be, and I may have seen him fifty times, but without having any idea of his name. A young farmer, whether on horseback or on foot, is the very last sort of person to raise my curiosity. The yeomanry[1] are precisely the order of people with whom I feel I can have nothing to do. A degree or two lower, and a creditable[2] appearance might interest me; I might hope to be useful to their families in some way or other. But a farmer can need none of my help, and is, therefore, in one sense, as much above my notice as in every other he is below it. ... I have no doubt of his being a very respectable young man. I know, indeed, that he is so, and, as such, wish him well. What do you imagine his age to be?"

"He was four-and-twenty the 8th of last June, and my birthday is the 23rd, just a fortnight and a day's difference – which is very odd."

"Only four-and-twenty. That is too young to settle[3]. His mother is perfectly right not to be in a hurry. They seem very comfortable as they are, and if she were to take any pains to marry him, she would probably repent it. Six years hence[4], if he could meet with a good sort of young woman in the same rank[5] as his own, with a little money, it might be very desirable."

"Six years hence! Dear Miss Woodhouse, he would be thirty years old!" ...

"I wish you may not get into a scrape[6], Harriet, whenever he does marry; – I mean, as to being acquainted with his wife – for though his sisters, from a superior education, are not to be altogether objected to[7], it does not follow that he might marry any body at all fit[8] for you to notice. The misfortune of your birth[9] ought to make you particularly careful as to your associates. There can be no doubt of your being a gentleman's daughter, and you must support your claim to that station[10] ... I say that if you should still be in this country[11] when Mr. Martin marries, I wish you may not be drawn in[12] by your intimacy with the sisters, to be acquainted with the wife, who will probably be some mere[13] farmer's daughter, without education."

"To be sure. Yes. ... if he marries a very ignorant, vulgar woman, certainly I had better not visit her, if I can help it."

Emma watched her through the fluctuations of this speech, and saw no alarming symptoms of love. The young man had been the first admirer, but she trusted there was no other hold[14], and that there would be no serious difficulty, on Harriet's side, to oppose any friendly arrangement of her own.

From *Emma*, Chapter 4

GLOSSARY

1 financially independent working-class people
2 respectable
3 make a home and get married
4 from now
5 social position
6 make an embarrassing mistake
7 are not completely unsuitable
8 suitable
9 *Harriet is illegitimate, and no-one knows who her parents are.*
10 make people believe that you really are a gentleman's daughter
11 county, region
12 led
13 humble
14 she believed that there wasn't any greater attachment

Austen's works

Austen's six major novels (*Sense and Sensibility, Pride and Prejudice, Mansfield Park, Emma, Persuasion* and *Northanger Abbey*) were all written between the years 1811 and 1817. They deal primarily with rural middle-class family life and relationships, and exhibit a strong sense of satire.

The text

Emma Woodhouse has decided to find a good husband for Harriet Smith, a new friend of hers with no social connections. Harriet has been staying with schoolfriends and is attracted to their brother, Robert Martin, a farmer. She is describing him to Emma.

Links 1c, 2e, 5c, 10a

Reading

1 Why is Emma interested in poor people, but not in farmers like Robert Martin?

2 Who does Emma think Robert Martin should marry, and when?

3 How does she think that Harriet should behave towards Robert's wife when he marries? Why?

4 Why is Emma satisfied at the end of the conversation?

Your analysis

5 What social class do you think Emma belongs to? What is her attitude to people from other social classes?

6 Why do you think Emma is so interested in Harriet?

Contemporary links

7 Are the differences in people's social class as wide today as they were in Jane Austen's day?

8 Do people still worry about social class when deciding who to marry?

James Fenimore Cooper (1789-1851)

Magua demands justice

"Listen," said the Indian …: "Magua was born a chief and a warrior among the red Hurons[1] of the lakes; he saw the suns of twenty summers make the snows of twenty winters run off in the streams before he saw a pale face; and he was happy! Then his Canada fathers came into the woods, and taught him to drink the fire-water[2], and he became a rascal[3]. The Hurons drove him from the graves of his fathers, as they would chase the hunted buffalo. He ran down the shores of the lakes, and followed their outlet[4] to the 'city of cannon'. There he hunted and fished, till the people chased him again through the woods into the arms of his enemies. The chief, who was born a Huron, was at last a warrior among the Mohawks[5]!"

"Something like this I had heard before," said Cora. …

"Was it the fault of Le Renard[6] that his head was not made of rock? Who gave him the fire-water? Who made him a villain? 'Twas the pale faces, the people of your own color."

"And am I answerable that[7] thoughtless and unprincipled men exist, whose shades of countenance[8] may resemble mine?" Cora calmly demanded of the excited savage.

"No; Magua is a man, and not a fool; such as you never open their lips to the burning stream[9]: the Great Spirit has given you wisdom!"

"What, then, have I do to, or say, in the matter of your misfortunes, not to say of your errors?"

"Listen," repeated the Indian, resuming his earnest attitude[10]; "when his English and French fathers dug up the hatchet[11], Le Renard struck the war-post of the Mohawks[12], and went out against his own nation. The pale faces have driven the red-skins from their hunting grounds, and now when they fight, a white man leads the way. The old chief at Horican, your father, was the great captain of our war-party. He said to the Mohawks do this, and do that, and he was minded[13]. He made a law, that if an Indian swallowed the fire-water, and came into the cloth wigwams[14] of his warriors, it should not be forgotten. Magua foolishly opened his mouth, and the hot liquor led him into the cabin of Munro. What did the gray-head? Let his daughter say."

"He forgot not his words, and did justice, by punishing the offender," said the undaunted[15] daughter.

"Justice!" repeated the Indian … "is it justice to make evil and then punish for it? Magua was not himself; it was the fire-water that spoke and acted for him! But Munro did not believe it. The Huron chief was tied up before all the pale-faced warriors, and whipped like a dog." …

"What would you have?" continued Cora. …

"What a Huron loves – good for good; bad for bad!" …

"What must I promise?" demanded Cora, still maintaining a secret ascendancy[16] over the fierce native by the collected and feminine dignity of her presence.

"When Magua left his people his wife was given to another chief; he has now made friends with the Hurons, and will go back to the graves of his tribe, on the shores of the great lake. Let the daughter of the English chief follow, and live in his wigwam forever."

From *The Last of the Mohicans*, Chapter 11

GLOSSARY

1 Magua's tribe
2 alcohol
3 villain, bad person
4 river that runs out of a lake
5 a rival tribe to the Hurons
6 Magua's other name ('The Fox')
7 Is it my fault
8 the colours of their faces
9 alcohol
10 becoming serious
11 started fighting again
12 promised to fight for the Mohawks
13 obeyed
14 tents
15 unafraid
16 superiority

Cooper's works

J. F. Cooper is best known for his stories of American frontier life and pioneer adventure. His most popular work is *The Last of the Mohicans* (1832), the second of five novels which centre around Natty Bumppo (known also as "Hawkeye"), a white man who has adopted the Indian way of life.

The text

Set in 1757, during the war between England and France for control of North America, *The Last of the Mohicans* tells the story of Cora and Alice Munro, daughters of the English commander, who are travelling to their father's fort. On the journey they are captured by Magua, a savage Indian who has changed allegiance between Indian tribes, and between the two European armies. Here, Magua explains to Cora why he wishes to be revenged against her father.

Links 3b, 3d

Reading

1 Put these events of Magua's life in the correct order.

a. He joined the Mohawk tribe.
b. He lived a peaceful life with his native tribe.
c. He fought against his native tribe with Munro as his leader.
d. The English and the French declared war on each other.
e. His native tribe rejected him.

2 The Huron rejected Magua, and Munro punished him for the same 'crime'. What was it?

3 How did Munro punish Magua, and how did it make him feel? How does Magua plan to use Cora to get revenge?

Your analysis

4 Who does Magua blame for the misfortunes of his life? Do you think that he is justified?

5 What impression do you get of Cora's character in this scene? How do you think she will react to Magua's final demand?

Contemporary links

6 How have Native Americans been treated in the USA since *The Last of the Mohicans* was written?

7 Can you think of any other races or cultures that have been dominated by colonising nations? What effect did the colonisation have on them?

Harriet Beecher Stowe (1811-1896)

Property and possessions

Stopping opposite to Tom, who had been attired[1] for sale in his best broadcloth[2] suit, with well-starched[3] linen and shining boots, he briefly expressed himself as follows: "Stand up."

Tom stood up.

"Take off that stock[4]!" and, as Tom, encumbered by his fetters[5], proceeded to do it, he assisted him, by pulling it, with no gentle hand, from his neck, and putting it in his pocket.

Legree now turned to Tom's trunk[6], which, previous to this, he had been ransacking[7], and, taking from it a pair of old pantaloons and dilapidated[8] coat, which Tom had been wont to put on about his stable-work[9], he said, liberating Tom's hands from the handcuffs[10], and pointing to a recess in among the boxes,

"You go there, and put these on."

Tom obeyed, and in a few moments returned.

"Take off your boots," said Mr. Legree.

Tom did so.

"There," said the former, throwing him a pair of coarse, stout[11] shoes, such as were common among the slaves, "put these on."

In Tom's hurried exchange, he had not forgotten to transfer his cherished Bible to his pocket. It was well he did so; for Mr. Legree, having refitted Tom's handcuffs, proceeded deliberately to investigate the contents of his pockets. He drew[12] out a silk handkerchief, and put it into his own pocket. Several little trifles[13], which Tom had treasured, chiefly because they had amused Eva, he looked upon with a contemptuous grunt, and tossed them over his shoulder into the river.

Tom's Methodist hymn-book[14], which, in his hurry, he had forgotten, he now held up and turned over.

Humph! pious[15], to be sure. So, what's yer name, - you belong to the church, eh?"

"Yes, Mas'r," said Tom, firmly.

"Well, I'll soon have that out of you. I have none o' yer bawling[16], praying, singing niggers[17] on my place; so remember. Now, mind yourself[18]," he said, with a stamp and a fierce glance[19] of his gray eye, directed at Tom, "I'm your church now! You understand, - you've got to be as I say." ...

He took Tom's trunk, which contained a very neat and abundant wardrobe, to the forecastle[20], where it was soon surrounded by various hands[21] of the boat. With much laughing, at the expense of niggers who tried to be gentlemen, the articles very readily were sold to one and another, and the empty trunk finally put up at auction[22]. It was a good joke, they all thought, especially to see how Tom looked after his things, as they were going this way and that; and then the auction of the trunk, that was funnier than all, and occasioned abundant witticisms[23]. This little affair being over, Simon sauntered up[24] again to his property.

"Now, Tom, I've relieved you of any extra baggage, you see. Take mighty good care of them clothes. It'll be long enough 'fore you get more. I go in for[25] making niggers careful; one suit has to do for one year, on my place."

From *Uncle Tom's Cabin*, Chapter 31

GLOSSARY

1 dressed
2 a high-quality fabric
3 made rigid
4 neckcloth
5 restricted by his chains
6 large suitcase
7 violently searching through
8 old and used
9 used to wear for working in the stables
10 metal rings that lock the hands together
11 strong
12 pulled
13 insignificant things
14 book of songs connected to the protestant Methodist church
15 religious
16 shouting
17 *very abusive term for a black person (from 'negro')*
18 behave correctly
19 putting his foot down heavily and looking angry
20 part of a boat where the crew's accommodation is
21 workers
22 a competition to buy something with different offers of money
23 was the cause of a lot of jokes
24 walked casually
25 like

Beecher Stowe's works

A committed American social reformer and Christian, Beecher Stowe published essays, religious poems and novels. Her anti-slavery novel *Uncle Tom's Cabin* (1852) sold half a million copies in the United States and was quickly translated into 37 languages.

The text

Tom, a black slave, has had to leave his home in New Orleans, where his kind master and his master's daughter, Eva, have died. He has just been bought by a plantation owner named Simon Legree and put on a riverboat with Legree's other slaves. Legree is inspecting his new purchases.

Links 3b, 3d, 3f

Reading

1 How is Tom dressed at the start of the scene? What changes does Legree make to Tom's clothes?

2 How does Legree discover that Tom is a religious man? What is Legree's attitude to this?

3 Why do the crew of the boat find Tom's possessions so amusing? What do they do with them?

4 What possessions is Tom left with at the end of the scene?

Your analysis

5 How would you describe Legree's treatment of Tom, and his attitude to slaves in general?

6 What is symbolised by this description of how Tom is gradually deprived of all his clothes and possessions?

7 Which of these words describe Tom's behaviour throughout the scene?

angry calm despairing passive resigned violent

Contemporary links

8 Do you think the slavery of black people has had a long-term effect on race relations in the USA?

Charles Dickens
(1812-1870)

An English lesson at Dotheboys

He could not but observe how silent and sad the boys all seemed to be. There was none of the noise and clamour of a schoolroom; none of its boisterous[1] play, or hearty mirth[2]. The children sat crouching and shivering[3] together, and seemed to lack the spirit to move about. … After some half-hour's delay, Mr Squeers reappeared, and the boys took their places and their books, of which latter commodity[4] the average might be about one to eight learners. A few minutes having elapsed[5], during which Mr Squeers looked very profound, as if he had a perfect apprehension of what was inside all the books, and could say every word of their contents by heart if he only chose to take the trouble, that gentleman called up the first class. Obedient to this summons there ranged themselves in front of the schoolmaster's desk, half-a-dozen scarecrows[6], out[7] at knees and elbows, one of whom placed a torn and filthy[8] book beneath his learned eye.

'This is the first class in English spelling and philosophy, Nickleby,' said Squeers, beckoning[9] Nicholas to stand beside him.

'We'll get up a Latin one, and hand that over to you. Now, then, where's the first boy?'

'Please, sir, he's cleaning the back-parlour window,' said the temporary head of the philosophical class.

'So he is, to be sure,' rejoined Squeers. 'We go upon the practical mode of teaching, Nickleby; the regular education system. C–l–e–a–n, clean, verb active, to make bright, to scour[10]. W–i–n, win, d–e–r, der, winder[11], a casement. When the boy knows this out of book, he goes and does it. It's just the same principle as the use of the globes. Where's the second boy?'

'Please, sir, he's weeding[12] the garden,' replied a small voice.

'To be sure,' said Squeers, by no means disconcerted. 'So he is. B–o–t, bot, t–i–n, tin, bottin, n–e–y, ney, bottinney[13], noun substantive, a knowledge of plants. When he has learned that bottinney means a knowledge of plants, he goes and knows 'em. That's our system, Nickleby: what do you think of it?'

'It's very useful one, at any rate,' answered Nicholas.

'I believe you,' rejoined Squeers, not remarking the emphasis of his usher[14]. 'Third boy, what's horse?'

'A beast, sir,' replied the boy.

'So it is,' said Squeers. 'Ain't it, Nickleby?'

'I believe there is no doubt of that, sir,' answered Nicholas.

'Of course there isn't,' said Squeers. 'A horse is a quadruped, and quadruped's Latin for beast, as everybody that's gone through the grammar knows, or else where's the use of having grammars at all?'

'Where, indeed!' said Nicholas abstractedly[15].

'As you're perfect in that,' resumed Squeers, turning to the boy, 'go and look after MY horse, and rub him down well, or I'll rub you down. The rest of the class go and draw water up[16], till somebody tells you to leave off[17], for it's washing-day tomorrow, and they want the coppers[18] filled.'

From *Nicholas Nickleby*, Chapter 8

GLOSSARY

1 rough
2 sincere happiness
3 bent and shaking with cold
4 *a reference to the books*
5 passed
6 figures made by farmers to frighten birds
7 with holes in their clothes
8 very dirty
9 indicating to
10 clean vigorously
11 *Squeers' misspelling of* window
12 pulling out the unwanted plants
13 *Squeers' misspelling of* botany
14 assistant
15 vaguely
16 pull water up from a hole in the ground
17 stop
18 large pans

Dickens' works

Dickens was one of the most prolific authors of the 19th century. His works, including some of the best-loved novels in the English language (*Oliver Twist* 1837-39, *Nicholas Nickleby* 1838-39, *David Copperfield* 1849-1850), were published in serial form in magazines, and his public reading tours of Britain and the US earned him huge popularity. His novels are populated by memorable, often comic, characters from all social classes, and many of his works criticise the social inequality of Victorian England.

The text

In the novel of the same name, 18-year-old Nicholas Nickleby's father has died, and Nicholas, his sister and his mother are dependent on the dead man's brother. Nicholas' uncle has secured him a job at Dotheboys Hall, a school for poor boys in Yorkshire run by Mr Squeers.

Links 5a, 8a

Reading

1 **How is the atmosphere of the classroom at Dotheboys Hall different to a normal classroom?**

2 **What do the boys there look like?**

3 **What does Squeers make the boys do when they have learned to spell a word?**

4 **What four tasks does Squeers make various boys do?**

Your analysis

5 **What details in the text show that:**
a. the school has no money?
b. Squeers is uneducated?

6 **What is Nicholas' reaction to Squeers' teaching methods? How does Dickens show this?**

7 **What serious message does Dickens intend to convey in this scene? Why, then, does he make it a humorous scene?**

Contemporary links

8 **How are today's classrooms and teaching methods different from the classrooms and methods of 100 years ago?**

9 **What do you think makes a good teacher? And a bad one?**

George Bernard Shaw
(1856-1950)

Eliza enters society

Mrs Higgins: Will it rain, do you think?
Eliza: The shallow depression in the west of these islands is likely to move slowly in an easterly direction. There are no indications of any great change in the barometrical situation.
Freddy: Ha! ha! how awfully funny!
Eliza: What is wrong with that, young man? I bet I got it right.
Freddy: Killing[1]!
Mrs Eynsford Hill: I'm sure I hope it won't turn cold. There's so much influenza about. It runs right through our whole family regularly every spring.
Eliza: My aunt died of influenza: so they said.
Mrs Eynsford Hill: *(clicks her tongue sympathetically)*
Eliza: But it's my belief they done the old woman in[2].
Mrs Higgins: Done her in?
Eliza: Y-e-e-e-es, Lord love you! Why should she die of influenza? She come through[3] diphtheria right enough the year before. I saw her with my own eyes. Fairly blue with it, she was. They all thought she was dead; but my father he kept ladling[4] gin down her throat til she came to[5] so sudden that she bit the bowl off the spoon.
Mrs Eynsford Hill: Dear me!
Eliza: What call[6] would a woman with that strength in her have to die of influenza? What become of[7] her new straw hat that should have come to me? Somebody pinched[8] it; and what I say is, them as pinched it done her in[9].
Mrs Eynsford Hill: What does doing her in mean?
Higgins: Oh, that's the new small talk[10]. To do a person in means to kill them.
Mrs Eynsford Hill: You surely don't believe that your aunt was killed?
Eliza: Do I not! Them[11] she lived with would have killed her for a hat-pin, let alone a hat.
Mrs Eynsford Hill: But it can't have been right for your father to pour spirits down her throat like that. It might have killed her.
Eliza: Not her. Gin was mother's milk to her. Besides, he'd poured so much down his own throat that he knew the good of it.
Mrs Eynsford Hill: Do you mean that he drank?
Eliza: Drank! My word! Something chronic[12].
Mrs Eynsford Hill: How dreadful for you!
Eliza: Not a bit. It never did him no harm what I could see. But then he did not keep it up regular. On the burst[13], as you might say, from time to time. … *(to Freddy, who is in convulsions of suppressed laughter)* Here! What are you sniggering[14] at?
Freddy: The new small talk. You do it so awfully well.
Eliza: If I was doing it proper, what was you laughing at? Have I said anything I oughtn't?
Mrs Higgins: Not at all, Miss Doolittle.
Eliza: Well, that's a mercy[15], anyhow. What I always say is …
Higgins: *(rising and looking at his watch)* Ahem!
Eliza: Well: I must go. So pleased to have met you. Good-bye.
Mrs Higgins: Good-bye.
Eliza: Good-bye, Colonel Pickering.
Pickering: Good-bye, Miss Doolittle.
Eliza: Good-bye, all.
Freddy: Are you walking across the Park, Miss Doolittle? If so …
Eliza: Walk! Not bloody likely[16] *(sensation)*. I am going in a taxi.

From *Pygmalion*, Act III

GLOSSARY

1 very funny
2 killed the old woman
3 survived
4 spooning
5 regained consciousness
6 why
7 what happened to
8 stole
9 the people who stole it killed her
10 insignificant conversation
11 the people who
12 excessively
13 sporadically
14 laughing
15 that's a relief
16 you must be joking (*'bloody' is a mild swear word these days, but the play's original audience would have been very shocked by its use*)

Shaw's works

The long career of George Bernard Shaw, the Irish dramatist and socialist campaigner, spanned both the Victorian age and the early 20th century. Shaw wrote over 50 plays (*Mrs Warren's Profession*, 1894, *Saint Joan*, 1924), most of which deal with moral and social problems.

The text

In *Pygmalion* (1913), Professor Higgins has been teaching Cockney flowerseller Eliza Doolittle to talk and act like a lady. For a bet with his friend Colonel Pickering, Higgins hopes to trick London's high society into believing that Eliza is an aristocrat. In this scene he introduces her to his mother and to her upper-class friends, the Eynsford Hills.

Links 5c, 8c, 8f

Reading

1 How does Eliza speak at the very start of the scene? How does she speak when she talks about her aunt's death?

2 Why does Eliza think that her aunt was murdered?

3 How does Higgins explain Eliza's use of slang?

4 How does the group react to Eliza's use of the word *bloody*?

Your analysis

5 What impression does Eliza make on Freddy Eynsford Hill in this scene? Do you think that the Eynsford Hills have guessed Eliza's true identity?

6 How do you think that Higgins is feeling during this scene? How should the actor playing him behave?

7 Does Shaw have any serious message to convey in this scene?

Contemporary links

8 Can you still tell a person's social class from the way that they speak? Do people still worry about revealing their class through their accents and vocabulary?

9 Have new methods of communication such as e-mail and texting made language more democratic?

Wilfred Owen
(1893-1918)

Parable of the Old Man and the Young

So Abram rose, and clave[1] the wood, and went,
And took the fire with him, and a knife.
And as they sojourned[2] both of them together,
Isaac the first-born spake[3] and said, My Father,
Behold[4] the preparations, fire and iron,
But where the lamb for this burnt-offering?
Then Abram bound[5] the youth with belts and straps,
And builded parapets and trenches[6] there,
And stretched forth the knife to slay[7] his son.
When lo![8] an angel called him out of heaven,
Saying, Lay not thy hand upon the lad[9],
Neither do anything to him. Behold,
A ram caught in a thicket[10] by its horns;
Offer the Ram of Pride instead of him.
But the old man would not so, but slew[11] his son,
And half the seed of Europe, one by one.

GLOSSARY

1 cut
2 stayed
3 spoke
4 look at
5 tied
6 low walls and ditches (typical of First World War battlefields)
7 kill
8 look!
9 do not touch the boy
10 a male sheep trapped in a bush
11 killed

Owen's works

Wilfred Owen is regarded as the greatest of the First World War poets. His poems reject nationalism and sentimentality and mix traditional romantic imagery with the bloody reality of war. In 1916, Owen became shell-shocked and was sent home to recover. He voluntarily returned to the army in 1918 and was killed a week before the end of the war.

The text

In this poem, Owen modernises the Christian story of Abraham and Isaac. In the Bible, God tests Abraham's loyalty by asking him to sacrifice his son to him. Abraham begins to follow God's instructions, but at the last minute God sends a ram to be sacrificed in Isaac's place.

Links 3c, 4f

Reading

1 Which lines in the poem refer specifically to soldiers' equipment and to the landscape of the First World War?

2 How does Owen's version of the Abraham and Isaac story differ from the version in the Bible?

Your analysis

3 Work out the symbolism of the poem.
Who do Abraham and Isaac represent?
Who are 'half the seed of Europe'?
Why is the ram called the Ram of Pride, and why won't Abraham kill it?

4 Find in the poem all the different terms used to refer to Abraham and Isaac. What is the significance of these terms, and the poem's title?

5 Which are the only two rhyming lines in the poem? How do they add to the poem's effect?

Contemporary links

6 How far is Owen's symbolic poem still relevant to war in our own times? Do old people and young people hold different opinions of war?

7 Is war always just a waste of life, or can it serve any purpose?

Virginia Woolf
(1882-1941)

Shakespeare's sister

... it would have been impossible, completely and entirely, for any woman to have written the plays of Shakespeare in the age of Shakespeare. Let me imagine, since facts are so hard to come by, what would have happened had Shakespeare had a wonderfully gifted[1] sister, called Judith, let us say. Shakespeare himself ... got work in the theatre, became a successful actor, and lived at the hub[2] of the universe, meeting everybody, knowing everybody, practising his art on the boards[3], exercising his wits[4] in the streets, and even getting access to the palace of the queen. Meanwhile his extraordinarily gifted sister, let us suppose, remained at home. She was as adventurous, as imaginative, as agog[5] to see the world as he was. But she was not sent to school. She had no chance of learning grammar and logic, let alone[6] of reading Horace and Virgil. She picked up a book now and then, one of her brother's perhaps, and read a few pages. But then her parents came in and told her to mend the stockings or mind[7] the stew[8] and not moon about[9] with books and papers. They would have spoken sharply but kindly, for they were substantial people who knew the conditions of life for a woman and loved their daughter – indeed, more likely than not she was the apple of her father's eye[10]. Perhaps she scribbled[11] some pages up in an apple loft on the sly[12] but was careful to hide them or set fire to them. Soon, however, before she was out of her teens, she was to be betrothed to[13] the son of a neighbouring woolstapler[14]. She cried out that marriage was hateful to her, and for that she was severely beaten by her father. Then he ceased to scold[15] her. He begged her instead not to hurt him, not to shame him in this matter of her marriage. He would give her a chain of beads or a fine petticoat[16], he said; and there were tears in his eyes. How could she disobey him? How could she break his heart? The force of her own gift alone drove her to it. She made up a small parcel of her belongings, let herself down by a rope one summer's night and took the road to London. She was not seventeen. The birds that sang in the hedge were not more musical than she was. She had the quickest fancy[17], a gift like her brother's, for the tune of words. Like him, she had a taste for the theatre. She stood at the stage door; she wanted to act, she said. Men laughed in her face. The manager – a fat, looselipped man – guffawed[18]. ... Yet her genius was for fiction and lusted to feed abundantly upon[19] the lives of men and women and the study of their ways. At last – for she was very young, oddly like Shakespeare the poet in her face, with the same grey eyes and rounded brows – at last Nick Greene the actormanager took pity on her; she found herself with child[20] by that gentleman and so – who shall measure the heat and violence of the poet's heart when caught and tangled[21] in a woman's body? – killed herself one winter's night and lies buried at some cross-roads where the omnibuses[22] now stop outside the Elephant and Castle[23].

That, more or less, is how the story would run, I think, if a woman in Shakespeare's day had had Shakespeare's genius.

From *A Room of One's Own*, Chapter 3

GLOSSARY

1 talented
2 centre
3 the stage of a theatre
4 intelligence
5 full of anticipation
6 not to mention
7 look after
8 a single pot of meat and vegetables
9 waste time, dream
10 her father's special favourite
11 wrote in a hurry
12 in secret
13 promised in marriage to
14 someone who sorts wool into different classifications
15 speak harshly to
16 underskirt
17 sharpest intelligence
18 laughed loudly
19 wanted very much to observe and make use of
20 pregnant
21 trapped
22 buses
23 an area of London

Woolf's works

Virginia Woolf was a key figure in the 'Bloomsbury Group' – a group of major English writers and artists of the early 20th century. Woolf's novels (*Mrs Dalloway*, 1925, *To the Lighthouse*, 1927) are known for their innovative "stream of consciousness" technique, concentrating not on plot, but on the interior workings of her characters' minds. Woolf was also a pioneer of feminist prose-writing.

The text

A Room of One's Own (1929) is a long essay about women writers and the position of women in society in general. Woolf concludes that, in order to achieve equality with men, women need fundamentals such as their own money, and time away from the domestic sphere.

Links 1c, 10d, 11a

Reading

1 Is Woolf's story about Shakespeare's sister real or imaginary?

2 What sort of education does Judith receive?

3 What forces her to run away from home, and where does she go?

4 What career does she want to follow, and what reaction does she receive from the men she meets?

5 Why does she kill herself?

Your analysis

6 What, precisely, makes it impossible for Judith to have the same kind of life as her brother?

7 Does Judith hate the man she is betrothed to, or the idea of marriage itself? Why do you think this is?

Contemporary links

8 How have attitudes towards women working changed since Shakespeare's (and Woolf's) day?

9 What problems can women still experience today if they want to have both a family life and a career?

John Steinbeck
(1902-1968)

A crime that goes beyond denunciation

The decay spreads over the State, and the sweet smell is a great sorrow[1] on the land. Men who can graft[2] the trees and make the seed fertile and big can find no way to let the hungry people eat their produce. Men who have created new fruits in the world cannot create a system whereby their fruits may be eaten, and the failure hangs over the State like a great sorrow. The works of the roots of the vines, of the trees, must be destroyed to keep up the price, and this is the saddest, bitterest thing of all. Carloads[3] of oranges dumped[4] on the ground. The people come from miles to take the fruit, but this could not be. How would they buy oranges at twenty cents a dozen if they could drive out and pick them up? And men with hoses[5] squirt[6] kerosene on the oranges, and they are angry at the crime, angry at the people who have come to take the fruit. A million people hungry, needing the fruit – and kerosene sprayed over the golden mountains. And the smell of rot[7] fills the country. Burn coffee for fuel in the ships. Burn corn to keep warm, it makes a hot fire. Dump potatoes in the rivers and place guards along the banks to keep the hungry people from fishing them out. Slaughter[8] the pigs and bury them, and let the putrescence[9] drip down into the earth. There is a crime here that goes beyond denunciation. There is a sorrow here that weeping cannot symbolize. There is a failure here that topples[10] all our success. The fertile earth, the straight tree rows, the sturdy[11] trunks, and the ripe fruit. And children dying of pellagra[12] must die because a profit cannot be taken from an orange. And coroners[13] must fill in the certificates – died of malnutrition – because the food must rot, must be forced to rot.

The people come with nets to fish for potatoes in the river, and the guards hold them back; they come in rattling cars to get the dumped oranges, but the kerosene is sprayed. And they stand still and watch the potatoes float by, listen to the screaming pigs being killed in a ditch[14] and covered with quicklime[15], watch the mountains of oranges slop down to a putrefying ooze[16]; and in the eyes of the people there is a failure; and in the eyes of the hungry there is a growing wrath[17]. In the souls of the people the grapes of wrath are filling and growing heavy, growing heavy for the vintage[18].

From *The Grapes of Wrath*, Chapter 25

GLOSSARY

1 sadness
2 blend one type of plant with another
3 quantities brought by car
4 abandoned
5 rubber tubes used to spray liquid
6 spray
7 decay
8 kill
9 rotting flesh
10 causes to fall
11 strong
12 vitamin deficiency
13 people who legally decide the cause of death
14 long narrow hole in the ground
15 a powder that helps things to rot
16 rot to liquid form
17 anger
18 the wine produced from a particular harvest

Steinbeck's works

Steinbeck is best remembered for his three novels of the Great Depression era of the 1930s: *Tortilla Flat, Of Mice and Men* and *The Grapes of Wrath.* These works all deal with the struggles of poor agricultural workers in the USA during that period.

The text

The Grapes of Wrath (1939) follows the Joad family as they join thousands of other farmers leaving their native Oklahoma during the Depression to try to make a living in Southern California. In the presence of the starving refugees, the produce growers of California destroy food to maintain scarcity and high prices.

Links 3e, 6c, 10c

Reading

1 The extract describes the destruction of five specific types of food. What are they, and how are they destroyed?

2 What effect does the destruction of the food have on the people in California?

Your analysis

3 Underline all the words connected with decay. Why do you think there are so many of them? What does the decay of the food symbolise?

4 What other words are repeated throughout the extract? Why do you think that Steinbeck uses this repetition?

Contemporary links

5 Is the world economy still based purely on profit-making?

6 What are the consequences of a world economy like ours? Who benefits from it and who suffers?

Dylan Thomas
(1914-1953)

Do Not Go Gentle Into That Good Night

Do not go gentle into that good night,
Old age should burn and rave[1] at close of day;
Rage[2], rage against the dying of the light.

Though wise men at their end know dark is right,
Because their words had forked no lightning[3] they
Do not go gentle into that good night.

Good men, the last wave by[4], crying how bright
Their frail deeds[5] might have danced in a green bay,
Rage, rage against the dying of the light.

Wild men who caught and sang the sun in flight,
And learn, too late, they grieved[6] it on its way,
Do not go gentle into that good night.

Grave men, near death, who see with blinding sight
Blind eyes could blaze[7] like meteors and be gay[8],
Rage, rage against the dying of the light.

And you, my father, there on that sad height,
Curse, bless me now with your fierce tears, I pray.
Do not go gentle into that good night.
Rage, rage against the dying of the light.

GLOSSARY

1 scream and shout
2 show violent anger
3 had no dramatic impact *(forked lightning is the flashing of light in the sky during a storm)*
4 when the last wave is near (i.e. when death is close)
5 weak actions
6 they missed the sun when it had disappeared
7 burn brightly
8 happy, merry

Thomas's works

Dylan Thomas, the unofficial national poet of Wales, is best remembered for his poems and for his 'play for voices', *Under Milk Wood.* The play was written for the radio and depicts the inner throughts of the inhabitants of a Welsh seaside town.

The text

In this poem, Dylan contemplates the approaching death of his father.

Links 10e

Reading

1 In verse 1, what three phrases does Thomas use to symbolise death? How does he think that old and dying people should react as death approaches?

2 In verses 2-6, Thomas examines different people's reactions to death. Match these people to the verses:
a. his father
b. serious people
c. fast-living people
d. good people
e. intelligent people

Your analysis

3 According to Thomas, which of the people identified in exercise 2:
a. feel that life has passed too quickly?
b. regret that their actions had no great effect or meaning (two groups of people)?
c. regret that they did not have a more exciting, intense life?

4 Does Thomas want his father to have a peaceful death? Why/Why not?

Contemporary links

5 How does your religion or culture view death, and advise people to react towards it? Is Thomas's reaction the same as this or different?

6 How does your society treat old people in the last few years of their lives? Do people pay attention to their thoughts and feelings?

Zadie Smith
(1975-)

A clash of cultures

Samad growled[1], 'I told you already. I don't want you participating in that nonsense. It has nothing to do with us, Magid. Why are you always trying to be somebody you are not?'

There was a mutual, silent anger as each acknowledged the painful incident that was being referred to. A few months earlier, on Magid's ninth birthday, a group of very nice-looking white boys with meticulous manners[2] had turned up on the doorstep and asked for Mark Smith.

'Mark? No Mark here,' Alsana had said, bending down to their level with a genial smile, 'Only the family Iqbal here. You have the wrong house.'

But before she had finished the sentence, Magid had dashed[3] to the door, ushering[4] his mother out of view.

'Hi, guys.'

'Hi, Mark.'

'Off to the chess club, Mum.'

'Yes, M – M – Mark,' said Alsana, close to tears at this final snub[5], the replacement of 'Mum' for 'Amma'. 'Do not be late, now.'

'I GIVE YOU A GLORIOUS NAME LIKE MAGID MAHFOOZ MURSHED MUBTASIM IQBAL!' Samad had yelled after Magid when he returned home that evening and whipped[6] up the stairs like a bullet to hide in his room. 'AND YOU WANT TO BE CALLED MARK SMITH!'

But this was just a symptom of a far deeper malaise[7]. Magid really wanted to be in some other family. He wanted to own cats and not cockroaches[8], he wanted his mother to make the music of the cello, not the sound of the sewing machine; he wanted to have a trellis[9] of flowers growing up one side of the house instead of the ever growing pile of other people's rubbish; he wanted a piano in the hallway in place of the broken door off cousin Kurshed's car; he wanted to go on biking holidays to France, not day trips to Blackpool[10] to visit aunties; he wanted the floor of his room to be shiny wood, not the orange and green swirled[11] carpet left over from the restaurant; he wanted his father to be a doctor, not a one-handed waiter; and this month Magid had converted all these desires into a wish to join in with the Harvest Festival like Mark Smith would. Like everybody else would.

From *White Teeth*, Chapter 6

GLOSSARY

1 made a noise like an angry animal
2 careful politeness
3 hurried
4 pushing
5 insult
6 ran
7 unhappiness
8 large beetles
9 wooden structure
10 a working-class seaside resort
11 mixed together

Smith's works

Zadie Smith astonished the British literary world with the publication, in 2000, of her first novel, *White Teeth*. The book won the Whitbread First Novel Award for that year and was described by many reviewers as the most outstanding writing début for years.

The text

White Teeth tells the story of three families, one Indian, one white, and one of mixed race, in North London and Oxford from World War II to the present day. In this extract, Samad Iqbal, a Bangladeshi immigrant to London, is asking his son Magid why he wants to take part in his school's Harvest Festival, a Christian celebration.

Links 1c, 3b, 10b

Reading

1 What did Magid tell his white friends that upset his parents?

2 What is his real full name?

3 What work does his father do?

4 What work does his mother do?

5 Why is Magid determined to participate in the Harvest Festival?

6 Why doesn't his father want him to go?

Your analysis

7 What do items like cats, pianos, holidays in France and wooden floors symbolise for Magid?

8 How is this text representative of the immigrant experience?

Contemporary links

9 What problems can immigrants experience in terms of clashes between their native culture and the culture of the country they live in?

10 Do you think that the older and younger generations of immigrants in your country have the same disagreements as Samad and Magid?

Pearson Education Limited,
Edinburgh Gate, Harlow
Essex CM20 2JE, England
and Associated Companies throughout the world

Third impression 2005

The Language & Culture pages were written by Claire Thacker.

Set in Blue Highway, Hanko, Nofret, Univers

Printed in Spain by Mateu Cromo, Pinto (Madrid)

ISBN - 13: 978-0-582-81797-5
ISBN - 10: 0582 81797-8

Design, pagination and cover by Apotema

Maps by Apotema

Illustrations by Lorena Canottiere

Picture research by Michela Piovesan and Cristina Rossi

Though every effort is made to ensure that information contained within this textbook is accurate and correct, occasional errors can occur. Any suggestions, corrections or observations on behalf of the reader will be gladly received and should be addressed to:
Pearson Education Italia
via G. Fara 28 - 20124 Milan, Italy

We are grateful to the following for permission to reproduce copyright material: Page 12: All US Census Bureau material for statistics on 'Families in the USA' and 'Families in the UK'; Page 17: charts taken from the Indian Health Service (IHS) website. Page 17: 'Kids need exercise, but what kind?' by Randi Hutter Epstein, copyright © 2003 The New York Times, Co. Reprinted with permission. Page 28, bottom left: © Crown copyright, Met Office. Reproduced under Licence Number Met0/IPR/2. Page 28, bottom right: © Crown copyright. Reproduced under Licence C02W0001598. Page 32: 'No Woman no Cry', reproduced by permission of International Music Publications Ltd, All Rights reserved. Page 38, bottom right: letter published in the Bristol Evening Post, May 2002. Reproduced by kind permission of Mr Tony Waite. Page 40, bottom left: letter by E J Poole. His letters written are held by the Department of Documents at the Imperial War Museum (ref 82/11/1). Page 46, middle left: text reproduced by permission of Christine Lampe, www.noquartergiven.net. Page 51: 'Peers stand in Lords by election' © The Guardian. Page 53, bottom right: 'A Jubilee sea of red, white and blue' by Caroline Davies © Telegraph Group Limited (2002). Page 55: © Pittsburgh Post-Gazette, November 27, 2003, all rights reserved. Reprinted with permission. Page 61: 'Shipbuilding' by Elvis Costello, 100% Warner/Chappell Print rights. Pages 64-65: 'Hothouse flowers' by Lucy Elkins © Telegraph Group Limited (2003). Page 67: by kind permission of Greenforce. Page 69: 'Parents must challenge high school culture', this article was written by Gerry Bowler and originally published in ChristianWeek magazine. Pages 70-71: by courtesy of Futures International High School. Page 72, left: by courtesy of Chetham School. Pages 80-81: 'Bread of Heaven' by Hester Lacey, courtesy of Country Living magazine © National Magazine Company. Page 83: 'Blossoming fields where poverty grows' by Alan Cowell copyright © 2003 The New York Times, Co. Reprinted with permission. Page 92: by kind permission of the Commonwealth Games Federation. Page 109: text from The Lord of the Rings reprinted by permission of Harper Collins Publishers Ltd. © J.R.R. Tolkien, 1974. Page 117: 'The best film soundtracks of all time' by kind permission of Classic FM. Page 120, top left: 'Sales figures taken from Guardian advertising report', 2003 © The Guardian. Page 121: '100 °F: Britain's hottest days', copyright The Independent, 2003. Page 127, right: copyright material by Turnitin and North High School. Page 137, right: 'Citizen to be a practical test' by Nicholas Watt © The Guardian. Page 139: Extract from 'No Logo' by Naomi Klein, reprinted by permission of Harper Collins Publishers Ltd. © Naomi Klein, 1999. Page 146: The Saga Story is from Dennis Barker's obituary of Sidney De Haan in The Guardian, London, February 23, 2001. Page 154: Extract from 'Pygmalion' by G.B. Shaw reprinted by permission of the Society of Authors. Page 156: Extract from 'A Room of One's Own' by Virginia Woolf reprinted by permission of the Society of Authors. Page 157: Extract from 'The Grapes of Wrath' by John Steinbeck (Penguin, 2001) Copyright 1939. Page 159: Extract from 'White Teeth' by Zadie Smith (Hamish Hamilton, 2000) Copyright © Zadie Smith, 2000.

We are grateful to the following for the permission to use copyright photographs: Agenzia Corbis/Contrasto (7, 8 middle right, 9 middle left, 10, 11 top right, 12 middle left, 13 middle left, 14, 15 top right, 16, 18, 19, 21, 22 middle 1st from top and 4th right from top, 23 top left and top right, 24 top left and bottom, 25, 26, 27, 28, 29, 30 2nd-5th right from top, 31, 33, 35 top, middle centre and right, bottom right, 36 middle and right, 37 top left, bottom left, middle 1st from top and bottom right, 38 left 1st and 2nd from top and bottom right, 39 bottom left and 1st and 2nd right, 40, 41 bottom, 42 bottom left, top and bottom right, 43, 44 top right and bottom, 45, 46, 47, 48, 49 top left and right, middle left, centre and right, bottom centre and right, 50 top right, 52 bottom, 53, 54, 56 top and bottom left, 58 top left and right, bottom, 60 top right, 62, 63, 66, 67 middle, 68 1st and 2nd right from top, 1st top left, 69, 71, 72, 73, 74, 75 middle left, 76, 77, 78, 79, 82, 83, 84, 85, 86 left, middle right, bottom, 88, 89 top left, 1st, 2nd and 4th right from top, 91 1st and 2nd left from top, 2nd right from top, 92 1st and 2nd from top, 93 bottom left and right, 94, 95 1st, 3rd and 6th top, middle and bottom, 96, 97, 100,101, 103, 105 top and middle left, middle right, 112 1st and 2nd left, 3rd right from top, 112 top left, 113 top left, 114, 117 top right, bottom, 119 bottom left, middle top and centre, right top and centre, bottom right, 120 middle left and bottom, 122, 124 bottom left and right, 126 1st and 2nd left from top, 128, 129, 130, 131, 132, 133, 136 2nd right from top, 138, 139 top right, 140 top left and right, 141 top left and right, 142 bottom left and right, 143, 146, 148, 149, 150, 153, 155 right, 156, 157, 159); Agenzia Empics/Contrasto (3rd, 4th, 5th and 6th from top); Agenzia Erich Lessing /Contrasto (35 middle left and bottom left); Agenzia Gamma/Contrasto (49 bottom left, 50 bottom left, 95 4th top, 135, 136 bottom left, 138-139, 139 middle left); The Artist and Haunch of Venison, London/© photograph: Tate, London 2003/copyright: The Artist and Haunch of Venison, London (106 bottom right); James Bareham – copyright trademark RUG Ltd 2002 (112 top right); Giancarlo Costa copyright photographs (52 top, 147 3rd left from top and 2nd right from top, 154); Elliot Right Way Books (80 bottom left); Farabolafoto (32 top left, 36 bottom left, 42 middle left and middle right, 44 top left, 56 top right, 68 2nd left from top, 89 3rd and 5th right from top, 93 top middle, 112 1st and 2nd right from top, 113, 116, 117 top left, 118, 125 middle left, 134 right, 144 left); Granata Images (9 top left, 13 top right, 15 middle left, 20, 22 left 2nd from top, right 3rd from top, 32 bottom left, 42 top left, 60 bottom left, 61 top left, 80 top left, 81 top left and top right, 91 top right and bottom left, 98, 102 top left,105 top and bottom right, 108 2nd , 3rd, 4th left from top, middle bottom, 1st, 2nd and 3rd right from top, 119 middle left, bottom centre, 123, 124 middle bottom, 145, 147 bottom left, 155 left, 158); Harper Collins Publishers Ltd (108 top left); ICP/Double's (8 top left, 12 top left, 22 left 1st from top and 4th right from top, 23middle bottom, 30 1st right from top, 32 middle left, 37 right bottom left, 50 middle, 56 middle left and right, 61 right, 80 middle, 81, 99, 102 top right, 103 top right and bottom right, 110 bottom left and middle right, 126, 127, 134 left , 136 middle top, 1st right from top, 137, 140 left 2nd from top, 141 middle right, 151, 152); Imperial War Museum (41 top right); Agenzia Marka (17, 22 1st, 2nd right from top, 5th middle bottom, 24 top right, 37 middle bottom, 38 right 1st from top, 39 right 1st from top, 75 middle centre, 86 top middle, 95 2nd and 5th top, 115, 139 top left, 141 bottom); Pearson Education Italia (8 bottom); Pearson Education Limited (11 left); Penguin Books (68 bottom); The Pittsburgh Post-Gazette, November 27, 2003, all rights reserved. Reprinted with permission (55); Room 13, Caol Primary School (106 top left and right, 107); Cristina Rossi (58 top right); David Sandison/The Independent (121).

All efforts have been made to trace all copyrights holders, however some remain unknown. We will happily remedy any unintentional mistakes or omissions, and would be grateful for any assistance in doing so.